German Poetry in Transition, 1945–1990

D1117941

German Poetry

in Transition

1945–1990

Bilingual Edition

EDITED AND TRANSLATED BY

Charlotte Melin

University Press of New England

Hanover and London

University Press of New England, Hanover, NH 03755
This collection, Introduction, English translations (with the exceptions noted below), Notes to the
Poems, Biographies, Select Bibliography, and Indexes © 1999 by University Press of New England
All rights reserved
Printed in the United States of America
5 4 3 2 1
CIP data appear at the end of the book

The following translations are reprinted here under separate copyright:

"Homecoming" and "When in My White Room at the Charité" by Bertolt Brecht copyright ©
1976, 1979 by Methuen London, Ltd. From *Bertolt Brecht Poems 1913–1956* edited by John Willett
and Ralph Mannheim. Reproduced by permission of Routledge, Inc.
"Two hands, born to give" and "Farewell" from *The Seeker and Other Poems* by Nelly Sachs,
translated by Ruth and Matthew Mead and Michael Hamburger. Copyright © 1970 by Farrar,
Straus & Giroux, Inc. Reprinted by permission of Farrar, Straus & Giroux, Inc.
"Only where find those words" from *O The Chimneys* by Nelly Sachs, translated by Michael
Hamburger, Christopher Holme, Ruth and Matthew Mead, and Michael Roloff. Translation copy-
right © 1967 and copyright renewed © 1995 by Farrar, Straus & Giroux, Inc. Reprinted by permis-
sion of Farrar, Straus & Giroux, Inc.

The following publishers and authors have generously given permission for the works appearing in
this anthology to which they hold copyright:

Arche Verlag AG, Zürich, for Silja Walter, "Mein kleiner weißer Hund und ich"/"My Small
White Dog and I" from *Gedichte*, © 1950 by Verlags AG Die Arche, Zürich.
Stiftung Hans Arp und Sophie Taeuber-Arp e.V., Rolandseck, for Hans Arp, "Reif zum Auss-
teigen"/"Ready to Get Off" and "Amerika"/"America," from *Gesammelte Gedichte II*, Limes Verlag,
© 1974.
Aufbau-Verlag GmbH, Berlin und Weimar, for Johannes R. Becher, "Die Jahre sind gezählt"/
"The Years Are Counted" from *Gesammelte Werke*, © 1967; Annerose Kirchner, "Sonntag"/"Sun-
day" from *Grenzfallgedichte*, © 1991; Karl Mickel, "Petzower Sommer"/"Petzow Summer" from
Nachrichten aus Deutschland © 1967; Inge Müller "Wie"/"How" and "Wir"/"We" from *Wenn ich
schon sterben muß* © 1985; Eva Strittmatter, "Bilanz"/"Balance Sheet" and "Vor einem Herbst"/"Be-
fore One Fall" from *Ich mach ein Lied aus Stille*, © 1974; "Nachts"/"At Night" from *Die eine Rose
überwältigt alles*, © 1977; Brigitte Struzyk, "Die Tochter des Sisyphos berichtet dem Vater"/"The
Daughter of Sisyphus Reports to Her Father" from *Der wild gewordene Tag: Gedichte*, © 1989.

(Copyright acknowledgments continued on p. 371)

Contents

1955–1965   Accomplishments and Rebellions

1965–1975   Poetry as Dialogue or Soliloquy

1975–1990 From New Subjectivity to a "New World Order"

Acknowledgments

This anthology, like many books, has developed with advice, assistance, and support from a number of individuals and institutions. I would like in particular to acknowledge my gratitude to Ingo Seidler, who inspired initial work on the translations and whose interest in the project, careful readings, and perceptive suggestions as things took form helped shape the collection in important ways. A grant from the National Endowment for the Humanities, an independent federal agency, provided resources for intensive work on the project in 1991–1992. Rebecca Raham, R. Blythe Inners, and Lisa Jennings, who aided me as research assistants, facilitated preparation of the manuscript with their careful attention to details and indefatigable efforts. Proofreading of one preliminary compilation of translations was capably executed by Frauke Lenckos, who examined both the German and English texts. Many others gave encouragement, information, and helpful comments along the way, including Reinhard Mayer, Cecile Zorach, Isolde Mueller, Edson Chick, Michèle Cloonan, and Marie-Luise Conen.

I would also like to express my appreciation to the many authors and publishing firms who corresponded with me concerning the poems and translations. Every effort has been made to contact all firms and individuals currently holding rights to the texts included in this collection. This was in itself a sizable undertaking, and I am grateful to those who have made this anthology possible by granting permission to include the various poems in bilingual presentation. Finally, I would like to thank my husband, Matthew Rohn, as well as my children, Eric and Anne, for their long patience, and my mother and late father for nurturing my earliest interests in poetry.

C.A.M.

German Poetry in Transition, 1945–1990

Introduction

A poem, in all its uniqueness, remains mindful of its dates, the poet Paul Celan observed in 1960.[1] His remark came at a time when postwar German poetry already seemed fundamentally shaped by the synchronous connection its language calls *Zeitgeist*, an ineffable spirit of the times that couples aesthetic life with historical context. Today, coherent readings of recent poetry written in German continue to turn on salient dates, for it is apparent in retrospect that around 1945, or 1968, or 1990—the years when political and social orders abruptly shifted in Europe—poetry was changing too. Beset by challenges to its aesthetic viability, German poetry enjoyed a renaissance that was animated in subtle, often unexpected ways, by its eerie prescience about and reaction to the events that occurred between the end of World War II and post–Cold War reunification. Yet the dates that define this poetic revival do not mark an abrupt end to one kind of writing and the beginning of another. Rather, they acknowledge an intrinsic but protean bond between each poetic text and its particular context.

The present collection encompasses the period's major poets, literary movements, and heterogeneous trends. Selected for their distinctive quality, the poems represent work by authors from the former East and West Germanies, Austria, Switzerland, and enclaves in Central Europe, as well as by expatriates. To provide a coherent context for this diversity, each poem is placed according to its respective period of composition and publication among contemporary texts. The division of the anthology into decades, too, follows both a gradual succession of themes that have preoccupied German writers and a parallel evolution of established styles alongside experimental forms. The translations themselves strive to complement this design by exhibiting each poem's distinct language, detail, and form. Complex existences, these poems and their language attend asynchronously to the echoes and overtones of history, those poetic dates to which Celan alluded. The historical events, then, that need to be mentioned in conjunction with postwar German poetry form no procrustean, chronological framework over which textual interpretations may be stretched, but they do

---

1. Paul Celan, "Der Meridian," *Ausgewählte Gedichte*, ed. Beda Allemann (Frankfurt am Main: Suhrkamp, 1972), 142.

stand as corroboration for experiences shared by the individual authors and they provide a background for the poems and translations that follow.

1945–1955: Ends, Continuities, and Beginnings

When the war ended in 1945, it left social turmoil, moral chaos, and horrific physical devastation in its aftermath. Millions of people had died; other millions were displaced or homeless. Dire money and food shortages prevailed, and under the destabilized conditions, black-market operations, rape, theft, and looting became commonplace. What had been Germany was now territory administered by the Allies (Britain, France, the United States), and the Soviet Union, who ran the country from 1945 to 1949. Austria was similarly divided among the victors, but would remain much less important than Germany in the postwar years, as would Switzerland, which had maintained neutrality during the war.

Soon the divided Germany became the focal point for the Cold War that developed between the United States and the Soviet Union, and their respective allies.[2] Mutual cooperation among the former allies halted by 1947, and tensions heightened as Stalin attempted to consolidate Soviet influence in Eastern Europe. Both sides had quickly initiated political and cultural reeducation programs in the areas they administered, but they pursued radically different approaches to reconstruction. While the Soviet Union laid claim to property as war reparations, confiscating land belonging to former Nazis and nationalizing industries under a program of economic socialism, the United States initiated the European Recovery Program (Marshall Plan) in 1947, to provide substantial economic assistance to Germany and promote capitalism. During the Berlin Blockade (1948–1949) when the Soviets attempted to gain full control of the former German capital by cutting off overland routes to the Western sectors, U.S. and British forces formed an "air bridge" to transport essential supplies to the city by plane.

By 1949, the forty-year division of Germany into East and West formally began. In May, the Western sectors formed the Federal Republic of Germany (FRG) by ratifying a provisional constitution or *Grundgesetz* that was in effect to become permanent. The Soviets countered by founding the German Democratic Republic (GDR). Further efforts to reunite the two countries in the early

2. For a history of the FRG see Dennis L. Bark and David R. Gress, *A History of West Germany* (Oxford: Basil Blackwell, 1989), and further Gordon Craig, *The Germans* (New York: Putnam, 1982), as well as *The Oxford Illustrated History of Modern Europe*, ed. T. C. W. Blanning (New York: Oxford UP, 1996).

1950s failed. The United States, locked in the Arms Race with the Soviet Union, faced the Korean War (1950–1953) and experienced a virulent wave of anti-Communist sentiment that witnessed such controversial cases as the Rosenberg trial, the Hiss affair, and the Oppenheimer scandal. McCarthyism—named after Joseph McCarthy, the U.S. senator from Wisconsin (1946–1957) whose House Un-American Activities Committee dramatically interrogated suspected Soviet sympathizers—eventually abated, yet suspicions about Communist attempts to undermine the West lingered.

Amid this Cold War atmosphere, Konrad Adenauer, the first chancellor (1949–1963) and a devout Catholic who envisioned a unified, Christian Europe, oriented the FRG firmly toward the West. The diplomatic initiatives of 1952, when Stalin surprisingly offered the possibility of a united, neutral Germany, were rejected under the suspicion that the Soviet Union merely wanted to delay German integration into the Western international community or sought to split the FRG from its new allies. Ten years after the end of the war, the occupation statutes were revoked and the FRG was admitted into NATO. The GDR, in reaction to these changes, joined the Warsaw Pact in 1956. Austria, where the Socialist party had faced diminishing influence, became free and neutral in 1955, led by conservative governments under Leopold Figl (leader of the Austrian People's Party and chancellor 1945–1953) and Julius Raab (chancellor 1953–1961).

The German literary landscape during this first postwar decade underwent a formidable reconstruction that in certain respects paralleled the changes that occurred in the political sphere. The Third Reich, labeling controversial works *entartete Kunst* (degenerate art), had through its cultural policies enervated or suppressed the avant-gardism that had flourished before the war with Expressionism, *Neue Sachlichkeit* (New Matter-of-Factness), Surrealism, and Dada. After the German capitulation, the mediocre poets who facilely produced *Heimatliteratur* (homeland literature) or propagandistic *Blut- und Bodendichtung* (race and soil poetry) quickly faded into obscurity. Of the *Innere Emigration* (inner emigration) poets who had remained in Germany under Fascist rule and retreated into silence to express their opposition to the Nazis, such as R. A. Schröder, Rudolf Hagelstange, and Oskar Loerke, few had publishable manuscripts stashed in their desks.

For much of the first postwar decade, the fate of German verse remained profoundly uncertain due to the utter disruption of literary life, the large number of poets who had become expatriates, and the immediate absence of an up-and-coming group of authors. Those who had emigrated—for instance, Nelly Sachs to Sweden, Bertolt Brecht to Scandinavia and the United States, Erich Arendt to Colombia, Erich Fried to England, and Karl Wolfskehl to New Zealand—remained abroad, contemplating whether to return, or deciding never to come back. One young writer, Franz Fühmann, who had packed a slim volume of Trakl poems in his soldier's knapsack, remained a prisoner of war and did not reach home from the Soviet Union for five years. The next generation of poets was still in their teens, like Ingeborg Bachmann in Austria, who welcomed the British liberating forces in halting high school English, or Hans Magnus Enzensberger, who began his literary education by snitching comic books and classics from the occupation troops.[3] Publishing houses, moreover, had to rebuild, reorganize, and obtain licenses from the Allies.

During this initial decade, writers who had established their reputations before the Nazi rise to power charted a variety of directions German poetry would take.[4] Wilhelm Lehmann and Elisabeth Langgässer, Gottfried Benn, Bertolt Brecht, and Hans Arp revived the modernist impulses that had thrived in the first third of the twentieth century with their respective work in nature, *l'art pour l'art*, political, and experimental poetry. Nelly Sachs, meanwhile, and a handful of emerging younger authors, developed a new trend, hermetic poetry, by fusing earlier traditions with their own individual outlook and voice.

At first rhymed nature poems enjoyed great popularity, rapidly becoming the most widely published type of verse. This poetry offered mainly clichéd, idyllic escapism from the bleak postwar present into the solace of an illusory, *heile Welt*, or snug, safe world.[5] Wilhelm Lehmann, however, pursued a line of stylistically subtle verse that combined rhyme with abundant, concrete biological details. Elisabeth Langgässer, on the other hand, developed complex poetic cycles characterized by a highly concentrated handling of intricate rhyme schemes, unexpected observations of nature, and mythical allusions, both classical and Biblical. Younger writers drawn to traditional verse and its postwar variations (Christine Busta, Günter Eich, Peter Huchel, Marie Luise Kaschnitz, and Karl Krolow, whose careers had been interrupted or delayed by the war) skirted sentimentality by combining rhymed forms with unvarnished perspicacity. Nature poetry, thus, increased in vigor well into the 1950s, though postwar uncertainties resulted in a growing dissatisfaction with effete, traditional content. Lehmann's naively optimistic prediction that the earth would simply awaken from the winter's spell seemed doubtful, for the world had unquestionably changed.[6]

3. Hans Magnus Enzensberger, "Mann, Kafka and the Katzenjammer Kids," *The New York Times Review of Books*, 17 Nov. 1985, p. 1, 37–39.

4. Cf. Peter Demetz, *Postwar German Literature* (New York: Pegasus, 1970).

5. Peter Rühmkorf, "Das lyrische Weltbild der Nachkriegszeit," *Bestandsaufnahme*, ed. Hans Werner Richter (München: Verlag Kurt Desch, 1962), 452.

6. See "German Times 1947" ("Deutsche Zeit 1947") in this anthology.

A loosely defined *Trümmerliteratur*, or "literature of the ruins," took shape by the late forties. *Trümmerlyrik*, which characteristically described the war's devastation, introduced fresh content while moving in the direction of new poetic form. The devastation, indeed, seemed to extend to language itself, for the poems virtually stuttered out their message in the broken phrases of a catastrophe's survivor. "This is my cap, / this is my coat" ("Dies ist meine Mütze / dies ist mein Mantel"), Eich's famous poem "Inventory" ("Inventur") repetitively begins. Its sharply reduced language, like the seemingly casual tone of Walter Höllerer's "He Lay So Strangely Relaxed by the Side" ("Der lag besonders mühelos am Rand"), abandoned the flowery rhetoric of epigonic, traditional verse in search of an authentic voice. This essential break with the past now became the focus of literary discussions that took up labels like *Kahlschlagliteratur* or *Stunde-Null* to describe the situation. While *Kahlschlagliteratur* (literature after the clearing of the forest) denotes a kind of writing that could theoretically coexist with nature poetry, the second concept, *Stunde-Null*, the "zero hour" represented by the year 1945, had an uncompromising ring that cast in absolute terms the psychological sense shared by many, especially younger writers, that German literature after the war had to rise from the ashes.

But in fact, poetry between 1945 and 1955 showed many continuities with what had preceded it, despite these agonistic formulations of its character.[7] The Nazis had tolerated some poets who worked outside the bounds of propagandistically correct verse because their vaguely edifying, readily accessible work posed no challenge to official culture. Hans Carossa, Hermann Hesse, Agnes Miegel, Börries von Münchhausen, or Georg Britting, for example, had continued to write idyllic poetry that tended to be provincial, conventional, and often about nature. Now poets who struggled to come to terms with history and to rediscover the literary heritage that had been suppressed during the Third Reich found polarizing rhetoric useful. It projected an invigorating sense of avant-gardism and mission by publicizing the German commitment to reenter the international literary community, even as it encouraged writers to become socially engaged intellectuals. Discussion about poetry and politics, begun under circumstances peculiar to the immediate postwar era, prevailed in German literary circles, and aesthetic dialogues among writers about poetic versus social impulses sustained a dynamic climate in which German poetry evolved through a constant reexamination of its own premises over the next four and a half decades.

---

7. See Hans Dieter Schäfer, "Zusammenhänge der deutschen Gegenwartslyrik," *Deutsche Gegenwartsliteratur*, ed. Manfred Durzak (Stuttgart: Reclam, 1981), 166–203; and Heinrich Vormweg, "Deutsche Literatur 1945–1960: Keine Stunde Null," *Die deutsche Literatur der Gegenwart*, ed. Manfred Durzak (Stuttgart: Reclam, 1971), 13–30.

The first major reassessment postwar German poetry experienced developed as a reaction against the political subordination of artistic autonomy. It originated with Gottfried Benn, a major figure in the Expressionist movement, who during the Third Reich had first discredited himself by publicly embracing the Nazis, and later, disillusioned with the regime, had lapsed into silence in the mid-1930s. After the Swiss publication of *Statische Gedichte* (Static Poems, 1949), his prestige grew enormously, reaching an apex in 1951, when he received the Georg Büchner Prize and delivered his widely influential lecture *Probleme der Lyrik* (Problems of Lyric Poetry).

At a time when writers tentatively searched for artistic identity in the postwar world, Benn outlined an impressive genealogy for modern poetry that extended back to Stéphane Mallarmé and Edgar Allen Poe. Forcefully asserting that poetry is absolute and monologic, Benn tried, as he had in the 1920s, to absolve the lyric genre from political responsibility and to declare it free to pursue purely aesthetic ends. Though questionable in light of the fact that political apathy among intellectuals had contributed to Hitler's rise to power, Benn's program possessed broad appeal because he challenged German literature to escape the provincialism and sycophancy to which it had been consigned. This conception of art as an autonomous activity and Benn's plea for the magic power of poetic language had an impact on an entire generation of younger writers, even those who objected to the apolitical stance he propounded or to the unsavory political engagement he had briefly practiced. His work introduced a new range of subjects and materials into the poetic vocabulary by mining the disciplines of medicine, psychology, and anthropology for inspiration, and assimilating prose elements, along with the postwar slang of Berlin pubs and cynical parlando diction.

Despite the aesthetically radical implications of Benn's call for a return to modernism, his position unfolded amid a conservative political and cultural climate that set the prevailing values.[8] A serious critique of this complacency of restoration and the progressive trivialization that was encroaching on poetry— the European equivalent of what Robert Lowell called the "tranquilized fifties"—came in 1951 from philosopher Theodor W. Adorno, who issued the famous pronouncement, "to write a poem after Auschwitz is barbaric" ("nach Auschwitz ein Gedicht zu schreiben, ist barbarisch").[9] For Adorno, the issue of the contemporary poem was not that it should cease to exist, but that it had to do more than just continue to exist, indeed that it needed to find aesthetically

8. Cf. James Rolleston, "Der Drang nach Synthese: Benn, Brecht und die Poetik der fünfziger Jahre," *Die deutsche Lyrik 1945–1975*, ed. Klaus Weissenberger (Düsseldorf: Bagel, 1981), 78–94.
9. Theodor W. Adorno, "Kulturkritik und Gesellschaft," *Aesthetische Theorie* (Frankfurt: Suhrkamp, 1970), 30.

adequate means to confront Fascism's inhumanity.[10] Hermetic poetry, which began to appear in the late 1940s, wrestled with this dilemma.

Sometimes mistakenly labeled esoteric, difficult to understand, or "dark" (dunkel), hermetic poetry had its roots in the modernist aesthetic of the late nineteenth and early twentieth century. In postwar German literature, a distinctive, lean style and trenchantly subjective origin defined hermetic verse. Succinct construction (mostly in unrhymed lines), an emphasis on individual voice and metaphor, and the articulation of a profound tension between private, poetic identity and public communication characterize this poetry. Notwithstanding the popular reproach that it is impossible to interpret, hermetic lyric simply demands an intense process of reading, employing extreme concentration and intimate familiarity with the literary past.

Without shirking the immediate political burdens, writers whose work showed hermetic tendencies—notably Nelly Sachs, Paul Celan, Ingeborg Bachmann, and Erich Arendt—helped elevate the German lyric genre again to the aesthetic heights it had reached in the early twentieth century. The agony of the Holocaust fills Sachs's poems with vivid, isolated images and clairvoyant allusions to the Cabbala, Old Testament, and mystical writings. Celan, the author of perhaps the most famous poem about the concentration camps, "Todesfuge" ("Fugue of Death"), employed recurrent themes, encoded content, dialogic construction, and literary allusions. His multilayered writing is permeated by grief over the fate of European Jews and by highly specific, often biographical elements that critics have only recently begun to decipher. Bachmann, a keenly intellectual poet appalled by war and skeptical about language's capacities to achieve expression, took as her subject an intense questioning of human relationships that anticipated later feminist developments. Arendt, who was influenced by the Expressionists and international modernism, crafted poetry with syntactically complex, rich language, mythical allusions, and increasing condensation.

By the mid-1950s, hermetic poetry on the one hand and Gottfried Benn on the other so dominated the German literary scene that they overshadowed Benn's contemporary, Bertolt Brecht, who published his *Buckower Elegien* (Buckow Elegies) in 1954 and laid the foundations for the poetically unencumbered, political verse that emerged after 1960. Brecht, an unorthodox Marxist, authored thousands of poems, but most of this poetry was not published until after his death. An important dramatist, the poet Brecht displayed a startling range of voice, extending from the anarchic and blatantly propagandistic to the lyrical and poignant. A masterful adapter of traditional forms and motifs, as

10. Cf. Otto Knörrich, *Die deutsche Lyrik der Gegenwart 1945–1970* (Stuttgart: Kröner, 1971), 19.

well as an innovative creator of fresh diction, he experimented with linguistic strategies such as dialectical construction and the interpolation of various types of language for the purpose of distancing the reader from the text.

Neglect of Brecht's poetic work in the first decade after 1945 also was connected to the conservative political and aesthetic climate that descended over both Germanies with the onset of the Cold War. Upon his return to Europe in 1947, Brecht, after some wavering, settled in East Berlin, where official policy favored Social Realism and regarded innovative modernism with suspicion. Yet when Brecht's works were published in the West, they at first received a lukewarm reception.[11] There, given the choice between the seemingly irreconcilable opposites of Brecht and Benn, the conservatism of the era favored the latter. Nonetheless, on both sides of the Iron Curtain, the vigor of Brecht's work strongly influenced younger poets, among them Günter Kunert, Hans Magnus Enzensberger, Günter Grass, Erich Fried, Helga Novak, and Wolf Biermann. As politics came to the fore in the 1960s, Benn's ascendancy gave way to Brecht's.

The postwar revival of experimental verse was similarly gradual, though for different reasons. One of the most important forerunners of this wing of German literature, Hans Arp, spent the war years in Switzerland and only began publishing poetry in German again in the early 1950s. Arp was a Dadaist sculptor and bilingual author who also wrote in French, but his international orientation and antiestablishment outlook did not make him a cult figure like Benn, or later Brecht. His playful handling of language and Surrealistic imagery attracted various Concrete and unconventional writers to his texts, yet in general, experimental poetry instead of coalescing around a single personality, appeared spontaneously in several locations in the early to mid-1950s. This experimentalism was prompted largely by a series of independent rediscoveries of avant-garde modernist texts—many of them in languages other than German—that had begun in the late forties.

One branch of experimental verse, "Konkrete Poesie" or "Concrete Poetry," took its name from a manifesto penned by German poet Eugen Gomringer and a Brazilian, Decio Pignatari, in 1953.[12] International in spirit, Concrete Poetry found inspiration in the visual arts, music, and writers such as Mallarmé, Arno Holz, Guillaume Apollinaire, Ezra Pound, e. e. cummings, and William Carlos Williams.[13] Typographical manipulation, a focus on isolated words or the image created by letters on the page, and sound experiments frequently appear as features of Concrete texts. A number of the group's practitioners lived in

---

11. Hermann Korte, *Geschichte der deutschen Lyrik seit 1945* (Stuttgart: J. B. Metzlersche Verlagsbuchhandlung, 1989), 66.

12. Eugen Gomringer, "Vorwort," *konkrete poesie* (Stuttgart: Philipp Reclam Jun., 1972), 5.

13. Ibid.

southwestern Germany, around Stuttgart and Ulm (notably Gomringer and Helmut Heissenbüttel), though the high degree of independence in their work counters definition of Concrete Poetry as a homogenous movement.

At approximately the same time, 1954–1964, the *Wiener Gruppe* (Viennese Group) was formed from a circle of befriended Austrian writers (including Friedrich Achleitner, H. C. Artmann, Konrad Bayer, Gerhard Rühm, and Oswald Wiener) who also staged happening-like performances as an "Art-Club." Reacting against the literary and social establishment, the Viennese Group looked to unconventional texts from baroque literature, Surrealism, and Dada as their models. Work by August Stramm, Gertrude Stein, and the philosopher Ludwig Wittgenstein provided particular inspiration. Its writers experimented with montage, sound poems, dialect texts, and collaborative projects, their efforts influencing authors peripheral to the circle itself, particularly Friederike Mayröcker and Ernst Jandl.

As the first decade after 1945 neared an end, the traditions that had nurtured poetry in the immediate postwar years began to give way to the kind of individualistic diversity that already characterized experimental literature. The premiere literary circle of the postwar era, *Gruppe 47* (Group 47), founded by Hans Werner Richter in 1947, reflected this altered situation. At the outset, the group had no fixed aesthetic agenda and served simply as a forum where authors read from their works and heard an immediate response (and sometimes sharp comment) from an audience of peers and critics. It did not have a fixed social program, although all of its members were more or less inclined to the left and many took part in pro-SPD (*Sozialdemokratische Partei Deutschlands* or Social Democratic Party) demonstrations, campaigns, and elections.[14] *Gruppe 47* eventually dissolved in 1968 after several years of decreased attendance and wrangling over political resolutions. Before its demise, however, it had attracted many of the best authors writing in German, and, through public recognition and prizes, had done much to encourage the emerging talents of the 1950s and 1960s.

1955–1965: Accomplishments and Rebellions

Vergangenheitsbewältigung, coming to terms with the past, intensely preoccupied German intellectuals in the second postwar decade. Even after the Nürnberg trials, the uncomfortable reckoning with history continued. Adolph Eichmann, the organizer of Hitler's "final solution," was captured in 1960,

---

14. Cf. K. Stuart Parkes, *Writers and Politics in West Germany* (New York: St. Martin's Press, 1986).

tried, and executed in 1962 for crimes against humanity, and Germany's future as two countries became more clearly defined. Construction of the Berlin Wall in 1961 caused a serious confrontation between East and West. Although GDR authorities claimed its intent was to keep Westerners out, its actual purpose was to keep Easterners in after they had received an education at state expense. Still, with internal political reshuffling in the FRG and encouragement from the United States, where President Kennedy favored détente after the Cuban missile crisis of 1962, rapprochement began.

The federal elections of 1957 in the FRG had given the conservative CDU/CSU (Christian Democratic Union/Christian Social Union) coalition an absolute majority in the *Bundestag*, or parliament; by the early 1960s, however, changes in the party coalitions were underway that would eventually result in Ludwig Erhard (chancellor 1963–1966) succeeding the aging Adenauer. The politically ambitious, conservative Defense Minister, Franz Josef Strauss, became embroiled in what was to be called the "*Spiegel* affair." After Strauss had won a libel suit against *Der Spiegel* over editorials depicting him as a warmonger, the news magazine published a damning exposé on German defense policy that cited classified sources. The *Spiegel* editors were summarily arrested, and their offices were illegally searched at Strauss' instigation, a move that provoked public protest against an abuse of power all too reminiscent of the Nazi era police state. Outrage over encroachments on freedom of the press and the nuclear defense strategy that many regarded as unacceptable had both immediate and long-term consequences. Political alliances were rearranged after the FDP (Free Democratic Party) temporarily split itself from the CDU/CSU coalition. The stature of the press was enhanced, and, most importantly, in the public sphere an attitude of liberalism emerged that favored more defined restrictions on the power of the state and greater protection of individual liberties.

For literature, the sharp polarization of Cold War politics and the very real threats posed by rearmament and the *Spiegel* affair rendered the question of authors' social responsibility all the more pressing. The *Wirtschaftswunder* (or "economic miracle") had brought phenomenal economic growth to the FRG, yet conservative pressures and rigidity by the government resulted in social stagnation that troubled intellectuals. Fiction became the preeminent genre in the hands of Heinrich Böll, Günter Grass, and Uwe Johnson, whose prose presented aspects of the Nazi era and its aftermath. By contrast, poetry, still dominated by nature poems, conventional, even devotional, texts, as well as hermetic verse, continued to struggle more privately with issues of conscience.

Between 1955 and 1960, Nelly Sachs (who was to receive the Nobel Prize for Literature in 1966) and Paul Celan each published two volumes of poetry. Their increasing preoccupation with the limitations of poetic language went hand in hand with their efforts to face memories of the Holocaust. When Celan received the prestigious Georg Büchner Prize in 1960, hermetic poetry reached its apogee. His acceptance speech, nonetheless, acknowledged that the contemporary poem seemed compromised because it showed "eine starke Neigung zum Verstummen" (a strong tendency to dissolve into silence).[15] Celan conceived of poetry as a "verzweifeltes Gespräch" (a desperate dialogue),[16] but the exchange the poem sought in the hermetic mode seemed to grow more and more tenuous.

Approaching poetry with quite different aesthetic assumptions, the era's "angry young men," writers born in the late 1920s, sought more radical alternatives, peppering their poems with public rhetoric, everyday subject matter, and aggressive irony.[17] Hans Magnus Enzensberger burst onto the literary scene with the publication of *Verteidigung der Wölfe* (Defense of the Wolves, 1957), a volume characterized by keen insight and caustic tone. Günter Grass showed an irreverent eye for mundane detail in *Vorzüge der Windhühner* (Advantages of the Greyhounds, 1956), and Peter Rühmkorf parodied the literary establishment in his *Irdisches Vergnügen in g.* (Worldly Pleasures in g., 1959, the title a pun on a work by the baroque poet Barthold Heinrich Brockes, with a mere letter replacing the word *Gott* or God used in the original title). Their work constituted both a challenge to the literary establishment and a reaction against the black-white definition of Cold War politics. By 1963, when Enzensberger became the youngest recipient of the Büchner Prize, the literary tide had clearly changed. The ascendancy of Benn and his autonomous aesthetic had begun to give way to the inspiration of Brecht and outspoken political *engagement*.[18]

What bridged the hermetic and iconoclastic outlooks was a "search for the lost language," as Enzensberger called the poetic quest for adequate means of expression.[19] Familiarity with the literary tradition became a prime route to this end; hence interest in French and Spanish Surrealism, modern American poetry (especially plain style), and avant-garde Russian verse grew as writers sought out international literature and translated it. Many young authors now fit the mold of the *Poeta doctus*, or "learned poet," the well-read writer with extensive academic training. Experimental literature flourished as well with the publication of major collections by Artmann, Achleitner, Franz Mon, Heissenbüttel, Claus Bremer, Mayröcker, and Jandl.

15. Paul Celan, *Ausgewählte Gedichte, Zwei Reden* (Frankfurt: Suhrkamp, 1972), 143.
16. Ibid., 144.
17. The label "angry young men" reflects the emulation of British and American verse during this era, and it was applied by Alfred Andersch to Enzensberger's early poetry in a review; Enzensberger at the time also used the phrase when describing his own work.
18. The term was coined by French Existentialist Jean Paul Sartre; cf. Gero von Wilpert, *Sachwörterbuch der Literatur* (Stuttgart: Alfred Kröner, 1969), 207.
19. Hans Magnus Enzensberger, "In Search of the Lost Language," *Encounter* 3 (1963): 44–51.

The relationship between literature and its audience was also changing as poets of all persuasions increasingly voiced opinions about the task of poetry in essays, public addresses, and verse. The University of Frankfurt initiated a highly acclaimed series of guest professorships for writers (1959–1968, resumed in 1979), with Ingeborg Bachmann as the first appointee. Literary discussions mirrored a growing sense that readers and writers interacted over texts, as in Hilde Domin's 1966 anthology, *Doppelinterpretationen* (Double Interpretations), where each poem in the volume was accompanied by comments from both its author and a critic, a presentation that invited reader reaction to the texts. Engaged writers, looking back to Brecht, emphasized the *Gebrauchswert* (utilitarian value) of verse. Concrete poets, on the other hand, contemplated the physical character of poetry and its potential aesthetic and social role in an age dominated by visual media. Poetry seemed poised to descend from its aesthetic pedestal and move into the public sphere of discourse.

Meanwhile, on the other side of the Iron Curtain, Cold War rigidity molded literature in its image. Many intellectuals and writers (in East and West alike) initially viewed Socialism as an unparalleled opportunity to alter society for the better. Some, like Elke Erb, Wolf Biermann, Peter Hacks, and Adolf Endler, had even emigrated *to* the GDR, although there utopian hopes often met with sharp contradiction.[20] Thus, while the initial confiscations of the Junkers' vast landholdings were cheered by the intellectuals in the 1950s, the later recollectivizations, which took the land away from the peasants and returned it to the state, raised doubts in the same circles. The government swiftly promoted a cultural policy that criticized the so-called "bourgeois decadence" of the West by declaring official opposition to "formalism" in 1951. Stalin's death in March 1953 did little to change the cultural climate, for in April the writers' union declared its intention to eliminate formalism, cosmopolitanism, bourgeois liberalism, and pacifism.[21] A workers' uprising in Berlin in June of that same year—uncomfortably mirrored in Brecht's poems "The Solution" ("Die Lösung") and "Wretched Morning" ("Böser Morgen")—precipitated repressive measures.

Johannes R. Becher, who had been an important Expressionist poet, but whose own late verse was rhymed and blandly conventional, became the first Minister for Culture (1954–1958) and exercised considerable power in shaping an official canon of literature that promoted Social Realism in combination with a new literary humanism. Ironically, his name was appropriated for the "Literaturinstitut Johannes R. Becher" (Becher Literature Institute), though

20. Cf. Heinz Ludwig Arnold, ed., *Literatur in der DDR, Rückblicke* (München: Text + Kritik Sonderband, 1991); Wolfgang Emmerich, *Kleine Literaturgeschichte der DDR* (Darmstadt: Luchterhand, 1981); and Uwe Wittstock, *Von der Stalinallee zum Prenzlauer Berg* (München: Piper, 1989).
21. Arnold, 283.

Becher himself opposed the idea of an official school patterned after Soviet models on the grounds that such an institution would merely foster formalist imitation.[22]

At the Becher Institute, where many of the second generation of GDR writers learned their art, a remarkably liberal climate prevailed, even during the hard-line period that extended from 1961 to 1971 (when Erich Honecker became head of state). Within the institute, broad-minded poets, such as Erich Arendt, Georg Maurer, and Stephan Hermlin, encouraged younger writers. The training that they received there accounts in part for the solid craftsmanship that distinguishes East German poets of that generation. Impulses from Russian, Czech, Hungarian, and Polish, but also Spanish and South American, poetry were incorporated into the poetic canon by way of translations. Other writers variously stemmed the official tendency toward cultural isolationism vis-à-vis the West. Franz Fühmann in his essays promoted the next generation of GDR poets, notably Sarah Kirsch, and later Uwe Kolbe. Peter Huchel managed *Sinn und Form* (Sense and Form) from 1949 to 1962, rendering it the foremost literary journal in the country by his editorial integrity and high standards. Such acts took courage, for, as was to be the case with Huchel, the government could ban an author from publishing.

The insidious effects of censorship—enforced through official statements, de facto self-censorship, and an intricate, unpredictable system of paid informers—have only begun to come to light since the end of the GDR and will take years to evaluate. From the outset, literature was held in high esteem in the GDR, and favored authors received various kinds of assistance and support, yet this high status presupposed at least relative adherence to the official cultural policy. A GDR author who could not appear in print in the East might nevertheless be able to publish in the West, but explicit permission was required to avoid penalties. Sanctioned conceptions of literature, moreover, often proved short-lived. Thus, the "Bitterfelder Weg" ("Bitterfeld Path," named for the city where the writers' conference met in 1959) promoted the notion that the division between art and life should vanish,[23] yet few authors joined workers on the production line, and even fewer workers rose from the workers' writers' circles to become authors who could be taken seriously.

For GDR authors born in the teens and even twenties, the erosion of prewar certainties and the postwar cultural whims of the GDR government impinged on literature.[24] Fühmann, for one, struggled throughout his life with the successive burdens of Nazism, Stalinism, and GDR Socialism; after Kruschchev's

22. Jürgen Deppe, "Literaturinstitut Johannes R. Becher," *Literatur in der DDR*, ed. Arnold, 64.
23. Emmerich, 85–87.
24. Cf. Wittstock, 13.

1956 denunciation of Stalin, he ceased writing poetry. Another poet, Hermlin, adopted a stance of largely unbroken public silence as a reaction to criticism leveled against him within the GDR, publishing no new poetry after 1958. A broad sense of loss pervaded the work of Johannes Bobrowski, who rooted his verse and prose in history and the Baltic landscape where he was born and raised. Younger writers living in the GDR shared doubts about the past and present similar to those of their counterparts in the West. Günter Kunert, who during the Nazi regime had been denied an education because his mother was Jewish, evinced a deep skepticism about politics and history. Volker Braun, ten years younger, admonished his country in poem after poem to get on with the tasks of the Revolution, though his work resisted utopian illusions, while Helga Novak cited unsolved social problems.

By 1965, literary pundits, taking their lead from Cold War geography, had separated German literature into "East" and "West." Such divisions reflected the profound structural differences between the two countries, but were in many respects artificial since writers rarely defined their work by politics alone. Stylistically, GDR literature resists categorization as a distinct entity because neither language, cultural heritage, state control, nor any particular consensus among its best authors rendered it wholly separate from other German writing. Moreover, though a convenient division of authors within the GDR into groups of "committed Socialists" and "courageous dissidents" might be appealing, the boundaries between the two often become indistinguishably blurred due to the complicated effects of censorship and other variables of public policy.

The question of whether there is, or ever was, a GDR literature raises the long-standing dilemma of how to square the seemingly incompatible tendencies toward cultural regionalism and internationalism throughout the German-speaking area. From 1955 to 1965, international spirits ran high, albeit slanted westward or eastward, depending on where an author resided. The prestige of West German publishers rose as they gathered authors from throughout Europe into their houses. Parallel to these highly publicized international strivings, less acclaimed regional impulses have always thrived in German literature. Thus, besides savvy cosmopolitans such as Ingeborg Bachmann, Hilde Domin, and Hans Magnus Enzensberger, postwar German poetry includes authors like the Swiss Erika Burkart and Kurt Marti, whose work poignantly reflects the loss of poetry's traditional origins in undisturbed nature, or an anomalous figure like the Austrian Christine Lavant, who wrote and eked out a precarious living with knitting and farm work. Though provincialism per se became suspect after 1945 because it carried with it the implicit threat of isolationism, regional diversity nevertheless continued and helped guarantee the vitality of German verse.

Around 1965 a paradigmatic shift in poetry began as the postwar literary establishment opened to a new generation of authors. Change marked the politics of the era as well throughout Europe. In the FRG, where Erhard had been unable to reconcile disagreements within his government, Kurt Georg Kiesinger became chancellor in 1966 and formed the "Grand Coalition," which included both the conservative CDU/CSU and the Socialists. This alliance precipitated heated protests because it effectively eliminated any opposition at the federal level and, hence, was widely viewed as a challenge to the democratic principles on which the FRG had been founded. Kiesinger's background as a former Nazi who had worked in Goebbels' propaganda ministry raised further suspicions about his intentions. Youthful leftists responded by organizing the APO or *Ausserparlamentarische Opposition* (Extraparliamentary Opposition, a concept articulated by Rudi Dutschke, a student at the Free University in Berlin). Student demonstrations over the next several years protested the ossified German university system, the ultraconservative Springer publishing firm, the Shah of Iran's government, and also the Vietnam War. This unrest provoked passage of federal *Notstandsgesetze* (emergency laws), raising the specter that civil turmoil would be used as a pretext to suppress democratic rights of assembly.

The election of Willy Brandt (chancellor 1969–1974) ushered in a new era of politics in the FRG. The SPD and moderate FDP (Free Democratic Party) broke with the "Grand Coalition." Brandt's government, following his motto, "Mehr Demokratie wagen!" (Let's dare to have more democracy!) subsequently introduced improvements in health, education, and pension programs. Most significantly, Brandt opened a dialogue with the GDR, despite the objections of the conservative opposition. Through his *Ostpolitik* (Eastern Policy), the East and West began to normalize relations with a series of agreements (1970–1973) that gave up territorial claims with respect to Poland, Czechoslovakia, and the Soviet Union, recognized existing boundaries, and eased trade and travel between the two Germanies. For his efforts, Brandt was awarded the Nobel Peace Prize in 1971. Both the FRG and GDR were admitted to the United Nations in 1973, and the United States granted the GDR diplomatic recognition in 1974.

In Austria, the conservative chancellor Josef Klaus organized the first single-party cabinet of the postwar era after the People's Party won the 1966 elections with an absolute majority. The Socialists, however, gained a narrow victory four years later that resulted in the appointment of Bruno Kreisky as chancellor (1970–1983). Kreisky (who in sharp contrast to his predecessor's wartime background was Jewish) led the government in undertaking various social reforms, and in the next two elections the Socialist majority grew steadily. In Switzerland, the 1945–1990 period was marked by great calm, with mild protests registered following both the decision to equip the Swiss army with nuclear weapons (1958) and a resolution to extend voting privileges to women (1971).

During this turbulent decade, the changes that affected poetry involved major reassessments of its form and content. In 1965, a controversy started over the long poem. The debate began with Walter Höllerer's "Thesen zum langen Gedicht" ("Theses on the Long Poem"),[25] a programmatic statement that demanded the democratization of poetry and a rejection of hermetic verse's internalized silence. A zealous advocate of contemporary literature, Höllerer looked to international poetry, especially American plain style verse and the Beat writers, as his models. His principle opponent in the debate, Karl Krolow, a consummate poet of terse, crafted verse, objected to the sloppy writing that the long poem genre seemed likely to encourage.[26] While formal assumptions were being questioned, content also came under scrutiny. Rhymed verse was to all but disappear from the literary mainstream between 1965 and 1975, while extended writing, prose poems, ballads, broken line forms, and documentary montages became increasingly popular. No significant long poem appeared until the 1970s, and even then the genre led to mixed results.[27] All the while, though, a radical "discovery of reality" *(Entdeckung der Wirklichkeit)*[28] was turning poetry's attention to concrete detail with an unprecedented exclusivity.

This fresh preoccupation with reality had begun almost inconspicuously among older writers, like Eich and Höllerer, and evolved with the generation that included Enzensberger, Grass, and Rühmkorf. In the mid-1960s it emerged full force in the work of Rolf Dieter Brinkmann. A precocious talent, Brinkmann, born in 1940, helped revolutionize the German literary scene by promoting Pop poetry that radically employed everyday diction and trivial or taboo subject matter. Unlike many of his contemporaries, Brinkmann showed a fine sense of language, a keen eye for detail, and an adept command of radical techniques, such as splicing and montage. Inspiration for his work derived from counterculture attitudes and an interest in American writers (including Frank O'Hara, Ted Berrigan, William Carlos Williams, Robert Creeley, Gregory

25. Walter Höllerer, "Thesen zum langen Gedicht," *Akzente* 12, no. 2 (1965): 128–30.
26. Karl Krolow, "Das Problem des langen und kurzen Gedichts heute," *Akzente* 13, no. 3 (1966): 277.
27. Harald Hartung, "Warten auf das lange Gedicht," *Deutsche Lyrik seit 1965* (München: Piper, 1985), 66–82.
28. Cf. the discussion of Peter Hamm's essay by this title in Hartung, 66.

Corso, Allen Ginsberg, and William S. Burroughs), whose work he anthologized for European audiences.

The heightened literary interest in the neo- and neon-realism advanced by Brinkmann and others accompanied increasing involvement by writers in political affairs. Grass and other authors had actively supported Willy Brandt in his election campaign of 1965, *Gruppe 47* drafted resolutions on domestic and international political issues, and intellectuals now regularly joined the APO demonstrations.[29] Indeed, a prime target for the authors' discontents became the United States, especially its involvement in Vietnam. The intense disillusionment with the United States is traceable to the idealized vision of America and its liberal democracy that had evolved over the first two postwar decades. The Marshall Plan had been greeted with emotions ranging from gratitude to euphoria, while America's affluence and life style had for German youth made it a dream of mythical proportions to which they aspired. The horror of Vietnam and the attending suspicion that the U.S. version of democracy was a mere sham evoked reactions in the opposite direction and produced dystopian literary depictions of America. Many writers now looked to Third World countries, especially China and Cuba, for models of how literature should serve society.

Disenchantment with the United States as a political entity, however, was mitigated by a continuing fascination with its culture. Among German poets, the two waves of interest in American verse extended even to some of the most outspoken critics of U.S. foreign policy. An initial phase of reception in the late 1950s and early 1960s had introduced or reintroduced German audiences to Walt Whitman, Emily Dickinson, and American and British Modernists (Marianne Moore, Pound, Williams, Stein, Robert Frost, T. S. Eliot, W. H. Auden, Robert Lowell, and Randall Jarrell). At that time, nearly every German poet of note had become involved with translation from one or more languages. Among the younger authors eventually translated from English were Sylvia Plath and Anne Sexton, Charles Olson and Robert Creeley, Gregory Corso and Ted Hughes. For some German poets the experience of working in translation decisively shaped their own writing, an ironic fact in the case of Enzensberger, a prime mediator of American literature, who in the 1960s became known as one of the sharpest critics of the United States. The second wave of interest in American verse, the one that revolved around Brinkmann and his promotion of Beat and Pop poets shared this contradictory character. A reception of Allen Ginsberg, Lawrence Ferlinghetti, Frank O'Hara, and Charles Bukowski started in the 1960s and continued during the very time when anti-U.S. sentiment over the Vietnam War peaked. Interest in this literature still informed some of the

29. Cf. Parkes, especially 72–73.

Agitprop (agitation and propaganda poetry) that was to develop after the "death of literature" *(Tod der Literatur)* had been declared.

Rumors about literature's demise circulated in 1968, a year that witnessed a series of unsettling political events. First, the Viet Cong launched the "Tet" offensive and U.S. involvement in the conflict escalated. Then the Soviet Union invaded Czechoslovakia in August to crush the fledgling "Prague Spring" reform movement. Student unrest was mounting in both Europe and the United States. On the German literary scene, *Gruppe 47* disbanded and the University of Frankfurt discontinued its guest lectures in poetry. In the January 1968 issue of the influential, left-oriented periodical *Kursbuch* (Time Table), Hans Magnus Enzensberger, its editor, observed that literature seemed to have reached a dead end. He proposed a new kind of socially functional writing designed to make the public politically literate.[30] A shrewdly incisive critic, Enzensberger himself sounded no simplistic death knell for literature and turned instead to publishing documentary texts, though privately he still wrote poetry. Nonetheless, amidst the turbulent rhetorical climate, literature's ostensible demise took hold as a convenient and damning slogan. Touting relevance, but all too often lacking artistic merit, *Agitprop* proliferated and eclipsed more subtle, introspective verse. The lyric genre, which now found itself judged according to the political correctness of the day, seemed to have fallen on hard times.

But the dogmatism and confrontational postures gave way to disillusionment. Though politically the counterculture movement and protest demonstrations had effected modest change, much of the original incentive for international agitation dissipated as the Vietnam War drew to a close. Terrorist organizations, spawned as protests during the epoch, carried out brutal assassinations on an international scale. Red Army Faction leaders Andreas Baader (1943–1977) and Ulrike Meinhof (1934–1976) were jailed in the early 1970s, then died in prison under controversial circumstances. In the FRG, where laws banned organizations hostile to the state, individuals who had joined the protest movement as students found themselves faced with a *Berufsverbot* (banning from professions, in other words intense job discrimination), which effectively barred them from jobs as state employees (including positions as teachers) by virtue of past association with a radical group, a situation similar to American McCarthyism. Subdued resignation dampened the intellectual climate, and for a while poetry seemed to shrink to a marginal activity of little significance in a conservative society.

Out of this mood of political resignation, a new kind of poem emerged.

30. Hans Magnus Enzensberger, "Commonplaces on the Newest Literature," trans. Michael Roloff, *Critical Essays*, ed. Reinhold Grimm and Bruce Armstrong (New York: Continuum, 1982), 35–45.

Largely sundered from its political roots, the lyric genre moved in the direction of private monologue and confession, enlarging on the discovery of reality that had recently altered the language and content of German verse. Known under a variety of rubrics that noted its penchant for the common place and a subjective outlook, this *Alltagslyrik* (quotidian poetry), *Neue Innerlichkeit* (New Inwardness), or *Neue Subjektivität* (New Subjectivity) did not, however, develop without controversy. For many, New Subjectivity implied a solipsistic outlook that, in Erich Fried's words, tended "to recognize more and more/of less and less/and finally/to see everything/of nothing."[31] The grief over lost utopias that never were, or the tedious preoccupation with life's trivia, seemed to these critics at best boring and at worst offensive. German literature never developed a true equivalent to American confessional poetry, but New Subjectivity insisted on the personal element to a degree uncomfortable for a lyric tradition rooted in lofty *Gedankenlyrik* (philosophical poetry) and rarefied *Erlebnisdichtung* (poetry of experience). Nonetheless, the best authors writing in this style, among them Jürgen Becker, Nicolas Born, Peter Handke, Rolf Haufs, Jürgen Theobaldy, and Christoph Meckel, displayed an ear for common language and an eye for detail that would have been unthinkable a decade earlier. Simultaneously, too, dialect poetry blossomed. Writers of political conscience, who had never quite disappeared altogether (like Helga Novak, who was now writing prose poems and ballads), turned to domestic issues, such as the tension created by the presence of *Gastarbeiter* (foreign workers), especially those from Turkey.

The advent of New Subjectivity, and the accompanying shift in the aesthetic climate, coincided with the more vigorous presence of women on the literary scene of the 1970s. Feminist periodicals and editions published their work and women poets began to figure more and more prominently in contemporary anthologies.[32] Though some women poets, for instance Hilde Domin, Ilse Aichinger, and Christa Reinig, had already sustained their work over the course of decades, the public careers of many female writers took off considerably later than men and experienced more interruptions. Certainly, too, as perpetually marginalized artists, women authors rarely fit into convenient categories, almost never became part of literary groups, and therefore did not enjoy even the passing successes of fashionable trends.

Sarah Kirsch's career offers a case in point. Born in 1935, she first majored in biology at the University of Halle, and then studied writing at the Becher

31. Erich Fried, "Neue Subjektivität," in *Lyrik-Katalog Bundesrepublik*, ed. Jan Hans et al. (München: Goldman, 1978), 115–16; for a translation of the poem in its entirety in English, see *100 Poems Without a Country*, trans. Stuart Hood (New York: Red Dust, 1980), 146.
32. Cf. Susan L. Cocalis, *The Defiant Muse* (New York: The Feminist Press, 1986), xx.

Institute (1963–1965). Married for a time, a mother, she had authored a variety of collaborative and independent works, including children's books, before she began to earn significant recognition as a poet at the age of nearly forty. Her poems, often written in a seemingly naive tone, are in fact intricate, multilevel weavings of biographical, political, naturalist, and literary allusions that demand exceptionally attentive reading. At first, however, GDR critics unreceptive to this approach simply dismissed her verse as overly personal. Her poem "Schwarze Bohnen" ("Black Beans") drew a vehement attack in 1969 for breaking the taboo against private writing, but Kirsch slowly won acclaim for her work, published in the East and in the West, beginning with *Landaufenthalt* (Stay in the Country, 1967), *Zaubersprüche* (Magic Incantations, 1973), and *Rückenwind* (Tailwind, 1976).

Like Kirsch, women poets throughout the German-speaking area—Elisabeth Borchers, Ilse Tielsch, Helga Novak, Eva Strittmatter, and others—achieved substantial recognition in the seventies. Put quite simply, women poets—and now not just a few—were responsible for some of the best contemporary writing. During the next decade, they would become an even more important presence on the German literary scene.

1975–1990: From New Subjectivity to a "New World Order"

From 1945 to the mid-1970s, German poetry had developed largely along lines of contest, swinging from one aesthetic position to a contrasting stance in the space of a decade. Beginning around 1975, a more disparate pattern of development took hold. Pluralism and heterodoxy, and arguably a leaning toward postmodernism, became commonplace. In place of clearly defined schools and movements, or binary aesthetic conceptions based on rejections of the past, the German literary scene expanded in the direction of multiple trends and teeming, coexistent diversity.[33]

The 1960s heritage persisted in the belated emergence of long poems, the proliferation of documentary writing, and the sustained emphasis on realism. Aleatory writing, however, began to give way to an open concern with craft in poetry by Sarah Kirsch, Helga Novak, Guntram Vesper, Karin Kiwus, and others. After 1980, a renaissance of traditional forms surprised literary critics. Thematically, poems again addressed existential questions and brooded about

33. Cf. Hanns-Josef Ortheil, "Perioden des Abschieds: Zum Profil der neuen und jüngsten deutschen Literatur," *The German Quarterly* 63, no. 3/4 (1990): 367–376. For an account of recent German literature see also Peter Demetz, *After the Fires: Recent Writing in the Germanies, Austria and Switzerland* (San Diego: Harcourt Brace Jovanovich, 1986).

themselves, as in late work by Enzensberger, Eva Strittmatter, Krolow, Domin, and Jandl. The mood of resignation continued with modifications. More writers remained outwardly estranged from the political sphere, yet poetry took up controversies, such as gender issues, German-American relations, and environmental concerns, while disquieting political events intruded on literary life with increasing frequency as the 1980s unfolded.

In the FRG, Helmut Schmidt replaced Willy Brandt as chancellor (1974–1982), maintaining a coalition of socialist and liberal parties that enabled passage of reform legislation, such as the laws legalizing abortion and no-fault divorce. The FRG became a central figure in the international community, a leader in the Common Market and a member of the European parliament first elected in 1979. Cooperation between France and Germany, traditional adversaries, grew. In 1982, at a time when conservative fortunes worldwide seemed on the rise with Reagan in the United States and Thatcher in England, the moderate FDP left the Schmidt coalition and joined the CDU/CSU. Helmut Kohl took over as chancellor, ushering in a conservative government. Despite this trend, the Green Party *(Die Grünen)*, which had been founded on a local level in 1980 to address environmental issues, won the necessary 5 percent of the popular vote in the 1983 elections to secure seats in the *Bundestag* (or parliament).

Notwithstanding the FRG's enhanced international prestige and Kohl's presentation of himself as a politician untainted by Fascism since he was born in 1930, the Nazi past remained a sensitive issue for Germans and Austrians alike, partly because a number of prominent politicians had questionable backgrounds. In the FRG, these included the conservative Karl Carstens (president 1979–1984). On the other hand, his successor Richard von Weizsäcker, whose father had been Hitler's representative to the Vatican, called upon his countrymen on the fortieth anniversary of the war's end to face the past honestly as the only route toward a credible future. Two years later, by contrast, Austria elected the former United Nations Secretary General, Kurt Waldheim, president (1986–1992), disregarding a storm of international protest over revelations concerning his much denied role in repression and deportations in Yugoslavia during the war.

The GDR, as well, was to experience its own crises. A cultural thaw began in 1971 when Erich Honecker became head of state, but soon a chill descended again. Wolf Biermann, known for his provocative songs, had his citizenship revoked by the GDR government while he was on a concert tour in the FRG in November 1976. The action prompted a quick response by GDR authors, who drafted a petition of protest. The signatories eventually included 150 writers and intellectuals, among them poets Sarah Kirsch, Volker Braun, Stephan

Hermlin, Günter Kunert, and Erich Arendt. In the wake of the "Biermann affair," the GDR instigated a variety of harsh measures. A number of authors were jailed, most were spied on or harassed by authorities, and still others expelled or unsubtly encouraged to remain abroad.

On both sides of the border, broadly related social and ecological issues gained public attention. As baby boomers came of age, housing shortages in the FRG grew so acute that *Hausbesetzer* (squatters) occupied vacant buildings. The oil crisis (1973–1974) necessitated curbed consumption and permanently raised energy prices, even as new construction of atomic energy facilities prompted antinuclear demonstrations. By the mid-1970s, Germany's beloved forests were visibly dying from the effects of acid rain. Then, too, the stationing of Pershing missiles in Europe proposed by the Reagan administration in 1983 provoked heated debates, a stronger peace movement, and renewed anti-American sentiments. GDR ecology groups comparable to those in the West became active in the mid to late 1980s and expressed concern over human rights violations, armament, and the appalling environmental pollution in cities like Berlin, Dresden, and Leipzig. Ultimately such protest gatherings formed one basis for the reform movement that challenged the East German government.

Amid these quite obvious threats to the world's environment, nature poetry experienced a resurgence. Unlike early postwar verse, it voiced the lament that the recourse to nature so fundamental to traditional conceptions of the lyric genre had been irrevocably lost. Günter Eich in 1955 could still draw a line of attachment between the poetic observer and the natural world by musing, "Who would want to live without the solace of trees!" By the 1980s, however, Erika Burkart in "Homo Faber" ("Man the Maker") described man's ineluctable estrangement from nature in an age of spreading commercial development. The state of the environment was also becoming an urgent topic in the GDR in poetry by Heinz Czechowski, Thomas Rosenlöcher, and Wolfgang Hilbig, to name representative authors. Concurrent with this thematic shift, poetry began to reflect the polarization of society along gender lines. A provocatively masculine stance colors work by Wolf Wondratschek, Jürgen Theobaldy, and others. Women poets recast legends in feminist versions, as in Helga Novak's rewritings of the Medea and Orpheus myths, or Novak's and Ilse Aichinger's accounts of the St. Martin legend. Others, notably Ursula Kreche and Hannelies Taschau, confidently defined the feminist position, or, like Karin Kiwus and Friederike Roth, explored the nuances and failures of cross-gender dialogue.

Given the conspicuous absence of coherent literary schools, the renaissance of form that began in the early 1980s seemed as startling as the "discovery of reality" that had occurred a decade earlier. This second debut of rhyme and traditional forms played to an equivocal audience. The new formalism was criticized for providing no fresh poetic insights, lapsing into conventionality, and super-imposing bald literary devices on the quotidian tone and prosaic language of the New Subjectivity it replaced. Ulla Hahn, a noteworthy example of this trend, met with highly mixed reviews for her collection *Spielende* (People Playing *or* Woman Playing *or* End of the Game, 1983). Some critics lauded its rhymed verse, while others viewed its poetic forms as hollow gesture and sus-pected studied traditionalism. The lyric genre also turned to a second tradi-tional source of inspiration, the realm of emotions, as in the work of Julian [Jutta] Schutting, who published *Liebesgedichte* (Love Poems, 1982). Such poetry had obvious pitfalls, but for older writers, unscathed by youthful dilem-mas about nostalgic content, the revival of form hardly represented any break in their careers. Peter Rühmkorf had penned rhymed verse even at the height of New Subjectivity, insistently maintaining his unique position as a satirist who believed in the magic and vitality of poetic device.[34] Karl Krolow, who had begun by writing exquisite rhymed verse, late in his career turned back to those origins. Eva Strittmatter, in the GDR, never deviated from short, tightly con-structed, rhymed texts. Besides this revival of formalism and intimate content, experimental verse prospered. Oskar Pastior, who had begun his career in the late 1960s, increasingly attracted attention among poets with his stunning lan-guage experiments. East German writers, too, such as Elke Erb and Kito Lorenc, independently worked on poetry that both manipulated and unmasked the manipulation of language.[35]

Such drastic pluralism—coupled with the blurring of boundaries between the mass media and literature and the renewed impact of international cultural influences—has transformed recent German literature and brought it into a phase of postmodernism.[36] In contemporary German poetry, as elsewhere, ap-propriative pastiche techniques abound[37] as writers create texts that overtly ac-knowledge the ahistorical discontinuities of contemporary life, the fragmenta-tion of traditions, and the artifice of artistic creation. Dramatic political events of the late 1980s, too, provided a foil for the sense of fragmentation infiltrating

34. Peter Rühmkorf, "Kein Apolloprogramm für Lyrik," *Lyrik-Katalog Bundesrepublik*, ed. Jans Hans et al. (München: Goldmann, 1978), 419–422.

35. Cf. Peter Geist, "Voices from No Man's Land: Recent German Poetry," trans. Friederike Ei-gler, *Cultural Transformations in the New Germany: American and German Perspectives*, Columbia, S.C.: Camden House, 1993, 132–53.

36. Cf. Ortheil, 376; Paul Michael Lützeler, "Einleitung: Von der Spätmoderne zur Postmod-erne—Die deutschsprachige Literatur der achtziger Jahre," *The German Quarterly* 63, no. 3/4 (1990): 351; Reinhold Grimm, "More Poetry from Germany," *Pembroke Magazine* 26 (1994): 126–30; and the Winter 1997 (vol. 21, no. 1) issue of *Studies in Twentieth Century Literature*, ed. James Rolleston, which was devoted to recent German poetry.

37. Fredric Jameson, "Postmodernism and Consumer Society," *The Anti-Aesthetic*, ed. Hal Fos-ter (Port Townsend: Bay Press, 1983), 113 ff.

literature. In 1986–1987, Romania expelled a number of authors who belonged to its German-speaking minority, including Rolf Bossert and Richard Wagner, whose work began to attract attention in the FRG. Meanwhile, a group of young GDR writers, many of whom lived in the *Prenzlauer Berg* section of East Berlin, had begun to create a name for themselves. The authors loosely associated with this group, Uwe Kolbe, Stefan Döring, Lutz Rathenow, Rainer Schedlinski, and Bert Papenfuss-Gorek, initially had little contact with each other, but were brought together for readings and gatherings under the encouragement of Elke Erb and Sascha Anderson, who, in a strange twist of fate, later turned out to have been a *Stasi* (GDR secret police) informer. Their stylistically diverse work shared an antiestablishment content and radical experimentation with language. All of them were born after 1945 and belonged to the generation that had grown up exclusively under socialism.

An exodus of GDR intellectuals had been underway since the Biermann affair. In the 1980s it continued with the emigration of poets Hilbig, Anderson, Kolbe, Gabriele Eckart, and many other writers, while a general crisis mounted in the East. Hungary began dismantling its border in May 1989, just days before a huge demonstration in Leipzig protested government tampering in recent communal elections. In August, a mass exodus through embassies and across southern borders began from the GDR to the West. The GDR's fortieth anniversary celebration ironically became its last. After months of tension, the border between East and West Berlin was opened on November 9, 1989.

But the jubilant crowds scanned by television cameras on that fall night were gone by 1990, the year that brought the reunification of the two Germanies. The intervening months had tempered the initial euphoria over the Communist collapse with pessimism about how the economic and social disparities between East and West would be resolved. Under the economic strain of reunification, latent social problems became more pressing in both Germanies, but particularly in the East, where hostility toward foreigners resulted in ugly attacks on asylum seekers. Literary debates simmered over the complicity or innocence of writers under the former GDR regime, the need for a new *Vergangenheitsbewältigung*, and earnest concerns about the economic future of authors and publishing firms in the East. At the time, for example, disinterest in GDR writers was so complete that bookstores in the East cleared their shelves, and in some cases simply dumped books in the trash.

German Poetry in Transition concludes with selections written at this point when Cold War political divisions were just ending. The fact that, as Celan advocated, these poems show so much mindfulness of their dates gives striking evidence of a continuity between recent verse and literature of the immediate postwar years. Yet poetry by authors writing in German has in other respects fundamentally changed since 1945. The lyric genre has moved beyond the pattern of agonistic stimulation that motivated its metamorphosis in the first postwar decades. To be sure, debate over the ethical responsibilities of writers was rekindled by revelations about the recent past. Nonetheless, one of the few discernible trends in German-language poetry has been a pronounced disinclination on the part of writers and anthologists to promote exclusive prescriptions for literature in the wake of the clear political transformations marked by the year 1990; as a result, an atmosphere of congenial tolerance for widely divergent forms of poetry gives every indication of persisting.

1945–1955

Ends, Continuities, and Beginnings

Hammering, she knocked the rust off the plow ...

Wilhelm Lehmann

Unberühmter Ort

Septemberpause, da schweigt der Wind.
Unter hohem Himmel, bei Hafergebind,
Chronist, memorier
Geschwindes Jetzt, veränderliches Hier.
Den unberühmten Ort
Bemerkte kein schallendes Wort.
Nie hat er Charlemagne gesehn,
Auch keine Schlacht is ihm geschehn.
Die Hecken tapeziert der Harlekin mit Flügelseide,
Sie stünde Kaiser Karl wie Hermelin zum Kleide.
Der Apfel bleibt liegen, wohin er fiel;
Den Sand des Weges schlitzt ein Bauernwagen;
Die Stare sammeln sich. Sie halten Konzil.
Hör zu, Chronist, schreib mit, was sie sagen.

Deutsche Zeit 1947

Blechdose rostet, Baumstumpf schreit.
Der Wind greint. Jammert ihn die Zeit?
Spitz das Gesicht, der Magen leer,
Den Krähen selbst kein Abfall mehr.

Verlangt nach Lust der dürre Leib,
Für Brot verkauft sich Mann und Weib.
Ich lache nicht, ich weine nicht,
Zu Ende gehr das Weltgedicht.

Da seine Strophe sich verlor,
Die letzte, dem ertaubten Ohr,
Hat sich die Erde aufgemacht,
Aus Winterohnmacht spät erwacht.

Wilhelm Lehmann

Unrenowned Place

September pause, the wind falls still.
With lofty sky, oat harvest near,
Chronicler, take up your quill
For the fleeting Now, the shifting Here.
Unrenowned place—
No sonorous word left its trace.
Never saw Charlemagne.
No battle befell its domain.
With dragonfly silk harlequin decks the hedges,
Befitting King Charles like garments with ermine edges.
The apple lies wherever it lands;
A farmer's wagon cuts the sands.
The starlings gather. They hold council day.
Listen well, chronicler, write down what they say.

German Times 1947

A tin can rusts, a tree stump whines,
The wind complains. About the times?
Stomachs empty, faces gaunt,
No garbage for the crows to haunt.

If skin and bones still lust for life
They're sold for bread by man and wife.
I cannot laugh, or cry, or moan,
The world's song strikes its final tone.

But when its stanzas disappear,
The last ones to the deafened ear,
The earth and every hill and dell
Awaken late from winter's spell.

Zwar schlug das Beil die Hügel kahl,
Versuch, versuch es noch einmal.
Sie mischt und siebt mit weiser Hand:
In Wangenglut entbrennt der Hang,
Zu Anemone wird der Sand.

Sie eilen, grämlichen Gesichts.
Es blüht vorbei. Es ist ein Nichts.
Mißglückter Zauber? Er gelang.
Ich bin genährt. Ich hör Gesang.

■ Elisabeth Langgässer

Vergehender Frühling

Abgeblüht ist schon das weiße
Ackerhornkraut, und das Zelt,
welches die Larve, die leise,
lila umschäumte, zerfällt.
Löwenzahn löschte die Lampe,
Lerchensporn samte geschwind,
Brennessel trat vor die Rampe,
Schwalbenflug schreibt in den Wind:
—Blaß wie auf brüchiger Seide—
lobe das Urbild und scheide!
Dulde Verwandlung und eile
von der Erscheinung zum Sinn.
Fürchte dich nicht vor der Feile
emsiger Grillen. Ich bin
noch überm Grab des Osiris,
aber du selbst bist schon fort,
wenn dich mit Schwertern der Iris
Hingang des Frühlings durchbohrt.
Unser die brüchige Seide
irdischer Dauer. Du scheide!

Though the ax laid bare that hill
Just try once more to try it still.
Earth mixed and filtered with wise hand,
The slope breaks out in purple blush,
Anemones bedeck the sand.

They rush on, faces old and grieved.
The bloom will pass, we are deceived.
A magic failed? No, not for long.
I have been fed. I hear the song.

■ Elisabeth Langgässer

Vanishing Spring

Already now the white is spent
of field chickweed, and the froth
that shaped the violet larva tent
decays around the silent moth.
Dandelion snuffed its lamp,
corydalis seeded there,
nettle walked the hillside ramp,
swallow flights trace the air:
—Pale as on silk they write—
laud the ideal and take flight!
Suffer renewal and hurry
from the mere semblance to sense.
Fear not the busy worry
of cricket rasp. I abide
still over the grave of Osiris
but you are already hence
when with the swords of iris
spring's passing pierces your side.
Ours the fragile silk weave
of earthly span. Take your leave!

■ **Günter Eich**

Inventur

Dies ist meine Mütze,
dies ist mein Mantel,
hier mein Rasierzeug
im Beutel aus Leinen.

Konservenbüchse:
Mein Teller, mein Becher,
ich hab in das Weißblech
den Namen geritzt.

Geritzt hier mit diesem
kostbaren Nagel,
den vor begehrlichen
Augen ich berge.

Im Brotbeutel sind
ein Paar wollene Socken
und einiges, was ich
niemand verrate,

so dient es als Kissen
nachts meinem Kopf.
Die Pappe hier liegt
zwischen mir und der Erde.

Die Bleistiftmine
lieb ich am meisten:
Tags schreibt sie mir Verse,
die nachts ich erdacht.

Dies ist mein Notizbuch,
dies meine Zeltbahn,
dies ist mein Handtuch,
dies ist mein Zwirn.

Günter Eich

Inventory

This is my cap,
this is my coat,
here is my shaving set
in a linen bag.

A tin can:
my plate, my cup,
in the metal
I have scratched my name.

Scratched it with this
precious nail,
which I hide
from greedy eyes.

In my haversack are
a pair of woolen socks
and some things I don't
tell anyone about,

it serves as a pillow
at night for my head.
The cardboard lies here
between me and the earth.

The pencil lead
I love the most:
by day it writes verses for me
that I have thought up by night.

This is my notebook,
this is my canvas,
this is my towel,
this is my thread.

Betrachtet die Fingerspitzen

Betrachtet die Fingerspitzen, ob sie sich schon verfärben!
Eines Tages kommt sie wieder, die ausgerottete Pest.
Der Postbote wirft sie als Brief in den rasselnden Kasten,
Als eine Zuteilung von Heringen liegt sie dir im Teller,
Die Mutter reicht sie dem Kinde als Brust.

Was tun wir,
Da niemand mehr lebt von denen, die mit ihr umzugehen wußten?
Wer mit dem Entsetzlichen gut Freund ist, kann seinen Besuch in Ruhe erwarten.
Wir richten uns immer wieder auf das Glück ein,
Aber es sitzt nicht gern aus unseren Sesseln.

Betrachtet die Fingerspitzen! Wenn sie sich schwarz färben,
Ist es zu spät.

Ende eines Sommers

Wer möchte leben ohne den Trost der Bäume!

Wie gut, daß sie am Sterben teilhaben!
Die Pfirsiche sind geerntet, die Pflaumen färben sich,
während unter dem Brückenbogen die Zeit rauscht.

Dem Vogelzug vertraue ich meine Verzweiflung an.
Er mißt seinen Teil von Ewigkeit gelassen ab.
Seine Strecken
werden sichtbar im Blattwerk als dunkler Zwang,
die Bewegung der Flügel färbt die Früchte.

Es heißt Geduld haben.
Bald wird die Vogelschrift entsiegelt,
unter der Zunge ist der Pfennig zu schmecken.

Watch Your Fingertips

Watch your fingertips, aren't they changing color already?
One day it will come back, that exterminated plague.
The postman drops it as a letter in your rattling mailbox,
As a herring ration it lies on your plate,
The mother gives it to her child with her breast.

What will we do,
Since no one of those who knew how to handle it is still alive?
Whoever is on friendly terms with the terrifying can calmly wait for its visit.
Again and again, we get ready for happiness,
But happiness doesn't like to sit on our chairs.

Watch your fingertips! When they turn black,
It's too late.

End of a Summer

Who would want to live without the solace of trees!

How good that they partake of dying!
The peaches are harvested, the plums color,
while under the bridge's arch time rushes on.

My despair I confide to the migrating flock.
It casually measures out its lot from eternity.
Its extents
become visible in the foliage as dark compulsion,
the movement of wings colors the fruits.

Patience is needed.
Soon the bird's calligraphy will be unsealed,
under the tongue you can taste the coin.

Karl Krolow

Mahlzeit unter Bäumen

Sitzen im gefleckten Schatten.
Luft kommt lau wie Milch gestrichen.
Kreis hat zaubrisch sich gezogen,
Und die Hitze ist gewichen.

Sicheln, die wie Nattern zischten,
Klirrten am erschrocknen Steine.
Grüne Glut drang aus der Wiese.
Distel biß am bloßen Beine.

Durch die Feuer der Kamille
Flohen wir auf blanker Sohle
Heuumwirbelt, in die Kühle
Von Lavendel und Viole.

Stille summt Käferflügel.
Ruhn, vom Ahorn schwarz umgittert.
Auge schmerzt vom Staub der Kräuter,
Der im lauten Lichte zittert.

Und wir schneiden Brot und Käse.
Weißer Wein läuft uns am Kinne.
Des gelösten Geists der Pflaume,
Werden wir in Fleische inne.

Hände wandern überm Korbe.
Fester Mund, er ward verhießen.
Welche Glieder, braun geschaffen,
Im bewegten Laube fließen.

■ Karl Krolow

Repast under Trees

Sitting in dappled shadows.
Milk-lukewarm breezes drift.
Circle magically inscribed,
And the heat begins to lift.

Sickles hissing like vipers
Clattered on startled stone.
Green swelled from the pasture.
Thistle bit bare ankle bone.

Through the chamomile fire
We fled on bare feet
In a whirlwind of hay
To lavender cool and sweet.

Beetle wing hums stillness.
Rest within black maple fence.
Eyes are smarting from weed pollen
Trembling bright and dense.

And we cut cheese and bread.
White wine runs down the chin.
Unfettered plum spirits spread,
Waken our flesh within.

Hands stray across the basket.
Firm mouth willing to surrender.
Flowing in rustled foliage,
Pliant limbs, brown and slender.

Worte

Einfalt erfundener Worte,
Die man hinter Türen spricht,
Aus Fenstern und gegen die Mauern,
Gekalkt mit geduldigem Licht.

Wirklichkeit von Vokabeln,
Von zwei Silben oder von drei'n:
Aus den Rätseln des Himmels geschnitten,
Aus einer Ader im Stein.

Entzifferung fremder Gesichter
Mit Blitzen unter der Haut,
Mit Bärten, in denen der Wind steht,
Durch einen geflüsterten Laut.

Aber die Namen bleiben
Im Ohre nur ein Gesumm
Wie von Zikaden und Bienen,
Kehren ins Schweigen um.

Vokale—geringe Insekten
Unsichtbar über der Luft,
Fallen als Asche nieder,
Bleiben als Quittenduft.

■ Gottfried Benn

Teils-teils

In meinem Elternhaus hingen keine Gainsboroughs
wurde auch kein Chopin gespielt
ganz amusisches Gedankenleben
mein Vater war einmal im Theater gewesen

Words

Candor of words invented,
Said behind doors out of sight,
From windows and to blank walls,
White-washed with patient light.

Reality of words spoken,
Of two syllables or three:
Cut from the riddles of heaven,
From a vein in the stone set free.

Deciphering of strangers' faces
With lightning under the skin,
With beards that the wind catches,
By a sound, whispered within.

And yet the names will remain,
A hum in the ear, so slight,
Like bees and cicadas, they return
Into the silence of night.

Vowels—those humble insects,
Invisible in the air,
Floating down like ashes,
Linger as quince scent there.

■ Gottfried Benn

Half Here, Half There

No Gainsboroughs hung in my parents' home
nobody played Chopin
the muses enjoyed no great status
my father had been to the theater once

Anfang des Jahrhunderts
Wildenbruchs »Haubenlerche«
davon zehrten wir
das war alles.

Nun längst zu Ende
graue Herzen, graue Haare
der Garten in polnischem Besitz
die Gräber teils-teils
aber alle slawisch,
Oder-Neiße-Linie
für Sarginhalte ohne Belang
die Kinder denken an sie
die Gatten auch noch eine Weile
teils-teils
bis sie weiter müssen
Sela, Psalmenende.

Heute noch in einer Großstadtnacht
Caféterrasse
Sommersterne,
vom Nebentisch
Hotelqualitäten in Frankfurt
Vergleiche,
die Damen unbefriedigt
wenn ihre Sehnsucht Gewicht hätte
wöge jede drei Zentner.

Aber ein Fluidum! Heiße Nacht
à la Reiseprospekt und
die Ladies treten aus ihren Bildern:
unwahrscheinliche Beauties
langbeinig, hoher Wasserfall
über ihre Hingabe kann man sich gar nicht erlauben
nachzudenken.

at the turn of the century
Wildenbruch's "Meadow Lark" or something,
our bit of culture
and that was it.

All gone now
gray hearts, gray hair
the garden in Polish territory
the graves half here, half there
but all Slavic,
Oder-Neisse line—
the contents of coffins couldn't care less
the children think of them
spouses, still too, for a while
half here, half there
until they have to move on.
Selah, thus ends the psalm.

Even tonight in the metropolis
a café terrace
summer stars,
from the next table
the quality of hotels in Frankfurt
comparisons,
the ladies dissatisfied,
if their frustrations had any weight
they would each weigh a ton.

But what atmosphere! Sultry night
à la travel folders and
the ladies step out of their pictures:
improbable beauties
long-legged, high waterfall
who would even dare think of them
in bed.

Ehepaare fallen demgegenüber ab,
kommen nicht an, Bälle gehn ins Netz,
er raucht, sie dreht ihre Ringe,
überhaupt nachdenkenswert
Verhältnis von Ehe und Mannesschaffen
Lähmung oder Hochtrieb.

Fragen, Fragen! Erinnerungen in einer Sommernacht
hingeblinzelt, hingestrichen,
in meinem Elternhaus hingen keine Gainsboroughs
nun alles abgesunken
teils-teils das Ganze
Sela, Psalmenende.

Fragment (1955)

30 x unter Qualen die Zähne plombieren lassen
100 x Rosen aus dem Süden gehabt
4 x an Gräbern geweint
25 Frauen verlassen
2 x die Tasche voll Geld u 98 x ohne Geld gehabt,
Schliesslich tritt man in eine Versicherung ein mit
12 50 pro Monat um
seine Beerdigung sicher zu stellen

Kann keine Trauer sein

In jenem kleinen Bett, fast Kinderbett, starb die Droste
(zu sehn in ihrem Museum in Meersburg),
auf diesem Sofa Hölderin im Turm bei einem Schreiner,
Rilke, George wohl in Schweizer Hospitalbetten,
in Weimar lagen die großen schwarzen Augen
Nietzsches auf einem weißen Kissen
bis zum letzten Blick—
alles Gerümpel jetzt oder gar nicht mehr vorhanden
unbestimmbar, wesenlos
im schmerzlos-ewigen Zerfall.

Married couples run a poor second
never make it somehow, balls land in the net
he smokes, she fiddles with her rings
worth a thought, incidentally:
the relation of marriage to a man's creativity—
paralysis or outpouring.

Questions, questions! Memories on a summer night
jotted down, scribbled over
no Gainsboroughs hung in my parents' home
all gone under now
half here, half there the lot
Selah, thus ends the psalm.

Fragment (1955)

30 x had your teeth filled in utter agony
100 x heard "Roses from the South"
4 x wept at graves
25 x left women
2 x pockets full of money, 98 x without money,
Finally you get insurance
for 5 bucks a month
to make sure your burial expenses are covered

Can Be No Mourning

In that tiny bed, a child's bed almost, Droste died
(on view in her museum in Meersburg),
on this sofa Hölderlin in a cabinetmaker's tower,
Rilke, George, it is true, in Swiss hospital beds,
in Weimar the large dark eyes
of Nietzsche rested on a white pillow
till his last glance—
all of it rubbish or no longer around,
indeterminable, insubstantial
in painless, permanent decay.

Wir tragen in uns Keime aller Götter,
das Gen des Todes und das Gen der Lust—
wer trennte sie: die Worte und die Dinge,
wer mischte sie: die Qualen und die Statt,
auf der sie enden, Holz mit Tränenbächen,
für kurze Stunden ein erbärmlich Heim.

Kann keine Trauer sein. Zu fern, zu weit,
zu unberührbar Bett und Tränen,
kein Nein, kein Ja,
Geburt und Körperschmerz und Glauben
ein Wallen, namenlos, ein Huschen,
ein Überirdisches, im Schlaf sich regend,
bewegte Bett und Tränen—
schlafe ein!

■ Walter Höllerer

Der lag besonders mühelos am Rand

Der lag besonders mühelos am Rand
Des Weges. Seine Wimpern hingen
Schwer und zufrieden in die Augenschatten.
Man hätte meinen können, daß er schliefe.

Aber sein Rücken war (wir trugen ihn,
Den Schweren, etwas abseits, denn er störte sehr
Kolonnen, die sich drängten) dieser Rücken
War nur ein roter Lappen, weiter nichts.

Und seine Hand (wir konnten dann den Witz
Nicht oft erzählen, beide haben wir
Ihn schnell vergessen) hatte, wie ein Schwert,
Den hartgefrorenen Pferdemist gefaßt,

We bear within us seeds of all gods,
the gene of death, the gene of lust—
who sundered them: the words, the objects,
who mixed them: the pains and the place
where they end, wood with streams of tears,
for a few short hours a miserable home.

Can be no mourning. Too far, too vast,
too far removed now bed and tears,
no No, no Yes,
birth and bodily pain and faith
a welling, nameless, a flicker,
something unearthly stirring in its sleep
moved bed and tears—
go to sleep!

■ Walter Höllerer

He Lay So Strangely Relaxed by the Side

He lay so strangely relaxed by the side
Of the road. His lashes hung
Heavy and content in the shadows under his eyes.
One could have thought he was asleep.

But his back was (we carried him, the heavy hunk,
A little aside because he sure disrupted
The columns that crowded past) this back
Was just a red rag, nothing more.

And his hand (we couldn't tell the joke
Often then, we both forgot
It quickly) had clutched like a sword
The solidly frozen horse dung,

Den Apfel, gelb und starr,
Als wär es Erde oder auch ein Arm
Oder ein Kreuz, ein Gott: ich weiß nicht was.
Wir trugen ihn da weg und in den Schnee.

■ Marie Luise Kaschnitz

Vater Feuerwerker

Zucker und Honig in Deinen Brei
Die Erde Dein Gärtchen Levkoi und Salbei
Deine Wangen Milch Deine Lippen Blut
Frag nicht, was Dein Vater tut
Nachts wenn du schläfst.

Er rührt im Tiegel
Hinter Schloß und Riegel
Aus Pulver und Blei
Einen anderen Brei.

Er sät im Dorn
Ein anderes Korn
Das wühlt und bebt
Und schießt gen Himmel in Garben.

Wohl denen die gelebt
Ehe sie starben.

Am Strand

Heute sah ich wieder dich am Strand
Schaum der Wellen dir zu Füßen trieb
Mit dem Finger grubst du in den Sand
Zeichen ein, von denen keines blieb.

The apple, yellow and rigid,
As if it were earth or else an arm
Or a cross, a god: I don't know what.
We carried him off and into the snow.

■ Marie Luise Kaschnitz

Pyrotechnist Father

Sugar and honey into your brew
The earth Your small garden sage and feverfew
Your cheeks milk Your lips blood red
Ask not what Your father does
At night when you sleep in bed.

In the crucible he concocts
Behind bolts and locks
From gunpowder and lead
Another brew instead.

He sows in the thorn
A different corn
To quake and rive
And shoot toward heaven afire.

Good for those who were alive
Before they expire.

At the Beach

Today again I saw you on the strand,
At your feet the wave's foam chased,
While you dug your fingers in the sand,
Drawing signs that left no trace.

Ganz versunken warst du in dein Spiel
Mit der ewigen Vergänglichkeit
Welle kam und Stern und Kreis zerfiel
Welle ging und du warst neu bereit.

Lachend hast du dich zu mir gewandt
Ahntest nicht den Schmerz, den ich erfuhr:
Denn die schönste Welle zog zum Strand
Und sie löschte deiner Füße Spur.

■ Ingeborg Bachmann

Alle Tage

Der Krieg wird nicht mehr erklärt,
sondern fortgesetzt. Das Unerhörte
ist alltäglich geworden. Der Held
bleibt den Kämpfen fern. Der Schwache
ist in die Feuerzonen gerückt.
Die Uniform des Tages ist die Geduld,
die Auszeichnung der armselige Stern
der Hoffnung über dem Herzen.

Er wird verliehen,
wenn nichts mehr geschieht,
wenn das Trommelfeuer verstummt,
wenn der Feind unsichtbar geworden ist
und der Schatten ewiger Rüstung
den Himmel bedeckt.

Er wird verliehen
für die Flucht von den Fahnen,
für die Tapferkeit vor dem Freund,
für den Verrat unwürdiger Geheimnisse
und die Nichtachtung
jeglichen Befehls.

Totally engrossed you were in play,
With that transience that's absolute;
Wave came in, and star and circle washed away
Wave went out, you followed your pursuit.

Laughingly you turned to me,
Could not guess the pain I knew:
For the fairest wave that rode the sea
Swept ashore and drowned your footprints too.

■ Ingeborg Bachmann

Every Day

War is no longer declared
but simply continued. The unheard of
occurs every day. The hero
stays far from the battles. The weakling
has moved into the firing zones.
The uniform of the day is patience,
the medal, the wretched star
of hope over the heart.

It is awarded
when nothing happens any more,
when the drum fire dies down,
when the enemy has become invisible
and the shadow of eternal armament
covers the sky.

It is awarded
for deserting the flag,
for courage in face of the friend,
for the betrayal of despicable secrets
and for the defiance
of every order.

Die gestundete Zeit

Es kommen härtere Tage.
Die auf Widerruf gestundete Zeit
wird sichtbar am Horizont.
Bald mußt du den Schuh schnüren
und die Hunde zurückjagen in die Marschhöfe.

Denn die Eingeweide der Fische
sind kalt geworden im Wind.
Ärmlich brennt das Licht der Lupinen.
Dein Blick spurt im Nebel:
die auf Widerruf gestundete Zeit
wird sichtbar am Horizont.

Drüben versinkt dir die Geliebte im Sand,
er steigt um ihr wehendes Haar,
er fällt ihr ins Wort,
er befiehlt ihr zu schweigen,
er findet sie sterblich
und willig dem Abschied
nach jeder Umarmung.

Sieh dich nicht um.
Schnür deinen Schuh.
Jag die Hunde zurück.
Wirf die Fische ins Meer.
Lösch die Lupinen!

Es kommen härtere Tage.

Fall ab, Herz

Fall ab, Herz, vom Baum der Zeit,
fallt, ihr Blätter, aus den erkalteten Ästen,
die einst die Sinne umarmt',
fallt, wie Tränen fallen aus dem geweiteten Aug!

Time Deferred

The days to come will be harder.
That time, deferred only until revoked,
appears on the horizon.
Soon you will have to lace your shoe
and chase the dogs back to the marshland farms.

For the fish entrails
have turned cold in the wind.
The light of the lupines burns poorly.
Your eyes make out in the fog:
that time, deferred only until revoked,
appears on the horizon.

Over there your lover is sinking in sand,
it rises around her blowing hair,
cuts her words short,
it assigns her to silence,
proves her mortal
and willing to part
after every embrace.

Do not look around.
Lace your shoe.
Chase the dogs back.
Throw the fish into the sea.
Snuff out the lupines!

The days to come will be harder.

Fall Off, Heart

Fall off, heart, fall from time's tree,
fall, you leaves, from the chilled branches
that once embraced the sun,
fall like tears from a widened eye!

Fliegt noch die Locke taglang im Wind
um des Landgottes gebräunte Stirn,
unter dem Hemd preßt die Faust
schon die klaffende Wunde.

Drum sei hart, wenn der zarte Rücken der Wolken
sich dir einmal noch beugt,
nimm es für nichts, wenn der Hymettos die Waben
noch einmal dir füllt.

Denn wenig gilt dem Landmann ein Halm in der Dürre,
wenig ein Sommer vor unserem großen Geschlecht.

Und was bezeugt schon dein Herz?
Zwischen gestern und morgen schwingt es,
lautlos und fremd,
und was es schlägt,
ist schon sein Fall aus der Zeit.

■ Silja Walter

Mein kleiner weißer Hund und ich

Mein kleiner weißer Hund und ich,
Wir gehn durch alle Türen.
Wir suchen dich. Wir suchen mich.
Wir weinen und wir frieren.

Der Regen kreiselt groß im See,
Wirft Ringe in die Runde.
Ich weiß nicht, wo ich geh und steh
Mit meinem kleinen Hunde.

Die Welt ist weit. Und weit bist du.
Wo enden Weg und Reise?
Ich hör dem großen Regen zu—
Mein kleiner Hund bellt leise.

The pastoral god's locks still fly in the wind
all day around his tanned brow,
but inside his shirt his fist is pressing
the already gaping wound.

So be firm when the tender back of the clouds
bends down to you one more time,
do not take it for granted when the Hymettus
fills your honeycombs once more.

For to the country man, one stalk in the drought,
to our vast human race, one summer means little.

And what does your heart attest?
Between yesterday and tomorrow it pendulates,
silent and strange,
and what makes it beat
is already its own fall out of time.

■ Silja Walter

My Small White Dog and I

My small white dog and I,
We walk through every door we see.
We shiver and we cry.
We look for you. We look for me.

The rain spins in the lake,
Grows larger casting rings and fog.
I lose the way I take
To wander with my little dog.

The world is far. And far are you.
Where will the journey go?
The heavy rain I listen to—
My little dog barks low.

Ich find dich nicht. Ich find mich nicht.
Mit dir ging ich verloren.
Mein Hund blickt trüb, und mein Gesicht
Preß ich an seine Ohren.

■ Hertha Kräftner

Auf den Tod eines Dichters

Mein Freund, der Dichter, ist gestorben.
Wir haben ihn unter einer Akazie begraben.
Seine Lebensgefährtin—ein böses Weib—
putzte die Gasthaussuppe aus seinem Smoking
(er trug ihn zum Begräbnis),
denn er hatte sich, sagte sie,
zeit seines Lebens nach Reinheit gesehnt.
Im übrigen fand sie, die Akazie dufte zu sehr,
er habe schon immer
über ihr schweres Parfum heimlich geklagt.
Sie aber habe gelitten, ach, gelitten
unter seinem Geruch
nach Tintenentferner und Bühnenstaub
und aufgeschnittnem Papier und manchmal
—leider—manchmal nach einer Sorte von Puder,
die sie niemals benützte.
Das sagte die Lebensgefährtin
auf dem Heimweg vom Grab,
und mehr war über sein Leben auch nicht zu sagen.

Indessen lag er still unter der süßen Akazie.
Hätt' ers gewußt, er hätte nächtelang nicht geschlafen
und sich um Verse gequält,
um Verse von weißen Akaziendolden
und graufeuchten Morgen
und bleichenden Knochen unter dem Gras.

I find no me. I find no you.
With you I was misled.
My dog looks sad, and I am blue,
My cheek on his soft head.

■ Hertha Kräftner

On the Death of a Poet

My friend the poet is dead.
We buried him under an acacia tree.
His companion—a real shrew—
scrubbed the restaurant soup out of his tuxedo
(he wore it for the funeral)
because all his life, she said,
he had longed for purity.
She also thought the acacia smelled too strong,
he had always complained privately
about her heavy perfume.
She in turn had suffered, o, suffered she had
from his smell
of ink remover and stage dust
and cut-open paper and sometimes
—unfortunately—sometimes of a kind of powder
that she never used.
That's what his companion said
on the way home from the grave,
and that was all that could be said about his life.

Meanwhile he lay quietly under the sweet acacia tree.
If he had known it, he would have stayed up for nights
and tortured himself over some verses,
verses about white acacia blossoms
and a gray, moist morning
and bones bleaching under the grass.

Hans Arp

Reif zum Aussteigen

In dem Zug der von A. nach B. fuhr
einer kurzen Fahrt von ungefähr dreiviertel Stunden
befand sich kaum ein echter Aussteiger im Wagen.
In B. der Endstation
stiegen wie notgedrungen
drei Reisende aus.
Die übrigen saßen traurig da.
Die meisten behaupteten
daß sie wenigstens noch drei- bis viermal
von A. nach B. fahren müßten
um reif zum Aussteigen zu sein.
Teils waren die Reisenden von der Zeitkrankheit
dem Hiersein und Dortsein befallen
und schauten mit kläglichen Augen in das Leere.
Es befanden sich unter den Nichtaussteigern
auch solche, die behaupteten
mehr oder minder tot zu sein
und sich unmöglich
von ihren Sitzen erheben zu können.
Diese baten um Blumenkränze und Blumenspenden.
Schließlich waren noch einige da
und diese waren nicht von der gewöhnlichsten Sorte
die sich zusammenrollten
fester und fester zusammenzogen
zusammenpreßten
so daß die Kleider krachten und platzten
und von der sich bildenden lebenden Kugel
aufgesogen wurden.
Mit diesen Nichtaussteigern
war überhaupt nichts anzufangen.
Sie beharrten darauf Kugel zu sein
und wurden langsam hart und härter.
An der Endstation wurden sie aus dem Wagen gerollt
und waren dort vor dem Bahnhofsgebäude
noch längere Zeit zu besichtigen.

Hans Arp

Ready to Get Off

In the train that ran from A. to B.
a short ride of about three quarters of an hour
there was hardly one real get-offer in the car.
In B. the terminus
three travelers got off
as if forced to.
The rest just sat there, looking sad.
Most of them maintained
that they would have to go from A. to B.
at least another three to four times
before they would be ready to get off.
In part the travelers suffered from the disease of the time
from being here and being there,
and stared into emptiness with doleful eyes.
Among the non-get-offers
there were also some who maintained
they were dead, more or less,
and could not possibly
get up from their seats.
They requested floral wreaths and bouquets.
Finally there were a few
and they were not of the most ordinary sort
who rolled themselves up
pulled and pressed together
tighter and tighter
until their clothes burst and split
and they were absorbed
by the live ball that was forming.
Now with these non-get-offers
nothing could be done at all.
They insisted on being a ball
and slowly grew harder and harder.
At the terminus they were rolled out of the car
and were for a time on display
in front of the station.

Amerika

Ein fadenscheiniger Clown
steigt einem fadenscheinigen Clown
auf den Buckel
und diesem fadenscheinigen Clown
steigt wieder ein fadenscheiniger Clown
auf den Buckel
und so fort.
Dem letzten fadenscheinigen Clown
steigt ein schwärmender Kolumbus
auf den Buckel
um nach seinen Karavellen Ausschau zu halten
die inzwischen in See gestochen sind
und zwar in der finsteren Richtung
aus der es stöhnt röchelt und gurgelt
und wo selbst die himmlischen Lichter
vor Angst zittern.

Ein Bettler mit einem Kopf wie eine Dörrbirne
entdeckt im Kleiderschrank
des schwärmenden Kolumbus
ein tadelloses ungetragenes Amerika.
Nicht weit von der Höhle des Bettlers
in der weiten sandigen Ebene
erhebt sich täglich einmal ein Erdteil
ein noch unbeschriebenes Blatt.
Dieser Erdteil hat vier gewaltige Adlerbeine
mit mächtigen rotlackierten pedikürten Krallen
Wie ein Raubvogel stürzt sich dieser Erdteil
in das himmlische Gewölbe
und schreit:
„Ich will das tadellose ungetragene Amerika haben."
Der Bettler zählt der Ordnung wegen
den Rest seiner Tage.

Ein brüchiges Clownsskelett
wird dick fett und reich
und kauft sich einen dressierten Esel.
Der Esel gerät unverhofft

America

A threadbare clown
climbs onto the humpback
of another threadbare clown
and this threadbare clown
has another threadbare clown
climb on his hump
and so on.
The last threadbare clown
has a raving Columbus climb
on his hump
to look for his caravels
which in the meantime have put to sea
and precisely in that dark direction
from which there comes moaning, groaning and gurgling
and where even the heavenly lights
tremble with fear.

A beggar with a head like a dried pear
discovers in the closet
of the raving Columbus
an impeccable, unworn America.
Not far from the beggar's cave
on the wide and sandy plain
there rises, once every day, a continent,
an as yet unwritten page.
This continent has four enormous eagle's legs
with mighty pedicured claws, painted red.
Like a bird of prey this continent rushes
into the heavenly vault
and shouts:
"I want to have the impeccable, unworn America."
The beggar counts, for order's sake,
the remainder of his days.

A brittle clown's skeleton
is turning gross, fat and rich
and buys itself a trained donkey.
Unexpectedly the donkey finds he is

in einen eigentümlichen Fall von guter Hoffnung.
Vier Beine wachsen diesem Esel über Nacht
aus dem Rücken.
Nun können sich die beiden
nicht mehr entschließen
auf welchen der vier Beine
ausgeritten werden solle.

Als der Bettler mit dem Kopf wie eine Dörrbirne
der Wehmut verfiel
versuchte der schwärmende Kolumbus
das Übermenschenmögliche.
Er versprach was die Sprache hergibt
und ließ noch während einer Woche
glattzüngige gleisnerische Onomatopoesien folgen.
Er versprach dem Bettler
die wunderjauchzende massiv diamantene
selbstgeigende Zigeunergeige.
Vor dieser Wundergeige
müßten selbst die altbekannten Himmel einpacken
die voller Geigen hängen.
Die Folge davon sei
daß beide
der Bettler und seine Wenigkeit der Kolumbus
hoch hoch oben
in den lichtesten Tiefen des Himmelsauges
mit allen fuchswild gewordenen Engeln
zu den jeder Beschreibung spottenden Klängen
der diamantenen Zigeunergeige tanzen würden
und aller Wehmut quitt wären.

a peculiar case of being in the family way.
Over night, four legs grow out of this
donkey's back.
Now the two can
no longer decide
on which of those four legs
to go out for a ride.

When the beggar with the head like a dried pear
fell into melancholy
the raving Columbus tried
the superhumanly possible.
He promised whatever the language would yield
and within a week had this followed
by smooth-tongued, hypocritical onomatopoetics.
He promised the beggar
the miracle-jubilant, massively diamond
self-fiddling gypsy fiddle.
Even the proverbial heavens, studded with rosy fiddles,
would have to pack up defeated
in the face of this miraculous fiddle.
From this would follow
that both
the beggar and humble Columbus himself
would—high high up
in the lightest depths of the heavenly eye
and with all the irate angels—
dance to the indescribable sounds
of the diamond gypsy fiddle
and be rid of all melancholy.

Bertolt Brecht

Rückkehr

Die Vaterstadt, wie find ich sie doch?
Folgend den Bomberschwärmen
Komm ich nach Haus.
Wo denn liegt sie? Wo die ungeheuren
Gebirge von Rauch stehen.
Das in den Feuern dort
Ist sie.

Die Vaterstadt, wie empfängt sie mich wohl?
Vor mir kommen die Bomber. Tödliche Schwärme
Melden Euch meine Rückkehr. Feuersbrünste
Gehen dem Sohn voraus.

Als ich in weißem Krankenzimmer der Charité

Als ich in weißem Krankenzimmer der Charité
Aufwachte gegen Morgen zu
Und die Amsel hörte, wußte ich
Es besser. Schon seit geraumer Zeit
Hatte ich keine Todesfurcht mehr. Da ja nichts
Mir je fehlen kann, vorausgesetzt
Ich selber fehle. Jetzt
Gelang es mir, mich zu freuen
Alles Amselgesanges nach mir auch.

Bertolt Brecht

Homecoming

My native city, however shall I find her?
Following the swarms of bombers
I come home.
Well, where is she? Where the colossal
Mountains of smoke stand.
That thing there amongst the fires
Is her.

My native city, how will she receive me?
Before me go the bombers. Deadly swarms
Announce my homecoming to you. Conflagrations
Precede your son.

Translated by Derek Bowman

When in My White Room at the Charité

When in my white room at the Charité
I woke up towards morning
And heard the blackbird, I understood
Better. Already for some time
I had lost all fear of death. For nothing
Can be wrong with me if I myself
Am nothing. Now
I managed to enjoy
The song of every blackbird after me too.

Translated by John Willett and Ralph Mannheim

■ Erich Arendt

Elegie IV

In memoriam Albert Einstein

Ein Weiser aber,
bevor er starb: Er
hob noch einmal
seine Hand . . . und angestrengt
vor Warnen war der Raum.
Das rote Cello seines Herzens
schwieg, das uns die Melodie
gestimmt der ungebrochnen Welt.
Da welkten schon und wie vom Rande
schmerzerregter See
die Schatten seines Mundes. Doch
voller Deutung war und ganz
im aufgefangnen Lichte dunkler Sterne
die letzte Stunde. Wie reifte da
im Weltgedichte seiner Zahlen
und voll Geheimnis uns
die Nacht!

Jedoch:
die Hand stand unbewegt.

Wind auf den Flächen
des Alls. Leben Tode
o Schmerz! Ausgerissen
die Schwingen Gottes, die Gedanken
lagen, verstreut.
Du aber im Nachtgrund,
Fliegender, fern
der weißen Wange deiner Erde,
dem Kinderstaunen
von Wipfel und grasleisem Mond:
todabgeschieden
unter den ferngesteckten
Gestirnen ahnt

Erich Arendt

Elegy IV

In memory of Albert Einstein

A wiseman though
before he died: He
lifted his hand
once more . . . and the room
was strained with warning.
The red cello of his heart that for us had intoned
the melody of the unbroken world
fell silent.
Soon the shadows of his mouth
withered from their edges
like an ocean roiled with pain. Yet
full of import was the last hour
and all in light
caught from dark stars. How the night
ripened there for us in the cosmic poem
of his numbers
and so full of mystery!

And yet:
the hand stood unmoved.

Wind on the plains
of the universe. Lives deaths
oh pain! Plucked out
the pinions of God, the thoughts
lay, scattered.
But you in the depth of the night,
flyer, far
from the white cheek of your earth,
from the childlike amazement
of tree tops and grass-quiet moon:
to death departed
among the far-flung
constellations, your heart

ein Walten dein Herz
Vernimm den Ton: Schweigen . . .
ein Denken, alterlos,
der Welt: die schmalgebogene
Brücke!

Oder schreckt es dennoch
tief um dich in dir
und du erinnerst den Schmerz
im altersgefurchten Rembrandtgesicht,
dies Wissen
unterm Lid, zurückgehalten,
wurzelhart, ein Schatten?
Wie schnell endet der Marsch . . . und wanken erst,
die ihn überdauern einen Atem lang,
die Berge, erlischt,
was menschlich war,
im Auge ihm . . . und zerdrückt ist
sein Stolz, Schmetterlingsflügel im Sturm.
Noch geht wie unter traumwärts
fliehenden Wolken still
dein Fuß, und
zerbrochen schon
ist, die dich trug,
die dünne Schale der Erde.

Blut quillt, ach,
immer wieder das Blut!

Verbirg, aschkalten Herzens, Bruder,
verbirg deine Hände! Deck zu
die Mitwissenden, die
zu schweigen verstehn:
Finger, die warfen Blatt um Blatt
auf den besudelten Tisch beim argen Spiel,
nicht aufzuschauen, da
der Würger umging. Deck zu,
Elender, daß schlafen du magst und,
inmitten des Todes,
gesichtlos.

suspects a rule.
Hark to the tone: silence . . .
a kind of thinking, ageless,
of the world: the narrowly arched
bridge!

Or does this knowledge yet
deeply alarm you
around you within
and you remember the pain
in the age-furrowed Rembrandt face
this knowledge
a shadow beneath the eye's lid,
held back, root hard?
How quickly the march ends . . . and once
the mountains reel which outlast him
by a breath, all that was human
is extinguished
in his eyes . . . and crushed is
his pride, butterfly wings in the storm.
Still your foot moves silently
as if beneath dreamward fleeing clouds
and crushed already
is what carried you,
the thin shell of the earth.

Blood wells, ah,
always again the blood!

Hide, brother, your heart ash cold,
hide your hands! Cover up
those accomplices who
know how to keep silent:
fingers that threw leaf after leaf
onto the soiled table at the evil game,
not to look up when
the strangler went around. Cover up
you miserable one, that you may sleep and be,
in the midst of death,
faceless.

Aber war nicht, sagt es,
sagt das gültige Wort: war,
wo im Buchenwald
der große Liebende, hier,
einem Herzschlag lauschte, nicht
der heile Ort? Und sang
er nicht einst?—Kahlgeschlagen
sein Berg. Sand und kaltes Erstarren:
die ungeschlossenen Wunden!
Und unter den Rinden
die fingerlose Angst!
Nacht du der Nacht:
felsennagender Schatten
an unserm Herzen!

Noch deine Bäume, Deutschland,
wissen zu viel.

■ Stephan Hermlin

Die einen und die anderen

In Ebenen, die qualmten von Regen,
Im gelben Wüstenglast,
In den Städten nächtlich
Von der Musik der Trauer durchrast,
Standen sie bloßen Hauptes
Vorm Block, an der Wand.
Aber das Geheimnis der einen und andern
War nur ihnen bekannt.

Die Türen des Sommers fallen
Mit fernen Gewittern zu.
Sie kommen mit den Sternen,
Stehn als Schatten vor Bett und Truh.

But was not, say it, all of you,
speak the true word: was not,
somewhere in the beech forest, at Buchenwald,
here, where the great lover
listened to a heart beat,
the sacred place? And did he not
sing then?—Deforested
his mountain. Sand and cold numbness:
the unclosed wounds!
And beneath the bark
the fingerless terror!
Night, you of the night:
cliff-gnawing shadow
at our heart!

Even your trees, Germany,
know too much.

■ Stephan Hermlin

The Ones and the Others

In flatlands, smoking with rain,
In the yellow desert glare,
In the cities flooded each night
With music of despair,
They stood, their heads uncovered,
On the block, against the wall.
But the secret of the ones and the others
Was known only to them of all.

The gates of summer fall shut
With distant thunder storms.
They come in with the stars,
Stand bedside like shadow forms.

Mit Gesichtern banal wie das eine,
Das grad in der Menge schwand,
Verkünden ihr Ende sie diesen
Und jenen das Zukunftsland.

Sie sind immer da, wie der harte
Blick des Himmels ist da,
Wie das Rauschen der Stille, das in
Blut und Muschel geschah.
Woher sie auch immer kommen,
Wohin sie auch immer gehn:
Sie sind da, bis die einen erliegen
Und die andern im Lichte stehn.

Da war einer im Dunkel.
Die Städte rauchten von Blut.
Über die einen und andern
Rollte die große Flut.
Er war allein. Er wußte: Wenn sich
Auch für mich kein Befreier fand:
Für die Meinen kommt die Morgenröte,
Und die andern verzehrt der Brand.

Unterm Dach der Donner geborgen,
Die Schläfe weiß von Zorn,
Schlagen sie an die Türen der Zukunft,
Stoßen die Zeiten nach vorn.
Legte sich der Sturm auch in den Ebenen
Neben die Toten. Wenn noch einer stand,
Wußte man: Ihretwegen hat man
Sein Schicksal in der Hand.

Weil die Gräser nach oben wachsen,
Weil die Ramme den Pflasterstein trifft,
Weil im Buch auf splittrigem Tische
Müd das Auge die Wahrheit umschifft,
Weil das Echo dem Ruf erwidert,
Weil der Halm nach der Sichel schreit,
Ist die Nacht für die einen nahe,
Der Tag für die andern nicht weit.

With faces of the crowd
Like the one that just vanished, bland,
They announce the end to these
And to those the promised land.

They are always there, like the skies
With their hard and merciless stare,
As in the coursing through blood and shells
The rushing of stillness is there.
Wherever they might come from,
Wherever they might go:
They are there till the ones stand defeated
And the others are in the light's glow.

There, one was in the darkness.
The cities were smoking with blood.
Over the ones and the others
Rolled the mighty flood.
He was alone. He knew: that
Though I might face my doom,
For my people will come rosy dawn,
And the others, the fire will consume.

Safe under the roof of thunder,
Their temples white with rage,
They hammer at the doors of the future
And push on ahead the age.
And when the storm laid itself down
By the dead, down in the flatlands,
If any still stood you knew:
For them he held fate in his hands.

Because the grasses grow high,
Because the jackhammer strikes stone,
Because in the book on the splintery table
The eye navigates the truth, weary to the bone,
Because the echo responds to the call
Because the blade screams for the scythe
Night is near for the ones,
For the others, the day is nigh.

Sitzen die noch auf den Richterstühlen,
Stehn jene zwischen Angel und Tür
Der unentschiedenen Jahre:
Für die schließt der Tag sich, für
Die andern rufen die Hähne,
Für alle fällt im Glas der Sand,
Der ist von den einen Ende,
Von den andern Anfang genannt.

■ ## Peter Huchel

Chausseen

Erwürgte Abendröte
Stürzender Zeit!
Chausseen. Chausseen.
Kreuzwege der Flucht.
Wagenspuren über den Acker,
Der mit den Augen
Erschlagener Pferde
Den brennenden Himmel sah.

Nächte mit Lungen voll Rauch,
Mit hartem Atem der Fliehenden,
Wenn Schüsse
Auf die Dämmerung schlugen.
Aus zerbrochenem Tor
Trat lautlos Asche und Wind,
Ein Feuer,
Das mürrisch das Dunkel kaute.

Tote,
Über die Gleise geschleudert,
Den erstickten Schrei
Wie einen Stein am Gaumen.
Ein schwarzes
Summendes Tuch aus Fliegen
Schloß ihre Wunden.

While these still sit in the judge's seat,
Those stand between the frame and door
Of the undecided years:
For those the day closes, for
The others, the cocks crow,
For both the sands in the hourglass fall,
But the ones will call it their doom,
The others, the beginning of all.

■ Peter Huchel

Roads

Strangled evening crimson
Of collapsing times!
Roads. Roads.
Crossways of flight.
Cart tracks across the field
That, with the eyes
Of slain horses,
Saw the burning sky.

Nights with lungs full of smoke,
With the hard breath of the fleeing,
When gunshots
Assaulted the twilight.
Stepping from the broken gate,
Silently, ashes and wind,
A fire,
Disgruntled, that chewed on the dark.

Dead people,
Flung across the rails,
The smothered scream
Like a stone at their palate.
A black
Cloth of buzzing flies
Closed their wounds.

Heimkehr

Unter der schwindenden Sichel des Mondes
kehrte ich heim und sah das Dorf
im wäßrigen Dunst der Gräben und Wiesen.

Soll ich wie Schatten zerrissener Mauern
hausen im Schutt, das Tote betrauern,
soll ich die schwarze Schote enthülsen,
die am Zaun der Sommer vergaß,
sammeln den Hafer rissig und falb,
den ein eisiger Regen zerfraß?
Fauliger Halm auf fauligem Felde—
niemand brachte die Ernte ein.
Nessel wuchert, Schierling und Melde,
Hungerblume umklammert den Stein.

Aber am Morgen,
es dämmerte kalt,
als noch der Reif
die Quelle des Lichts überfror,
kam eine Frau aus wendischem Wald.
Suchend das Vieh, das dürre,
das sich im Dickicht verlor,
ging sie den rissigen Pfad.
Sah sie schon Schwalbe und Saat?
Hämmernd schlug sie den Rost vom Pflug.

Da war es die Mutter der Frühe,
unter dem alten Himmel
die Mutter der Völker.
Sie ging durch Nebel und Wind.
Pflügend des steinigen Acker,
trieb sie das schwarzgefleckte
sichelhörnige Rind.

Homecoming

Under the moon's vanishing sickle
I returned and saw the village
in the watery mist of ditches and meadows.

Am I, like the shadows of burnt walls,
to live in the rubble, mourn the dead,
am I to shuck the black pod
that the summer forgot at the fence,
gather the oats, yellow and coarse,
that an icy rain gnawed?
Rotten stalk in a rotten field—
no one brought in the harvest.
Nettles are rampant, hemlock, and pigweed,
Hunger blossoms strangle the stone.

But in the morning,
the dawn was cold,
when the hoarfrost
still froze out the source of light,
a woman came from the Wendish woods.
Looking for the wasted cattle
that had gone lost in the thicket,
she walked the cracked path.
Did she already see swallows and crops?
Hammering, she knocked the rust off the plough.

The mother of dawn she was,
under the old sky
the mother of the peoples.
She walked through fog and wind.
Ploughing the stony field
she drove the black-spotted,
sickle-horned cattle.

Michael Guttenbrunner

Die Bodenständlinge

Die Sänger dieser Lande
sind des heimatlichen Speckes Sänger,
und sie vergleichen sich ein jeglicher
mit einem Baum;
ich hab es oft gehört und weiß es nun wohl,
daß ihre Wurzeln erdverbunden sind.
Wenn aber große Zeiten anbrechen,
die das dicke Ende in sich tragen,
dann feiern sie, um nicht vors Gewehr zu müssen,
die besoffenen Eintagsworte
der jeweiligen Tyrannen.
Wenn's aber vorbei ist,
dann singen sie wieder, als ob nichts gewesen wäre,
die Sau am Spieß
und Kraut und Rüben der Heimat.
Ihnen fehlt jedes Wort
für die Geschlagenen und Entrechteten,
von deren Blute Europas Henker trieften.
Ich allein singe heute vom Krieg.
Denn ungetilgter Schulden Samen ist wieder gereift,
und neue Drohung verdunkelt die Welt.
Als die Partisanen zum Kampfe aufbrachen
und die Freiheit ihre Morgensterne
im Dunkel der Wälder entzündete,
da rüsteten sich die Wüsten,
da griffen Wälder
mit grüner Kraft zu den Waffen.
Aber die Landsknechte und ihre Schreibknechte
sprachen nur von Banditen.
Von Ratten zerfressen
wurde des deutschen Schlachthauses
babylonischer Turm.
Aber höher von Jahr zu Jahr
hob die Menschheit ihr Haupt voll Blut und Wunden,

Michael Guttenbrunner

The Homeland Singers

The singers of these lands
are the ethnic bacon bards,
and they compare themselves, one and all,
to a tree;
I have heard it often and now know for sure
their roots are fully grounded in the soil.
But whenever Great Times emerge,
complete with their own bitter ends,
they celebrate, lest they have to face guns,
the drunken, fleeting words
of the tyrant in charge.
Still, when it's over and done
they sing again, as if nothing had happened,
of the pig on the spit
and of cabbage and turnips at home.
They lack any words
for the downtrodden and disinherited
whose blood drips from Europe's henchmen.
I alone sing of war today.
For the seed of old unredeemed debts has ripened,
and new threats darken the world.
When the partisans went to battle
and lit the freedom of their morning star cudgels
in the dark of the forests
the deserts themselves went to arms
the forests in green strength
reached for weapons.
But the hired soldiers and their hired scribblers
could speak only of bandits.
The Babylonian tower
of the German slaughterhouse
was eaten by rats.
Yet from year to year mankind
lifted its head higher covered with blood and wounds,

bestrahlt von Siegeshoffnung.
Nun aber blickt neue Gefahr
medusenhäuptig auf West und Ost.
Wen müßte man nicht alles
zum Teufel jagen?
Von den heimatlichen Sängern
werdet ihr's nie erfahren.

■ Günter Kunert

Über einige davongekommene

Als der Mensch
unter den Trümmern
seines
bombardierten Hauses
hervorgezogen wurde,
schüttelte er sich
und sagte:
Nie wieder

Jedenfalls nicht gleich.

■ Nelly Sachs

Auch dir, du mein Geliebter

Auch dir, du mein Geliebter,
Haben zwei Hände, zum Darreichen geboren,
Die Schuhe abgerissen,
Bevor sie dich töteten.
Zwei Hände, die sich darreichen müssen

illuminated with the hope of victory.
But now new danger looks
with its Medusa head to West and East.
Whom shouldn't you send packing
to the devil?
From the homeland singers
you will never learn it.

■ Günter Kunert

About Some Who Survived

When the man
was pulled out
from
under the debris
of his bombed house,
he shook himself
and said:
Never again

At least not right away.

■ Nelly Sachs

Two hands, born to give

Two hands, born to give,
Tore off your shoes
My beloved,
Before they killed you.
Two hands, which will have to give themselves up

Wenn sie zu Staub zerfallen.
Deine Schuhe waren aus einer Kalbshaut.
Wohl waren sie gegerbt, gefärbt,
Der Pfriem hatte sie durchstochen—
Aber wer weiß, wo noch ein letzter lebendiger
Hauch wohnt?
Während der kurzen Trennung
Zwischen deinem Blut und der Erde
Haben sie Sand hineingespart wie eine Stundenuhr
Die jeden Augenblick Tod füllt.
Deine Füße!
Die Gedanken eilten ihnen voraus.
Die so schnell bei Gott waren,
So wurden deine Füße müde,
Wurden wund um dein Herz einzuholen.
Aber die Kalbshaut,
Darüber einmal die warme leckende Zunge
Des Muttertieres gestrichen war,
Ehe sie abgezogen wurde—
Wurde noch einmal abgezogen
Von deinen Füßen,
Abgezogen—
O du mein Geliebter!

Abschied

Abschied—
aus zwei Wunden blutendes Wort.
Gestern noch Meereswort
mit dem sinkenden Schiff
als Schwert in der Mitte—
Gestern noch von Sternschnuppensterben
durchstochenes Wort—
Mitternachtgeküßte Kehle
der Nachtigallen—

When they turn to dust.
Your shoes were made of calfskin.
They were well tanned and dyed,
The awl had pierced them—
But who knows where a last living breath
Still dwells?
During the short parting
Between your blood and earth
They trickled sand like an hourglass
Which fills each moment with death.
Your feet!
The thoughts sped before them.
They came so quickly to God
That your feet grew weary,
Grew sore in trying to catch up with your heart.
But the calfskin
That the warm licking tongue
Of the mother-cow once stroked
Before the skin was stripped—
Was stripped once more
From your feet,
Torn off—
Oh my beloved

Translated by Ruth and Matthew Mead and Michael Hamburger

Farewell

Farewell—
word bleeding from two wounds.
Yesterday still a word of the sea
with the sinking ship
as a sword in the middle—
Yesterday still a word
pierced by the dying of shooting stars—
midnight-kissed throat
of the nightingales—

Heute—zwei hängende Fetzen
und Menschenhaar in einer Krallenhand
die riß—

Und wir Nachblutenden—
Verblutende an dir—
halten deine Quelle in unseren Händen.
Wie Heerscharen der Abschiednehmenden
die an deiner Dunkelheit bauen—
bis der Tod sagt: schweige du—
doch hier ist: weiterbluten!

■ Hilde Domin

Vor Tag

Der Kuß aus Rosenblättern
immer neue weiche kleine
Blätter der sich öffnenden Blüte.

Nicht jenes Wenig von Raum
für die Spanne des Wunschs
zwischen Nehmen und Geben.

Du hobst die Decke von mir
so behutsam
wie man ein Kind nicht weckt
oder als wär ich
so zerbrechlich
wie ich bin.

Ich wurde nicht wirklicher
als ein Gedicht
oder ein Traum
oder die Wolke
unter der Wolke.

Today—two hanging shreds
and human hair in a clawing hand
that tore—

And we who bleed in aftermath—
bleeding to death because of you—
hold your source in our hands.
We hosts who bid farewell
who build your darkness—
until death says: be silent—
but here it is: go on bleeding!

Translated by Ruth and Matthew Mead and Michael Hamburger

■ Hilde Domin

Before Daybreak

The kiss of rose petals
always new soft small
petals of the blossom opening up.

Not that smallness of space
for the span of the wish
between taking and giving.

You lifted the cover from me
so cautiously
as if not to waken a child
or as if I were
as fragile
as I am.

I did not become more real
than a poem
or a dream
or a cloud
under the cloud.

Und doch, als du fort warst,
der zärtliche Zweifel:
Ist es tröstlich
für einen Mann
mit einer Wolke zu schlafen?

■ Christine Busta

Winter über den Dächern

Diese Tage sind anders geschrieben:
rot auf weiß,
mit den Füßen grauer, verlauster Tauben.
Botschaften der Geduld, hingeduckt unterm Schneewind.
wachsam äugend vorm Dickicht der erfrorenen Fenster.

Ungelesene Zeichen mählich verharschten Vertrauens;
aber noch kreisen die Flüge über dem Abgrund.
Vielleicht doch
streut vor Nacht eine Hand
das Korn der Gnade, das harte.

■ Paul Celan

Todesfuge

Schwarze Milch der Frühe wir trinken sie abends
wir trinken sie mittags und morgens wir trinken sie nachts
wir trinken und trinken
wir schaufeln ein Grab in den Lüften da liegt man nicht eng
Ein Mann wohnt im Haus der spielt mit den Schlangen der schreibt
der schreibt wenn es dunkelt nach Deutschland dein goldenes Haar Margarete

And yet, when you were gone,
the tender doubt:
Is it consoling
for a man
to sleep with a cloud?

■ Christine Busta

Winter on Roof Tops

These days have been written differently:
red on white,
with the feet of gray, lice-infected doves.
Messages of patience stooped beneath the snowy wind,
attentively looking before the jungle of frozen windows.

Unread signs of trust gradually crusted with scabs;
but still the flock circles over the abyss.
Perhaps still
before night a hand will strew
the seed of grace, that hard grain.

■ Paul Celan

Death Fugue

Black milk of dawn we drink it at dusk
we drink it at midday and morning we drink it at night
we drink and we drink
we shovel a grave in the air there no one lies cramped
A man lives in the house he plays with the serpents he writes
he writes when darkness descends to Germany your golden hair Margareta

er schreibt es und tritt vor das Haus und es blitzen die Sterne
    er pfeift seine Rüden herbei
er pfeift seine Juden hervor läßt schaufeln ein Grab in der Erde
er befiehlt uns spielt auf nun zum Tanz

Schwarze Milch der Frühe wir trinken dich nachts
wir trinken dich morgens und mittags wir trinken dich abends
wir trinken und trinken
Ein Mann wohnt im Haus der spielt mit den Schlangen der schreibt
der schreibt wenn es dunkelt nach Deutschland dein goldenes Haar Margarete
Dein aschenes Haar Sulamith wir schaufeln ein Grab in den Lüften da liegt
    man nicht eng

Er ruft stecht tiefer ins Erdreich ihr einen ihr andern singet und spielt
er greift nach dem Eisen im Gurt er schwingts seine Augen sind blau
stecht tiefer die Spaten ihr einen ihr andern spielt weiter zum Tanz auf

Schwarze Milch der Frühe wir trinken dich nachts
wir trinken dich mittags und morgens wir trinken dich abends
wir trinken und trinken
ein Mann wohnt im Haus dein goldenes Haar Margarete
dein aschenes Haar Sulamith er spielt mit den Schlangen

Er ruft spielt süßer den Tod der Tod ist ein Meister aus Deutschland
er ruft streicht dunkler die Geigen dann steigt ihr als Rauch in die Luft
dann habt ihr ein Grab in den Wolken da liegt man nicht eng

Schwarze Milch der Frühe wir trinken dich nachts
wir trinken dich mittags der Tod ist ein Meister aus Deutschland
wir trinken dich abends und morgens wir trinken und trinken
der Tod ist ein Meister aus Deutschland sein Auge ist blau
er trifft dich mit bleierner Kugel er trifft dich genau
ein Mann wohnt im Haus dein goldenes Haar Margarete
er hetzt seine Rüden auf uns er schenkt uns ein Grab in der Luft
er spielt mit den Schlangen und träumet der Tod is ein Meister aus Deutschland

dein goldenes Haar Margarete
dein aschenes Haar Sulamith

he writes it and steps from the house and then the stars glitter
    he whistles his dogs together
he whistles his Jews out he has a grave dug in the earth
he tells us now strike up the dance

Black milk of dawn we drink you at night
we drink you at morning and midday we drink you at dusk
we drink and we drink
A man lives in the house he plays with the serpents he writes
he writes when darkness descends to Germany your golden hair Margareta
Your ashen hair Sulamith we shovel a grave in the air there no one lies
    cramped

He shouts dig deeper into the earth you there you others sing and make music
he grabs for the iron in his belt he waves it his eyes are blue
dig the spades deeper you there you others play on for the dance

Black milk of dawn we drink you at night
we drink you at midday and morning we drink you at dusk
we drink and we drink
a man lives in the house your golden hair Margareta
your ashen hair Sulamith he plays with the serpents

He shouts play that death sweeter for death is a master from Germany
he shouts bow more darkly those fiddles then rise as smoke in the air
then you have a grave in the clouds there no one lies cramped

Black milk of dawn we drink you at night
we drink you at midday death is a master from Germany
we drink you at dusk and morning we drink and we drink
death is a master from Germany his eye is blue
he shoots with a leaden bullet he shoots with precision at you
a man lives in the house your golden hair Margareta
he drives his dogs at us gives us a grave in the air
he plays with the serpents and dreams for death is a master from Germany

your golden hair Margareta
your ashen hair Sulamith

Mit wechselndem Schlüssel

Mit wechselndem Schlüssel
schließt du das Haus auf, darin
der Schnee des Verschwiegenen treibt.
Je nach dem Blut, das dir quillt
aus Aug oder Mund oder Ohr,
wechselt dein Schlüssel.

Wechselt dein Schlüssel, wechselt das Wort,
das treiben darf mit den Flocken.
Je nach dem Wind, der dich fortstößt,
ballt um das Wort sich der Schnee.

Corona

Aus der Hand frißt der Herbst mir sein Blatt: wir sind Freunde.
Wir schälen die Zeit aus den Nüssen und lehren sie gehn:
die Zeit kehrt zurück in die Schale.

Im Spiegel ist Sonntag,
im Traum wird geschlafen,
der Mund redet wahr.

Mein Aug steigt hinab zum Geschlecht der Geliebten:
wir sehen uns an,
wir sagen uns Dunkles,
wir lieben einander wie Mohn und Gedächtnis,
wir schlafen wie Wein in den Muscheln,
wie das Meer im Blutstrahl des Mondes.

Wir stehen umschlungen im Fenster, sie sehen uns zu von der Straße:
es ist Zeit, daß man weiß!
Es ist Zeit, daß der Stein sich zu blühen bequemt,
daß der Unrast ein Herz schlägt.
Es ist Zeit, daß es Zeit wird.

Es ist Zeit.

With Changing Key

With changing key
you open the house in which
the snow of the unsaid is drifting.
And with the blood that may run
from your eye, or your mouth, or your ear,
your key will be changing.

Changing the key is changing the word
that may drift with the snowflakes.
And in the wind that rejects you,
round the word gathers the snow.

Corona

From my hand autumn is eating his leaf: we are friends.
We shell time out of the nuts and teach it to walk:
and time then returns to the shell.

In the mirror it's Sunday,
in dreams there is sleeping,
the mouth speaks the truth.

My eye descends to the sex of my lover:
We look at each other,
we speak only darkly,
we love one another like poppies and memory,
we sleep like wine in the seashells,
like the sea in the moon's blood red beam.

We stand in the window embracing, they look at us from the street:
It is time that they knew!
It is time that the stone deigned to blossom,
that a heart beat for unrest.
It is time that the time come.

It is time.

1955–1965

Accomplishments and Rebellions

. . . could you toss the lyre down to me?

Johannes Bobrowski

Die Jura

Deine Wasser
hart vor dem Wald,
unterströmig,
voll der weißen Kälte der Quellen
sommers.
Nur um Mittag
steigt an die Fläche leise
mit den glänzenden Flossen
der Fisch, ein alter
Räuber. Er kehrt
wieder unterm Mond. Und er eilt nicht,
wenn der wilde Otter
im Wurzelgewirr,
tief im Geflecht der Finsternis lärmt.

In der großen Stille
komm ich zu dir,
schöner Bruder der Wälder, der Hügel,
mein Fluß.
In der Stille des jungen Tags
im Beerengesträuch
komm ich den Sandpfad. Mein Kahn
folgt deinem Herzlaut, dem immer
jähen Wassergeräusch
unter der Kühle.

Uferweide, bittrer Geruch,
ein Grün wie aus Nebeln.
Und der Tau. Es hockt im verwachsnen Hang
vor dem Dorf im Gebüsch
der Graukopf, mit klammen Fingern
malt er deine Röte, dein Grün, die fremde
Bläue, den Silberlaut:

Johannes Bobrowski

The Jura

Your waters
hard by the forest,
with undercurrents,
full of the white cold of springs
in summer.
Only toward noon
the surface rises quietly
with the shining fins
of the fish, an old
robber. He returns
again under the moon. And he does not hurry
when the wild otter
in the tangle of roots
cries, deep in the mesh of the darkness.

In the vast stillness
I come to you
handsome brother of the forests, the hills,
my river.
In the stillness of the young day
in the berry bushes
I come on the sandy path. My boat
follows the sound of your heart, that always
precipitous rush of water
beneath the coolness.

Bank willow, bitter smell,
a green as if made of fog.
And the dew. Something crouches on the overgrown slope
before the village in the bushes
the gray-head, with clammy fingers
he paints your reds, your greens, the foreign
blues, the silver tone:

Einst
erhob ein großer
Gott der Fluren, ein Hartmaul,
das Gesicht. Über dem Uferwald
stand er
in der Schwärze der Opferstatt,
glänzte vom Fett,
sah in den Wiesen das rötliche Erz,
und die Quellen
schossen hervor, seiner Blicke
sandige Spur.

Wer entzündet die späten
Feuer des Jahrs, wo der Strom,
Nemona, geht, aus breiten
Lungen schreit vor dem Eis,
das herabfällt? Aus offenen Himmeln
stürzt es, es fährt ein gelber
Rauch vor ihm her.

Memorial

Schwarz vor den Horizont
geschüttet, die Stadt. Ich zähl die Gewitter
über ihr. Morgen geh ich, ich will ein Grab
schließen, verlassen wie diese
Stadt, die zerstört ist
bis in den Grund, die die Vögel
meiden. Ein Baum
steht mir am Weg. Der gibt mir
von seinem Laub.

Ode auf Thomas Chatterton

Mary Redcliff, rot, ein Gebirge, unter
deinen Türmen, unter der Simse Wirrung
und den Wänden, steilem Geschneid der Bögen,
träufend von Schatten . . .

Once
a great god of the plains,
a hard-mouthed one, raised
his face. Over the forest on the bank
he stood
in the blackness of the sacrificial place,
gleamed with oil,
saw in the meadows the reddish ore,
and the springs
shot forth, sandy spoor
of his glance.

Who kindles the late
fires of the year, where the current,
Nemona, goes, from broad
lungs screaming with the ice
that plunges? From the open sky
it plummets, a yellow
smoke rushes in front of it.

Memorial

Black poured out in front
of the horizon, the city. I count the thunderstorms
above it. Tomorrow I go, I want to close
a grave, abandon it like this
city, which is destroyed
down to the ground and which the birds
avoid. A tree
stands in my path. It gives me
some foliage.

Ode to Thomas Chatterton

Mary Redcliff, red, a mountain range, under
your towers, under the chaos of the cornices
and the walls, steep crosscut of the vaults,
dripping with shadows . . .

aufwuchs hier das Kind mit dem Wort allein wie
mit den Händen, ratlos; ein Nächtewandler
oft: der stand auf hangender Brüstung, schaute
blind auf die Stadt hin,

schwer vom Monde, wo sich ein Gräber mühte
seufzend im Gelände der Toten — , rief die
hingesunkne Zeit mit verblichnen Namen.
Ach, sie erwachte

nie doch, da er ging, in der Freunde Stimmen
Welt zu finden, in seiner Mädchen sanfter
Schläfenschmiegung, da er in schmalen Stuben
lehnte das Haupt hin.

Nie mehr nahte, da er es rief, das Alte.
Nur der Zweifel, einziges Echo, flog im
Stiegenknarren stäubend, im Klang der Turmuhr
eulenweich auf nur.

Hinzusprechen: daß er verging so, seine
dämmervollen Lieder — Wir zerren immer,
täglich ein Undenkliches her, doch was wir
hatten der Zeit an,

immer gilt's ein Weniges, das Geringste,
den und jenen rührend: dann einmal ist's ein
Baum, ergrünt, ein zweigendes, tausendfaches,
rauschendes Laubdach;

Schatten wohnt darunter — der schattet nicht die
schmale Spur Verzweiflung: dahingefahren,
falber Blitz, wo kaum ein Gewölk stand, in die
Bläue gekräuselt,

über jener Stadt, die in Ängsten hinfuhr,
Bristol, da der Knabe gesungen, draußen
an dem Avon, wo ihn der Wiesentau noch,
endlos noch kannte.

here the child grew up as alone with the word as
perplexed with his hands; a sleepwalker
often: he stood on suspended breastwork, stared
at the town blindly,

moon encumbered, where gravedigger toiled
sighing in the terrain of the dead—, summoned
with faded names a time sunken away.
Alas, she awakened

never, when he left to find in voices
of friends the world, in his girls' gently
arching temples, when he in narrow chamber
his head inclined.

Never again neared, when he summoned it, that past.
Only the doubt, sole echo, blew up dusty
in the stair's creaking, in the tower clock's sound
soft as on owl wing.

To be said: that this is how he vanished, his
songs twilight filled—Always we drag along
daily one memory, yet of what
we had at the time,

always a little holds true, a trifle,
affecting this and that: all at once it's a
tree, turned green, a branching, thousand-fold,
rustling leaf roof;

shadows dwell beneath—it shades not the
slim trace of despair: departed,
dun-colored lightning, when hardly a cloud stood
curled in the blue skies

above that city, anxiously rushing,
Bristol, where the lad sang, out
by the Avon, where the meadow dew still
endlessly knew him.

Ach, die Eulenschwingen der Kindheit über
seinen Schritten, da er in fremden Straßen,
bei der Brücke fand unter wind'gem Dach ein
jähes Umarmen

und den Tod; der kam wie ein Teetrunk bläßlich,
stand am Tisch, in raschelnde Blätter legend,
auf die Schrift den knöchernen Finger, „Rowley"
las er, „Aella".

■ Johannes R. Becher

Die Jahre sind gezählt

Die Jahre sind gezählt, die dir verbleiben.
Die Jahreszeiten sind gezählt.
Was du geschrieben hast, was du wirst schreiben,
Ist schon gesichtet und ist ausgewählt.

Die Jahre sind gezählt, die bittern Jahre.
Die Tränen spärlich und zu spät,
Und auch das schöne Jahr, das wunderbare,
Ist schon vergangen und wie fortgeweht.

Die Wochen sind gezählt. Fürs Wochenende
Ist „Eintrübung" vorhergesagt,
Und schweigend blicken an dich deine Hände,
Als hätten sie um einen Rat gefragt.

Die Tage sind gezählt. O wie sie eilen
Dem Ende zu, unaufhaltsam.
Die Schrift ist müd. Es zittert in den Zeilen.
Der Abschied kam, bevor man Abschied nahm.

Alas, childhood's owl pinions over
his steps, when in foreign streets he found
by the bridge under windy roof a
sudden embrace

and death; it came like a sip of tea palish,
stood at the table, at rustling papers pointed
its bony finger at the writing, "Rowley,"
he read, "Aella."

■ Johannes R. Becher

The Years Are Counted

The years are counted that for you remain.
The seasons left are counted too.
What you have written, writing you'll attain,
Already is selected, winnowed through.

The years are counted out, the bitter years.
The tears were sparse and came too late,
And likewise that brief year of love and cheers,
Is passed already on the winds of fate.

The weeks are counted out. For next weekend
Predictions call for overcast,
With silent looks your hands seem to perpend,
As if to ask for some advice at last.

The days are counted. How they quickly race
On toward the end unchecked they fly.
The script is tired. Lines tremble in their place.
The good-bye came before one said good-bye.

Die Stunden sind gezählt, zu Tod gehetzte,
Schon wie voraus berechenbar,
Naht sie, die Stunde, deine allerletzte.
Vielleicht wirst ihrer du nicht mehr gewahr.

Es zählen nicht die Freuden, nicht die Qualen.
Es zählt nicht der, nicht jener Schritt.
Es aber zählt, unausdrückbar in Zahlen,
Vielleicht ein Lied in ferner Zeit noch mit.

■ Stephan Hermlin

Die Vögel und der Test

> Zeitungen melden, daß unter dem Einfluß der Wasserstoffbombenversuche die
> Zugvögel über der Südsee ihre herkömmlichen Routen ändern.

Von den Savannen übers Tropenmeer
Trieb sie des Leibes Notdurft mit den Winden,
Wie taub und blind, von weit- und altersher,
Um Nahrung und um ein Geäst zu finden.

Nicht Donner hielt sie auf, Taifun nicht, auch
Kein Netz, wenn sie was rief zu großen Flügen,
Strebend nach gleichem Ziel, ein schreiender Rauch,
Auf gleicher Bahn und stets in gleichen Zügen.

Die nicht vor Wasser zagten noch Gewittern
Sahn eines Tags im hohen Mittagslicht
Ein höhres Licht. Das schreckliche Gesicht

Zwang sie von nun an ihren Flug zu ändern.
Da suchten sie nach neuen sanfteren Ländern.
Laßt diese Änderung euer Herz erschüttern . . .

The hours are counted, hunted unto death,
Reckoned with well in advance,
It nears, the hour of your final breath,
You will not be aware of it perchance.

They do not count, the joys and not the pain.
They do not count, the one or other choice.
Yet counting what the numbers don't contain,
Perhaps one day a song will add its voice.

■ Stephan Hermlin

The Birds and the Bomb

Newspapers report that hydrogen bomb tests have caused migratory birds to change
their accustomed routes over the South Pacific Ocean.

From savannas across the tropical sea
As if blind and deaf over distances and time
Driven by winds and physical necessity
They flew in search of food and better clime.

No thunder could divert them, no typhoon
Nor net when they were called to great migrations,
Strove toward their goal, a screaming, smoking plume
Along the same paths, in congregations.

Those undeterred by water, storm or night
Saw one day in the highest midday light
A greater light. That awesome sight

Compelled them from then on to change their chart
To seek a new and a more tranquil flight.
Let this grave change be pondered in your heart . . .

■ Karl Krolow

Historie

Männer trugen über den Platz eine Fahne.
Da brachen Centauren aus dem Gestrüpp
Und zertrampelten ihr Tuch
Und Geschichte konnte beginnen.
Melancholische Staaten
Zerfielen an Straßenecken.
Redner hielten sich
Mit Bulldoggen bereit,
Und die jüngeren Frauen
Schminkten sich für die Stärkeren.
Unaufhörlich stritten Stimmen
In der Luft, obwohl sich
Die mythologischen Wesen längst
Zurückgezogen hatten.

Übrig bleibt schließlich die Hand,
Die sich um eine Kehle legt.

■ Christa Reinig

Robinson

Manchmal weint er, wenn die Worte
Still in seiner Kehle stehn,
Doch er lernt an seinem Orte
Schweigend mit sich umzugehn,

Und erfindet alte Dinge,
Halb aus Not und halb in Spiel,
Splittert Stein zur Messerklinge,
Schnürt die Axt an einen Stiel,

Karl Krolow

History

Men carried a flag across the square
Then the centaurs broke out of the bushes
And trampled on the cloth
And history could begin.
Melancholy states
Crumbled at street corners.
Orators stood ready
With bulldogs
And the younger women
Made up their faces for the stronger party.
Ceaselessly voices argued
In the air, even though
The mythological creatures
Had long since returned.

What remains in the end is a hand
Closing around a throat.

Christa Reinig

Robinson

Sometimes he cries when the words
Stand still in his throat,
But he learns in his place
To occupy himself in silence,

And invents old things,
Half out of need and half in play,
Splinters stones into knife blades,
Ties the ax to a handle,

Kratzt mit einer Muschelkante
Seinen Namen in die Wand,
Und der allzu oft genannte
Wird ihm langsam unbekannt.

■   Kurt Marti

Das Herz der Igel

Was soll ich die Wälder
besingen?
Was soll ich das Herz der Igel
preisen?
Das Herz einer Frau, das Herz eines Mannes
ist größer.
Aber sie weigern sich strikte,
in meine Gedichte zu treten.
So hocke ich auf der Schwelle,
warte auf einen, der einkehrt
und singe indessen
die Wälder und auch
das Herz der Igel.

■   Wulf Kirsten

Kyleb

Kyleb,
he, du mein dorf dort
am fuße niemals geschorener kälberrohrhänge,
stirb nicht mit deinen

Scratches with a mussel's edge
His name on the wall,
And that name, too often mentioned,
Slowly grows strange to him.

■ Kurt Marti

The Heart of the Hedgehogs

Why should I sing a hymn to
the forests?
Why should I praise
the heart of the hedgehogs?
The heart of a woman, the heart of a man
is larger.
But they strictly refuse
to step into my poems.
And so I squat on the threshold,
wait for someone to enter
and meanwhile sing
about the forests and also
the heart of the hedgehogs.

■ Wulf Kirsten

Kyleb

Kyleb,
hey you village of mine, over there
at the foot of never-sheared calf-ear slopes,
don't die with your

klapprigen mühlen
am rauschenden bach!
letztes klipp-klapp noch
wird verbacken zu gnadenbrot.

dorf, du mein dorf, ich müßt
deiner spotten und führ'n üble nachrede,
heißen
faulen jakob oder trantute dich,
anachronistischen winterschläfer
und liebhaber von mehlmotten.

hör auf, so romantisch
mit holzpantoffeln zu scheppern
so störrisch zu zuckeln
ochsigen gemüts!
mein altes Kyleb, komm mir nicht länger
mit greisenallüren,
gestützt auf krücken!
ausgeschlummert! los einen galopp!

verruhn mag der kapphahn,
ort des gerichts
im spinnenwinkel
hinter schattenmorellen
als sinnbild grausiger saecula.

sesam öffne dich
für mein altes klappriges dorf!
mit dem lehmbuden-klarschlag
in die verlassenen steinbrüche,
wo die zerscherbten jahrzehnte
verrotten
in abgelegten galoschen.

rickety mills
beside the rushing stream!
the last clip-clop will still be baked
into the bread of charity.

village, you village of mine, i should
make fun of you and spread ugly rumors about you
call you
lazy bones or sluggish hag
anachronistic winter sleeper
and connoisseur of flour weevils.

stop romantically
clomping your wooden clogs
dawdling obstinately
an oxen temperament!
my old Kyleb, don't come to me any more
with airs of octogenarians,
propped up on crutches!
enough of this napping! off at a gallop!

the capon may rest,
place of justice
in the spiderweb corner
behind black morels
as a symbol of horrid centuries.

open sesame
for my rickety village!
put those clay huts
into the abandoned quarries
where the splintered decades
rot
in discarded galoshes.

fuderweise der hölle ins sperrmaul
gestopft altbacknen dreck!
nicht länger *lotweise* soll
holen der teufel
die denkmäler der fron:
schäbige hungerkornspeicher
und krähwinklerhütten.

he, du mein stilles Kyleb
leg los!
schnell und laut
kommt ins altväterliche dorf
das neue jahrtausend.
hinter dem mond gilt
nicht mehr.

■ Ingeborg Bachmann

Exil

Ein Toter bin ich der wandelt
gemeldet nirgends mehr
unbekannt im Reich des Präfekten
überzählig in den goldenen Städten
und im grünenden Land

abgetan lange schon
und mit nichts bedacht

Nur mit Wind mit Zeit und mit Klang

der ich unter Menschen nicht leben kann

by the cartload stuff ancient junk
into hell's gaping mouth!
no longer by the ounce
let the devil take
the monuments of old slavery:
shabby corn cribs for times of famine
and Podunk shanties.

hey, you peaceful Kyleb of mine
get going!
fast and loud
the new millennium
is coming to the antiquated village.
"behind the moon"
won't wash any more.

■ Ingeborg Bachmann

Exile

A dead body I am, wandering about
no longer registered anywhere
unknown in the realm of the prefect
redundant in the golden cities
and the greening countryside

passed up long ago
not provided with anything

Except wind and time and sound

who cannot live among people

Ich mit der deutschen Sprache
dieser Wolke um mich
die ich halte als Haus
treibe durch alle Sprachen

O wie sie sich verfinstert
die dunklen die Regentöne
nur die wenigen fallen

In hellere Zonen trägt dann sie den Toten hinauf

Freies Geleit

Mit schlaftrunkenen Vögeln
und winddurchschossenen Bäumen
steht der Tag auf, und das Meer
leert einen schäumenden Becher auf ihn.

Die Flüsse wallen ans große Wasser,
und das Land legt Liebesversprechen
der reinen Luft in den Mund
mit frischen Blumen.

Die Erde will keinen Rauchpilz tragen,
kein Geschöpf ausspeien vorm Himmel,
mit Regen und Zornesblitzen abschaffen
die unerhörten Stimmen des Verderbens.

Mit uns will sie die bunten Brüder
und grauen Schwestern erwachen sehn,
den König Fisch, die Hoheit Nachtigall
und den Feuerfürsten Salamander.

Für uns pflanzt sie Korallen ins Meer.
Wäldern befiehlt sie, Ruhe zu halten,
dem Marmor, die schöne Ader zu schwellen,
noch einmal dem Tau, über die Asche zu gehn.

I, with the German language
this cloud around me
and which I keep as a house,
drift through all languages

O how it turns dark
those somber those rain tones
only the few will fall

Up into brighter zones it will then carry the corpse

Safe Conduct

With sleep-drunk birds
and wind-shot trees
the day gets up, and the sea
empties a foaming goblet to him.

The rivers course to the great water,
and the land puts promises of love
into the mouth of the pure air
with fresh flowers.

Earth wants no mushroom of smoke,
no spitting up of creatures against the sky,
with rain and angry lightning bolts she wants to
stop the unspeakable voices of destruction.

With us she wants to see the motley brothers
and the gray sisters awake,
king fish, her highness the nightingale
and the fire prince salamander.

For us she plants corals in the sea,
commands woods to keep quiet,
the marble to swell its beautiful vein,
the dew once more to walk across ashes.

Die Erde will ein freies Geleit ins All
jeden Tag aus der Nacht haben,
daß noch tausend und ein Morgen wird
von der alten Schönheit jungen Gnaden.

■ Nelly Sachs

Wo nur finden die Worte
die Erhellten vom Erstlingsmeer
die Augen-Aufschlagenden
die nicht mit Zungen verwundeten
die von den Lichter-Weisen versteckten
für deine entzündete Himmelfahrt
die Worte
die ein zum Schweigen gesteuertes Weltall
mitzieht in deine Frühlinge —

■ Hilde Domin

„Seids gewesen, seids gewesen!"

Die letzte Erde
der Erde letzter Tag
die letzte Landschaft
die eines letzten Menschen Auge sieht
unerinnert
nicht weitergegeben
an nicht mehr Kommende
dieser Tag
ohne Namen ihn zu rufen
ohne Rufende

Earth wants safe-conduct into the universe,
receiving each day from its night,
so that another thousand and one mornings will be
of the old beauty by youthful graces.

◼ Nelly Sachs

Only where find those words
those illumined by the first sea
those opening their eyes
those not wounded by tongues
those hidden by the light-wise
for your inflamed ascension
those words
which a universe piloted into silence
draws along with it into your Springs—

Translated by Michael Hamburger, Christopher Holme,
Ruth and Matthew Mead, and Michael Roloff

◼ Hilde Domin

"Be as you were, be as you were!"

The last earth
the earth's last day
the last landscape
that the last human eye sees
unremembered
not passed on
to those no longer to come
this day
no name to call it by
no one to call

nicht grüner
nicht weißer
nicht blauer
als die Tage die wir sehn
oder schwarz
oder feuerfarben
er wird einen Abend haben
oder er wird keinen Abend haben
seine Helle sein Dunkel
unvergleichbar.

Die Sonne die leuchtet falls sie leuchtet
unbegrüßt
nach diesem Tag
wird es sich unter ihr öffnen?
Werden wir
als Staunende
wieder herausgegeben
unter einem währenden Licht?

Zünder der letzten Lunte
Maden der Ewigkeit?

Schöner

Schöner sind die Gedichte des Glücks.

Wie die Blüte schöner ist als der Stengel
der sie doch treibt
sind schöner die Gedichte des Glücks.

Wie der Vogel schöner ist als das Ei
wie es schön ist wenn Licht wird
ist schöner das Glück.

Und sind schöner die Gedichte
die ich nicht schreiben werde.

not greener
not whiter
not bluer
than the days we see
or black
or fire colored
it will have an evening
or it will have no evening
its brightness its darkness
incomparable.

The sun that shines if it shines
ungreeted
after this day
will anything open beneath it?
Will we
astonished people
issue forth again
under an enduring light?

Igniter of the last fuse
maggots of eternity?

More Beautiful

More beautiful are the poems of joy.

Just as the blossom is more beautiful than the stalk
that still brings it forth
the poems of joy are more beautiful.

Just as the bird is more beautiful than the egg
as it is beautiful when light breaks
joy is more beautiful.

And more beautiful are the poems
that I will not write.

Christine Busta

Biblische Kindheit

Damals bist du oft zu mir gekommen,
und das Dunkel war von deinem frommen
Koboldnamen heimlig, Habakuk!
Denn zum Essenträger unter den Propheten
brauchte man nicht feierlich zu beten,
und von deinem Brei bekam man nie genug.
Immerzu warst du umsummt von Bienen
und dein Brotsack stak mit Mandeln und Rosinen
voll und Kringeln, die man nur im Himmel buk.
Bartlos warst du, Gott nahm dich beim Schopfe,
Windroßreiter mit dem Struwelkopfe,
der die wunderbare Schüssel nie zerschlug,
jedem Kinderkummer, der noch wachte,
Daniels sanfte Schlummerlöwen brachte
und die Monduhr unterm Bauernkittel trug.
Geh ich in der Welt nicht ganz verloren,
ist's, weil manchmal nachts die tauben Ohren
treu dein Echo tröstet, Habakuk.

Erika Burkart

Als ich ein Kind war und Kronen verteilte,
das Wasser mich trug, der Spiegel mich einließ,
vogelgestaltig der Dämon mich anflog,
mit Himmel die Wand tapeziert und der Himmel
Decke und Wandung der Rundstube Welt,
der Hirte ein Gott
und die Gottheit ein Hirt war,

Christine Busta

Biblical Childhood

Back then you often came to me
and made the dark snug with the piety
of your elfish name, Habakkuk!
For one had no need for solemn prayer
among those prophets who provisions bear
yet of your gruel one never got enough.
Always bees around you buzzed
and your sack crammed with almonds, raisins, leaven
biscuits only baked in heaven.
Beardless you, God grabbed your crowning fuzz,
wind horse rider with the unkempt mop
who never made the magic dishes drop,
to the cares of each still wakeful child
you brought Daniel's slumbering lions mild
and wore your moon watch beneath a peasant smock.
If I do not get lost in this world below
it is because at night your faithful echo
comforts my deaf ears, old Habukkuk.

Erika Burkart

When I Was a Child

When I was a child and gave out crowns,
the water bore me, the mirror admitted me,
bird shaped demons flew to me,
the walls were carpeted with the sky and the sky
was ceiling and wall to the world's round room,
the shepherd a god
and the godhead a shepherd,

Notenbilder aus Vögeln und Drähten
im Gegenlicht tönten,
die Ähren an Sterne rührten, das Gras
Wanderblumen und Schlafengel barg,
der Strahl aus dem Brunnen
kristallene Grotten höhlte in mir,

überfloß die Zeit —
schäumte in Faltersträußen und Frühschnee,
gerann — immer war eine Glocke dabei —
zu breiten Röten und Eisvogelblau.
Der Himmel trug auf der Schulter
den zweiten Himmel, der stürzte, als ich

nicht mehr ein Kind war,
die Erde sich drehte,
die Herzen sich drehten,
das Kreuz vom Baum,
der Baum sich vom Wald,
die Liebe sich trennte
in ich du er sie,
die Sonne im Kind,
das Kind in der Sonne verschwand.

■ Paul Celan

Sprachgitter

Augenrund zwischen den Stäben.

Flimmertier Lid
rudert nach oben,
gibt einen Blick frei.

Iris, Schwimmerin, traumlos und trüb:
der Himmel, herzgrau, muß nah sein.

musical notes made of birds and wires
sounded against the back lighting,
the wheat touched the stars, the grass
sheltered migrating flowers and angels of sleep,
the jet of water from the well
carved out crystal grottos in me,

time overflowed—
foamed up in butterfly bouquets and early snow,
curdled—a bell always pealed—
into broad reds and kingfisher blue.
The sky bore on its shoulders
a second heaven that tumbled down when I

no longer was a child,
the earth turned,
hearts turned,
the cross detached itself from the tree,
the tree from the woods,
and love separated
into I you he she,
the sun disappeared in the child,
the child in the sun.

■ Paul Celan

Confessional Grate

Eye round between the lattice.

Undulating creature lid
rows upward
sets one glance free.

Iris, swimmer, dreamless and cloudy:
heaven, heart gray, must be near.

Schräg, in der eisernen Tülle,
der blakende Span.
Am Lichtsinn
errätst du die Seele.

(Wär ich wie du. Wärst du wie ich.
Standen wir nicht
unter *einem* Passat?
Wir sind Fremde.)

Die Fliesen. Darauf,
dicht beieinander, die beiden
herzgrauen Lachen:
zwei
Mundvoll Schweigen.

Zürich, zum Storchen

Für Nelly Sachs

Vom Zuviel war die Rede, vom
Zuwenig. Von Du
und Aber-Du, von
der Trübung durch Helles, von
Jüdischem, von
deinem Gott.

Da-
von.
Am Tag einer Himmelfahrt, das
Münster stand drüben, es kam
mit einigem Gold übers Wasser.

Von deinem Gott war die Rede, ich sprach
gegen ihn, ich
ließ das Herz, das ich hatte,
hoffen:
auf
sein höchstes, umröcheltes, sein
haderndes Wort —

Diagonal, in the iron tulle,
the span turning soot black.
By its bent toward light
you divine the soul.

(Were I like you. Were you like me.
Didn't we stand
beneath one trade wind?
We are strangers.)

The flagstones. On them,
close to each other, both the
heart gray puddles:
two
mouthfuls of silence.

Zürich, Sign of the Stork

For Nelly Sachs

Of too much we talked, of
too little. Of you
and you again, of
the clouding of things with light, of
things Jewish, of
your God.

Of
that.
On the day of an ascension,
the cathedral stood across the way, it came
with touches of gold across the water.

Of your God we talked. I spoke
against him, I
let the heart that I had
hope:
for
his highest, death rattled, his
wrathful word—

Dein Aug sah mir zu, sah hinweg,
dein Mund
sprach sich dem Aug zu, ich hörte:

Wir
wissen ja nicht, weißt du,
wir
wissen ja nicht,
was
gilt.

■ Peter Huchel

Psalm

Daß aus dem Samen des Menschen
Kein Mensch
Und aus dem Samen des Ölbaums
Kein Ölbaum
Werde,
Es ist zu messen
Mit der Elle des Todes.

Die da wohnen
Unter der Erde
In einer Kugel aus Zement,
Ihre Stärke gleicht
Dem Halm
Im peitschenden Schnee.

Die Öde wird Geschichte.
Termiten schreiben sie
Mit ihren Zangen
In den Sand.

Your eyes looked at me, looked away,
your mouth
spoke to my eyes, I heard:

We
really don't know, you know,
we
really don't know
what
counts.

■ **Peter Huchel**

Psalm

That from the seed of man
No man
And from the seed of the olive tree
No olive tree
Will come—
This can be measured
With the yardstick of death.

Those who live
Under the earth
In a dome of cement—
Their strength is like
The reed's
In the whipping snow.

Bareness becomes history.
Termites write it
with their pincers
In the sand.

Und nicht erforscht wird werden
Ein Geschlecht,
Eifrig bemüht,
Sich zu vernichten.

■ Christine Lavant

Es riecht nach Schnee, der Sonnenapfel hängt
so schön und rot vor meiner Fensterscheibe;
wenn ich das Fieber jetzt aus mir vertreibe,
wird es ein Wiesel, das der Nachbar fängt,
und niemand wärmt dann meine kalten Finger.
Durchs Dorf gehn heute wohl die Sternensinger
und kommen sicher auch zu meinen Schwestern.
Ein wenig bin ich trauriger als gestern,
doch lange nich genug, um fromm zu sein.
Den Apfel nähme ich wohl gern herein
und möchte heimlich an der Schale riechen,
bloß um zu wissen wie der Himmel schmeckt.
Das Wiesel duckt sich wild und aufgeschreckt
und wird vielleict nun doch zum Nachbar kriechen,
weil sich mein Herz so eng zusammenzieht.
Ich weiß nicht, ob der Himmel niederkniet,
wenn man zu schwach ist, um hinaufzukommen?
Den Apfel hat schon jemand weggenommen . . .
Doch eigentlich ist meine Stube gut
und wohl viel wärmer als ein Baum voll Schnee.
Mir tut auch nur der halbe Schädel weh
und außerdem geht jetzt in meinem Blut
der Schlaf mit einer Blume auf und nieder
und singt für mich allein die Sternenlieder.

And there will be no inquiry about
A race
Eagerly bent
On destroying itself.

■ Christine Lavant

It smells like snow, the round sun apple sets
so beautiful and red outside my window pane;
when now the fever in my body wanes
it turns into a weasel that the neighbor gets
and then no one will warm my icy fingers.
Today throughout the village go star-singers
and surely come to where my sisters hide.
I am a little sadder now than yesterday,
but not by far enough to learn to pray.
The apple I would like to bring inside
and secretly would like to smell the skin,
just to know what is the heaven's flavor.
The weasel, wild and frightened, now ducks in
and maybe will yet creep off to the neighbor
because my heart so tightly does contract.
I don't know if the heavens ever bend
when one has grown too feeble to ascend?
Already someone took the apple back . . .
But actually my room is very fine
and warmer than a tree that's full of snow.
Only half my skull still's aching though,
and then there runs within this blood of mine
the sleep with its one flower near and far
and sings for me alone the songs of every star.

In uns allen hat er vielleicht noch nichts

In uns allen hat er vielleicht noch nichts,
worauf er auch nur eine einzige Nacht
das Haupt seiner Leiden einschläfern könnte
und das brennende Herz sich bewahren.

In uns allen leidet das eigene Haupt,
in uns allen lauert das eigene Herz,
und wird schläfern diebisch mit seinem Namen
in bittern Nächten uns ein.

Wir schleifen ihn mit bis zum Höllenrand,
wir geben ihn auf im Vorhof der Liebe,
und später — zu spät! — mit versteintem Herzen
bieten wir ihn uns als Obdach an.

■ ## Hans Magnus Enzensberger

Isotop

Reffen wir ruhig die Regenschirme!
Die nächste Sintflut wird seicht sein.
Das alte Verfahren, Majore und Kühe
auf Hochspannungsmasten, der allgemeine
Andrang zum Ararat, zu den Alpenvereinen,
das Inlett plötzlich geplatzt, Panik
unter den Klempnern und pampige Tauben
mit oder ohne Ölzweig, das alles
hat sich nicht recht bewährt: Immer
dieselben Gerechten entstiegen der Arche
und begaben, den Wasserleichen zum Hohn,
Wandelanleihen und Päpst al pari.

In all of us he has perhaps nothing yet

In all of us he has perhaps nothing yet
on which he could for just one night
put the head of his suffering to sleep
and shelter his burning heart.

In us all it's our own head that suffers,
in us all it's our own heart that lurks,
and thievishly we lull ourselves to sleep
with his name on bitter nights.

We drag him about over to the brink of hell,
we give up on him in the anteroom of love
and later—too late!—with hearts turned to stone
we offer him as a refuge to ourselves.

■ Hans Magnus Enzensberger

Isotope

Let's blithely reef the umbrellas!
The next deluge won't be deep.
The same old stuff, majors and cows
on high tension towers, the public
rush to Ararat, to Alpine Clubs,
the bedtick suddenly burst, panic
among the plumbers and cheeky doves
with or without olive branch, a lot
didn't quite stand the test in the end: Always
the same righteous people disembarked from the ark
and negotiated, in scorn of the drowned corpses,
adjustable loans and popes at cost.

Heute sind im Ural und in Arizona
Nobelpreisträger in Rudeln dabei,
den Wirkungsgrad zu verbessern,
um die Knöchel der Damen zu schonen.
Zuversicht herrscht in den Labors,
aus den Türritzen dringt ein Tau,
ein Ausschlag, feucht und human,
bomben-, tod- und betriebssicher, fett,
ein heiserer hauchdünner Schweiß.

Vorbei ist die Zeit der Versuche,
aus den Poren der Welt kriecht längst
eine dürre Flut, und wir ersaufen,
diszipliniert vor den Fahrkartenschaltern
kniend in Kuckucksuhren und Jod.

Abendnachrichten

Massaker um eine Handvoll Reis,
höre ich, für jeden an jedem Tag
eine Handvoll Reis: Trommelfeuer
auf dünnen Hütten, undeutlich
höre ich es, beim Abendessen.

Auf den glasierten Ziegeln
höre ich Reiskörner tanzen,
eine Handvoll, beim Abendessen,
Reiskörner auf meinem Dach:
den ersten Märzregen, deutlich.

Fremder Garten

Es ist heiß. Das Gift kocht in den Tomaten.
Hinter den Gärten rollen versäumte Züge vorbei,
das verbotene Schiff heult hinter den Türmen.

Today in the Urals and in Arizona
Nobel Prize winners in droves are busy
improving the degree of effectiveness
to spare the ladies' knuckles.
Confidence reigns in the labs,
a dew seeps through the door cracks,
a rash, damp and human,
bomb-, death-, and foolproof, fat,
a hoarse sweat, thin as breath.

Gone is the age of experiments,
from the pores of the world
a sterile flood has long since oozed out, and we drown,
well disciplined in front of the ticket counters
knee-deep in cuckoo clocks and iodine.

Evening News

Massacres for a handful of rice,
I hear, for everyone every day
a handful of rice: drumfire
on thin huts, indistinct
I hear it, at supper.

On the glazed tiles
I hear rice grains dancing,
a handful at supper,
rice grains on my roof:
the first March rain, distinct.

Strange Garden

It is hot. The poison boils in the tomatoes.
Behind the gardens missed trains roll past,
the forbidden ship howls behind the towers.

Angewurzelt unter den Ulmen. Wo soll ich euch hintun,
Füße? Meine Augen, an welches Ufer euch setzen?
Um mein Land, doch wo ist es? bin ich betrogen.

Die Signale verdorren. Das Schiff speit Öl in den Hafen
und wendet. Ruß, ein fettes rieselndes Tuch
deckt den Garten. Mittag, und keine Grille.

Karl Heinrich Marx

Riesiger Großvater
jahvebärtig
auf braunen Daguerreotypien
ich seh dein Gesicht
in der schlohweißen Aura
selbstherrlich   streitbar
und die Papiere im Vertiko:
Metzgersrechnungen
Inauguraladressen
Steckbriefe

Deinen massigen Leib
seh ich im Fahndungsbuch
riesiger Hochverräter
displaced person
in Bratenrock und Plastron
schwindsüchtig   schlaflos
die Galle verbrannt
von schweren Zigarren
Salzgurken   Laudanum
und Likör

Ich seh dein Haus
in der rue d'Alliance
Dean Street   Grafton Terrace
riesiger Bourgeois
Haustyrann
in zerschlissnen Pantoffeln:

Rooted under the elms. Where am I to put you,
feet? My eyes, on what shore set you?
Out of my own land, but where is it? I have been cheated.

The signals dry up. The ship spews oil into the harbor
and turns. Soot, a greasy trickling cloth
covers the garden. Noon, and not a cricket.

Karl Heinrich Marx

Giant grandfather
Yahweh-bearded
on brown daguerreotypes
I see your face
in the snow white aura
tyrannical   pugnacious
and the papers in vertigo
butchers' bills
inaugural addresses
arrest warrants

Your massive body
I see on the wanted lists
giant traitor
displaced person
in frock coat and wide tie
consumptive   sleepless
your bile singed
with heavy cigars
salt pickles   laudanum
and liqueur

I see your house
in the rue d'Alliance
Dean Street   Grafton Terrace
giant bourgeois
household tyrant
in worn-out slippers;

Ruß und „ökonomische Scheiße"
Pfandleihen „wie gewöhnlich"
Kindersärge
Hintertreppengeschichten

Keine Mitrailleuse
in deiner Prophetenhand:
ich seh sie ruhig
im British Museum
unter der grünen Lampe
mit fürchterlicher Geduld
dein eigenes Haus zerbrechen
riesiger Gründer
andern Häusern zuliebe
in denen du nimmer erwacht bist

Riesiger Zaddik
ich seh dich verraten
von deinen Anhängern:
nur deine Feinde
sind dir geblieben:
ich seh dein Gesicht
auf dem letzten Bild
vom April zweiundachtzig:
eine eiserne Maske:
die eiserne Maske der Freiheit.

■ Ilse Aichinger

Nachruf

Gib mir den Mantel, Martin,
aber geh erst vom Sattel
und laß dein Schwert, wo es ist,
gib mir den ganzen.

soot and "economic shit"
pawning things "as usual"
coffins of children
tales of back stairs

No mitrailleuse gun
in your prophet hand:
I see it
in the British Museum
under the green lamp
with terrifying patience calmly
wreck your own house
giant founder
for the sake of other houses
in which you never awoke

Giant zaddik
I see you betrayed
by your followers:
only your enemies
remain to you:
I see your face
on the last picture
from April eighty-two:
an iron mask:
the iron mask of liberty.

■ Ilse Aichinger

Petition to St. Martin

Give me that coat, Martin,
but first get off your horse
and leave your sword where it is,
give me the whole coat.

■ Inge Müller

Wie

Wie kann man Gedichte machen
Lauter als die Schreie der Verwundeten
Tiefer als die Nacht der Hungernden
Leiser als Atem von Mund zu Mund
Härter als Leben
Weich wie Wasser, das den Stein überlebt?
Wie kann man keine Gedichte machen?

Wir

Wir, sagte einer, der dazugehört
Sind die verlorne Generation
Sie haben uns um unsre Ration geprellt
Das uns Zustehende war schon verteilt
Wir wurden mit der Lügenflasche aufgezogen
Gefüttert mit dem Brei der Heuchelei
Gezüchtigt mit der Peitsche der Vergangenheit
Geängstigt mit dem Teufel an der Wand
Bis wir das Gängelband zerrissen aus Furcht
Und stolpernd über unsre eignen Füße fielen
Im Namen unsrer Väter schrien wir Heil
Und glaubten unser eigenes
(Und wer von uns den Mund nicht auftat
Würgend an unverdaubaren Schalen
Spie hin und wieder aus ins Gebüsch: der Magen
War gesünder als der Kopf)
Wir lernten Preußens Gloria und drei vier:
Ein Lied und Deutschland, Deutschland über alles
Über die eigne Leiche gehn fürs Vaterland
Marsch, marsch: Volk ans Gewehr, Deutsch sein
Heißt treu sein; Kopf ab zum Gebet
Humanismus heißt: JEDEM DAS SEINE
(Die Mauer steht noch, wo das steht).

Inge Müller

How

How can one make poems
Louder than the cries of the wounded
Deeper than the night of the starving
Quieter than breath from mouth to mouth
Harder than life
Soft as the water that outlives the stone?
How can one not make poems?

We

We, someone said, who's included
Are the lost generation
They swindled us out of our ration
Our share was already divvied up
We were nursed with a bottle of lies
Fed with the gruel of hypocrisy
Flogged with the whip of the past
Intimidated by the devil sketched on the wall
Until we tore off the lead strings in fear
And tripping over our own feet fell
In the name of our fathers we screamed Heil
And believed we hailed ourselves
(And anyone among us who did not open his mouth
Gagging on indigestible peels
Spit out now and again into the bush: the stomach
Was healthier than the head)
We learned Prussia's Gloria and one two sing:
A song and Deutschland, Deutschland über alles
Walk over your own corpse for the fatherland
March, march: the people to arms! To be German
Is to be true blue, heads off for prayer
Humanism means: TO EACH HIS OWN
(The wall still stands, where that stands).

■ Helga Novak

Mein Staat — Der heilige Martin

mein Staat baut lichte Schulen
mein Staat garantiert kostenlose
Gesundheitsfürsorge
und Hochschulstipendien
mein Staat baut Wohnhäuser
und Altersheime und zahlt
Kindergeld und Renten
mein Staat hat die Fabrik-
und Hausbesitzer enteignet
er gibt mir Arbeit
und verlangt niedrige Mieten

mein Staat verbietet mirs Maul
und steckt mich ins Heer
und macht die Haushaltspläne
und die Außenpolitik
ohne mich

mein Staat gleicht dem heiligen Martin
der seinen Mantel zerschlitzt
was soll ich denn mit dem halben Lumpen
dem einen Ärmel anfangen
ich — der ich nackt und bar
unterm Großen Wagen bin
und er — der Fette
in drei Pullovern und Filzstiefeln
satt unterm Hut

mein Staat verlangt daß ich ihn heilige
und drückt sich beiseite
um den andern halben Lumpen
in den Abort zu stopfen

Helga Novak

My State—Saint Martin

my state builds bright schools
my state guarantees medicare
free of charge
and university scholarships
my state builds apartment houses
and homes for the aged it pays
subsidies for children and pensions
my state has disowned the factory
and real estate owners
it gives me work
and takes low rent

my state tells me to shut up
and drafts me into the army
it makes the national budget
and foreign policy
without me

my state is like Saint Martin
who cuts his coat in two
what am I supposed to do with that half rag
that one sleeve
I—naked and bare
under the big dipper
and he—old fatso
in three sweaters and felt boots
gorged under his hat

my state demands that I canonize him
and he slips out
to stuff the other half rag
into the john

Kain oder Abel

Deutschland
schalkhafte Nutte
nenne dich nicht
Europa Wertarbeit
Hochkonjunktur Kronprinz
der Wirtschaftsgemeinschaft

nenne dich nicht
sozial
Land der Werkleute
human gebildet
rote Nation
deine Röcke sind Fahnen
im Wind der Großmächte

rechts mit Geld und
links mit Transparenten
bekleidet bettelst du
vor der Toren
um die Atombombe

du schläfst in den
Seidenkissen der Diebe
in den Matratzen der
Pharisäer nein
du wälzt dich nicht
mit Grobianen Kohleschippern
Knütteln und Kreaturen
deinen Neugeborenen verhängst du
statt sie abzutreiben
Kain oder Abel zu sein

Cain or Abel

Germany
wily whore
don't call yourself
Europe quality work
boom market crown prince
of the economic community

don't call yourself
social-minded
land of the working people
humanely educated
red nation
your skirts are flags
in the winds of the superpowers

right draped in money and
left in banners
you beg
before the portals
for the atom bomb

you sleep on the
silk pillows of thieves
on the mattresses of the
Pharisees no
you don't trundle
with the ruffians, the coal miners
cudgels and creatures
you destine your newborns
instead of aborting them
to be Cain or Abel

Volker Braun

Anspruch

Kommt uns nicht mit Fertigem. Wir brauchen Halbfabrikate.
Weg mit dem Rehbraten — her mir dem Wald und dem Messer.
Hier herrscht das Experiment und keine steife Routine.
Hier schreit eure Wünsche aus: Empfang beim Leben.
Zwischen die Kontinente, zu allen Ufern
Spannt seine Muskeln das Meer unserer Erwartungen
An alle Küsten trommeln seine Finger die Brandung
Über die Uferklinge läßt es die Wogen springen und aufschlagen
Immer erneut hält es die Flut hoch und gibt es sie auf.

Für uns sind die Rezepte nicht ausgeschrieben, mein Herr.
Das Leben ist kein Bilderbuch mehr, Mister, und keine peinliche Partitur,
    Fräulein.
Hier wird ab sofort Denken verlangt.
Raus aus den Sesseln, Jungs. Feldbett — meinetwegen.
Nicht so feierlich, Genossen, das Denken will heitere Stirnen.
Wer sehnt sich hier nach wilhelminischem Schulterputz?
Unsere Schultern tragen einen Himmel voll Sternen.

Hier wird Neuland gegraben und Neuhimmel angeschnitten —
Hier ist der Staat für Anfänger, Halbfabrikat auf Lebenszeit.
Hier schreit eure Wünsche aus: an alle Ufer
Trommelt die Flut eurer Erwartungen!
Was da an deine Waden knallt, Mensch, die tosende Brandung:
Das sind unsere kleinen Finger, die schießen nur
Bißchen Zukunft vor, Spielerei.

Volker Braun

Claim

Don't come to us with things finished. We need half-made pieces.
Out with the roast venison—in with the forest and the knife.
Here experiment reigns and not a fixed routine.
Here scream out your wishes: let life provide!
Between continents, toward every shore
— The sea of our expectations stretches its muscles
On every coast its fingers drum the surf
Over the shore's knife edge it makes waves jump and break
Over and over it raises the flood waters up and abandons them.

For us the prescriptions were not spelled out, sir.
Life is no longer a picture book, mister, nor a painstaking musical score, miss.
From now on thinking is demanded here.
Up out of the easy chairs, boys. Campcots—for all I care.
Don't be so solemn, comrades, thinking needs cheerful brows.
Who here longs for Wilhelminian shoulder insignias?
— Our shoulders bear a sky full of stars. —

Here new land is dug and new skies cut—
Here is a state for beginners, half-made and for life.
Here scream out your wishes: toward every shore drum
ʹ The flood of your expectations.
— What bangs against your calves, man, the raging surf:
That's our little fingers, they shoot out just
A little future, child's play.

■ Günter Kunert

Edgar Lee Masters

Hier ruht ein verhungerter Gott, der Menschen
schuf, sie zu begraben in einem Ort, den
er erbaute im Geiste und nannte:
Spoon-River.

Der Grabsteine säte, darauf eingeschrieben
stand die harte, böse Zeit, und der nichts
erntete davon, denn Schweigen, Schweigen.

Starb selbst
nach Schluß des Weltkriegs Nummer zwei,
vergessen,
in der Steinstadt New York im Armenhaus an
unheilbarer Magenleere.

Weil er jene, in deren Kontobüchern nichts steht
von der Menschlichkeit, auf seinen Kirchhof
brachte und dort verscharrte neben Bettlern,
Huren, Rebellen.

■ Helmut Heissenbüttel

Einfache grammatische Meditationen

c [konjunktivisch]
bis zur Mittel der Hälfte
weniger als zu wenig
am wenigsten
als ob als ob

■ Günter Kunert

Edgar Lee Masters

Here rests a famished god who created
men only to bury them in a place that
he constructed in his mind and named:
Spoon River.

Who sowed gravestones on which stood
written the hard, evil times and who harvested
nothing from this except silence, silence.

Died himself
after the close of World War number two,
forgotten,
in the stone city New York in the poor house
of an incurably empty stomach.

Because he brought to his graveyard
those whose account books are empty of humanity
and there buried them beside beggars,
whores, rebels.

■ Helmut Heissenbüttel

Simple Grammatical Meditations

c [subjunctively]
up to the middle of the half
less than too little
the least
as if as if

wahrscheinlich wahrscheinlich
auf sich genommen nicht auf sich genommen
unentschieden
vorläufig vorläufig

f [partizipial]
wartend warten gewartet haben
gewartet werden
rumgekriegt nicht rumgekriegt rumgekriegt worden sein
widerrufene Widerrufe
quergespannte Geräusche
quergespannte Geräusche aus endlichen Zeitpunkten
widerrufene Widerrufe auf Widerruf richtend auf
aufgerichtet gerichtet auf aufgerichtete Richtung
aufgerichtete Richtungen aus unendlichen Zeitpunkten

das Sagbare sagen
das Erfahrbare erfahren
das Entscheidbare entscheiden
das Erreichbare erreichen
das Wiederholbare wiederholen
das Beendbare beenden

das nicht Sagbare
das nicht Erfahrbare
das nicht Entscheidbare
das nicht Erreichbare
das nicht Wiederholbare
das nicht Beendbare

das nicht Beendbare nicht beenden

probably probably
taken upon himself not taken upon himself
undecided
provisionally provisionally

f [participially]
waiting to wait to have waited
to be waited
won around not won around have been won around
retracted retractions
diagonally stretched noises
diagonally stretched noises from finite points in time
retracted retractions until retracted rising up
rising up directed at risen up direction
risen up directions from infinite points in time

to say the sayable
to experience the experienceable
to decide the decidable
to reach the reachable
to repeat the repeatable
to end the endable

the unsayable
the unexperienceable
the undecidable
the unreachable
the unrepeatable
the unendable

not to end the unendable

■ Eugen Gomringer

worte sind schatten
schatten werden worte

worte sind spiele
spiele werden worte

sind schatten worte
werden worte spiele

sind spiele worte
werden worte schatten

sind worte schatten
werden spiele worte

sind worte spiele
werden schatten worte

■ Ernst Jandl

diskussion

ist das a) lyrik?
ist a) das lyrik?
a) ist das lyrik?
ist das lyrik a)?

das ist a) lyrik
das a) ist lyrik.
a) das ist lyrik.
das ist lyrik a).

■ Eugen Gomringer

words are shadows
shadows become words

words are games
games become words

if shadows are words
words become games

if games are words
words become shadows

if words are shadows
games become words

if words are games
shadows become words

■ Ernst Jandl

discussion

is that a) lyric?
is a) that lyric?
a) is that lyric?
is that lyric a)?

that is a) lyric.
that a) is lyric.
a) that is lyric.
that is lyric a).

peter frißt seinen weg ins schlaraffenland

petermilchbreiberg
eterpilchbreiberg
tereplchbreiberg
ertepchbreiberg
retephbreiberg
retepbreiberg
mretepreiberg
miretepeiberg
milretepiberg
milcretepberg
milchreteperg
milchbreteprg
milchbrretepg
milchbreretep
milchbreiretep
milchbreibretpe
milchbreiberepet
milchbreiberrpete
milchbreibergpeter

■　Friederike Mayröcker

Tod durch Musen

(modell 1 / cleo):

erheitern erzürnen bis an die stirn
es geht auh ohne
900 kilo herz
barfusz über dem meeresspiegel
cleo cloistered
bundschuh & schweiz / hopfgarten blauer käse
schaut mir neugier auge blaut
in forchtenstein ach
strasz burg

(goebbels „. . wollt ihr den totalen krieg . . !" JAAA)

peter eats his way into the land of milk and honey

petermilkandhoney
 eterpilkandhoney
  tereplkandhoney
  ertepkandhoney
   retepandhoney
    mretepndhoney
    miretepdhoney
    milretephoney
    milkreteponey
    milkaretepney
    milkanretepey
    milkandretepy
    milkandhretep
    milkandhoretpe
    milkandhonrepet
    milkandhonerpete
    milkandhoneypeter

■ Friederike Mayröcker

Death by the Muses

(model 1/cleo):

cheer provoke up to the brow
it also works without
900 kilos of heart
barefoot over the sea surface
cleo cloistered
bundschuh & switzerland/hopfgarten blue cheese
looks at me curiosity the eye blues
in forchtenstein ah
strasz burg

(goebbels: ". . do you want all out war . . ! YESSS)

(modell 2 / kalliope):

alle die jahre grünes septett
schon goethe sagte
die differenzierung des orts
die diskriminierung der noten-gräber
die d. der toten-schrift
immer eines himmels
minderen fuszes bei trauben stadt
abend voll dämmer zu sterben
eine wüste voll
und die künstlichen paradiese mit den augen eines lamms

(modell 3 / melpomene):

in rhein-mein-schlinge-gelockt; die tolle
zugezogen; hochgehalten; gehängt; mit
        dem bürzel nach oben;
versenkt —
ausruf totalen schmerzes (mit zusammengepreszten lippen
    hervorgebrachter laut)

(poet.) knallen; schnuppe am lampendocht / gebrüll
weintoll
entfesselte dame!
und schon sind wir mitten drin in der suspekten abstraktion

(modell 4 / thalia):

random eines kurfürstlichen molochs (wärest besser
    ein mädchen geworden!)
hast-schon-recht-
hinter ihnen geht eener / hinter ihnen steht eener
dölln-seä-seech-neech-om
durch den abtritt im schweizerhaus(stil)
schweizerischer burgen-verein /
(„. . hölfzt dö ooch d'burg' & schlöss'
vor untergang und sch. zu bewahr'n . . ")

(model 2/calliope):

for all those years green septet
goethe said even then
the differentiation of the place
the discrimination of the note-diggers
the d. of the obit-uary
always of one heaven
of lesser footing in clustered city
evening full of dusk to die
a desert full
and the artificial paradises with the eyes of a lamb

(model 3/melpomene):

enticed into the rhine-mine trap; glamour wave
pulled down, brushed back, hung; with
        the rump up;
drooping—
outcry of total pain (with lips pressed together
    sound brought forth)

(poet.) detonate; snuff on the lampwick/roaring
madly drunk
unchained lady!
and already we are in the midst of the suspect abstraction

(model 4/thalia):

randomness of an elector's moloch (it would have been better
    if you had been a girl!)
you-are-right-already
some guy follows behind you/some guy stands behind you
don't turn around
through the lavatory in the swiss house (style)
swiss society of castles/
(". . d'ya also help keep th' forts & castles
w'll keep ya frum wrack and ruin . .")

— l'association suisse pour
la protection des chateaux
et des RUINES/vous nous aidez à conserver nos chateaux! —

(„ . . könnt ihr mir die lyra 'runterwerfen?")

(modell 5 / urania):

das ablegen mehrerer prothesen
das anschnallen guten mutes
die vertilgung von milden gaben / konfrontation mit der milchstrasze —
„. . nur die schräg-bilder . ."

schweigen: ein ergusz nach unten
eine flocke zeit
blendung des gehörs

golfplatz der sterne / rothschild über den seriösen morgenstern

(modelle 6 & 7 / terpsichore & erato):

schaut mich an aus seinen silberblauen /
pop-schüler kaut siringen /

     — hatte keine ahnung von nottingham —
     — gisbornes försterin —
     — kleiner john in sherwood —
     — ah du bist es mozgo —
     — beim heiligen john von verneuil —
     — bestellt gisborne viele grüsze von ivanhoe —
     — die sachsen jagen direkt auf den w. zu —
     — flieh ehe sie die tore schlieszen —
     — der teufel soll den glöckner holen —
     — ja ich bin es leute von nottingham ich bringe euch
          die grüsze der gesetzlosen —

(alles in sprechblasen)

—l'association suisse pour
la protection des chateaux
et des RUINES/vous nous aidez à conserver nos chateaux!—

(". . could you toss the lyre down to me?")

(model 5/urania):

the casting aside of several artificial limbs
the buckling on of good spirit
the eradication of mild gifts/confrontation with the milky way—
". . only the lopsided pictures . ."

silence: a discharge downward
a flake of time
hearing blinded

golf course of the stars/rothschild about the serious morgenstern

(models 6 & 7/terpsichore & erato):

looks at me from his silverblues/
pop-student chews syringa/

> —had no idea of nottingham—
> —gisborne's forestress—
> —little john in sherwood—
> —oh so it's you mozgo—
> —at st. john's of verneuil—
> —sends gisborne greetings from ivanhoe—
> —the sachsens are charging right toward the w.—
> —flee before they close the gates—
> —the devil take the bell ringer—
> —yes people of nottingham it's me i bring you
>   greetings from the outlaws—

(everything in comic strip balloon speech)

(modell 8 / polyhymnia):

durch gesang weissagen
personen die etwas tun können
mündel / wonne
prolongiertes saiteninstrument
mit sturm
mit ohnedies
(".. und haben jeden dank schon in der tat empfangen .. ")
eine bö
        aus dem stegreif
ein hirn voller
geigen
nur mit den lippen lachen

zerreiszen —

(modell 9 / euterpe):

den reptilismus der musen
anzweifeln
archaisch verschleudern / tanzschritte
im „metropol"
petro-chemie mit purpurrotem kamm
rotharig
braunrückig
purpurwangig
purpurfüszig
von rosen rot
abtasten / aufheben / straucheln
— zu sterben

tod durch musen

(model 8/polyhymnia):

prophesy through song
people who can do something
minor/bliss
prolonged string instrument
with storm
with moreover
(". . and have already received every thanks indeed . .")
a squall
        off the cuff
a brain full of
fiddling
to laugh only with your lips

rip to shreds—

(model 9/euterpe):

to call into question
the reptilism of the muses
archaically squander/dance steps
in the "metropol"
petrochemistry with purple-red crest
red-haired
brown-backed
purple-cheeked
purple-footed
red with roses
pick up/stumble/feel out
—to die

death by muses

Rose Ausländer

Alice in Wonderland

Wenn das Gras aus dem Schlaf steigt
klopfen grüne Finger an meine Schläfe
ALICE
      und es geht durch Kiefernschacht
ins Gebiet der Hirsch und Hasen

Ich trinke Milch aus dem Pilz
und schrumpfe zusammen
Käferklein erklimm ich einen Halm
Deutlich rieselt Bienengespräch Vogelgespräch
meine Muttersprachen

Ein flüchtendes Wiesel warnt mich
vor dem lauernden Luchs
Hier kommt meine schüchterne Freundin
das Reh
und gibt mir Bescheid

Ich esse Pilzfleisch
und wachse waldweit

Spiegel waschen sich im Tau
Der Regenbogen in jedem Tropfen
färbt siebenfach das Geheimnis des Kreises

Wann bist du Baum
wann bist du Vogel
wann bist du Lied
ALICE

■ Rose Ausländer

Alice in Wonderland

When the grass rises from sleep
green fingers rap on my temples
ALICE
      and off we go through the pine gorge
into the range of the stags and hares

I drink milk from the mushroom
and shrink
beetle small I scale a grass blade
Plainly the conversations of bee of bird ripple
my mother tongues

A fleeing weasel warns me
of the lurking lynx
Here comes my shy friend
the deer
and tells me what's what

I eat mushroom flesh
and grow forest wide

Mirrors wash themselves in the dew
The rainbow in each drop
colors sevenfold the secret of the circle

When are you tree
when are you bird
when are you song
ALICE

Franz Fühmann

Die Richtung der Märchen

Die Richtung der Märchen: tiefer, immer
zum Grund zu, irdischer, näher der Wurzel der Dinge,
ins Wesen.

Wenn die Quelle im Brunnen nicht springt
und ratlos die Bürger sich stauen:
Held Hans hebt den Stein, der im Wasser liegt,
da hockt eine Kröte darunter,
die Kröte muss man töten,
dann springt der Quell wieder rein.

Die Spindel fiel in den Brunnen,
das Mädchen sprang in die Tiefe,
unten tat sich ein Pfad auf,
der führte zur weisen Frau,
die lohnte gerecht mit Gold oder mit Pech
im Lande tief unter dem Brunnen.

Als er gegen den Drachen zog,
musste der Held den Schacht hinab,
den Drachen in der Höhle zu treffen.

Er sagte: „Lasst mich hinunter, und wenn ich
vor Angst an den Strängen zerre, dann folgt meinem Zerren nicht,
lasst mich noch tiefer hinunter, und je mehr ich zerr,
    desto tiefer lasst mich hinunter." Und
sie liessen ihn hinunter, und er zerrte, und sie liessen ihn tiefer hinab,
und er kam, zerrend, in die Höhle,
und er besiegte den Drachen.

Dem Grund zu, die Richtung der Märchen,
dem Grund zu, wir zerrn an den Strängen,
dem Grund zu, wir zerrn an den Strängen,
dem Grund zu: Wir zerrn an den Strängen . . .

■ Franz Fühmann

The Direction of Fairy Tales

The direction of fairy tales: deeper, always
toward the center, more earthly, closer to the roots of things,
toward essence.

If the spring in the well does not gush
and the inhabitants are stymied:
Hans the hero lifts the stone that lies in the water,
a toad squats beneath it,
the toad must be killed,
then the spring flows pure again.

The spindle falls into the well,
the girl leaps into the depths,
below a path opens up
that leads to a wise woman
who rewards justly with gold or with pitch
in the land deep under the well.

When he went out to fight the dragon
the hero had to descend into the shaft,
to meet the dragon in the cave.

He said: "Let me down, and when I pull
on the line out of fear, never mind my pulling,
but let me down deeper, and the more I pull,
    the farther you should let me down." And
they let him down, and he pulled, and they let him down deeper,
and he came, pulling, into the cave
and he defeated the dragon.

Toward the center, the direction of the fairy tales,
toward the center, we pull on the lines
toward the center, we pull on the lines
toward the center: we pull on the lines . . .

■ **Georg Maurer**

Die Romantiker und die Dekadenten

Längst war der Himmel geräumt,
und die Madonnen sassen auf Wiesen,
zeigten den schneeweissen Busen und tränkten den Knaben.
Auf dem Plan erschienen die Dichter und suchten ihre Geliebten,
jeder seine Madonna. Und die Mädchen erschrocken
sahn sich auf Wolken gesetzt, auf denen sie nicht sitzen konnten,
selbst die Engelhafteste, Schwebendste fiel
durch den glänzenden Dunst. Schwermütig
wandelten die Dichter, besangen nur tote Jungfraun,
machten das kühle Grab, das weisse Sterbelaken
zu ihrem Himmel und feierten dort die Feste
in mächtigen Hymnen der Nacht —
bis einer im Grabgewölbe schauernd
den Sargdeckel hob: Entsetzt sah er die Würmer
die Leckerbissen sich neiden
vom Leib der Geliebten. — Und alle Dichter
waren nun aufgeklärt, nahmen auf ihre Knie
schnell die Dirnen und vom Wirte die Drogen.
Doch den Absinth im Blut, taumelten sie
in die Morgenluft und bekehrten sich weinend
zur Madonna oben, an deren unendlichem Lager
längst die Physiker sassen mit nüchternen Instrumenten.

Georg Maurer

Romantics and Decadents

The heavens had long been cleared out,
and the madonnas sat in fields,
displayed snow white bosoms and nursed their sons.
On the plain the poets appeared and sought their lovers,
each his madonna. And the girls, to their horror,
saw themselves set on clouds where they could not sit,
even the most angelic who hovered best fell
through the shining steam. Downcast
the poets promenaded, sang only about dead virgins,
made the cool grave, the white shrouds
into their heaven and there celebrated the festivities
in forceful hymns of the night—
until one shuddering in the grave vault
raised the coffin lid: horrified he saw the worms
coveting tasty morsels
from the body of the beloved.—And all the poets
were suddenly enlightened, quickly took whores
on their knees and drugs from the innkeepers.
But with absinthe in their blood they staggered
into the morning air and converted weeping
to the Madonna above, at whose infinite bedside
the physicists had long been sitting with sober instruments.

■ Günter Grass

Goethe

oder eine Warnung an das Nationaltheater zu Mannheim

Ich fürchte Menschen,
die nach englischem Pfeifentabak riechen.
Ihre Stichworte stechen nicht,
sondern werden gesendet,
wenn ich schon schlafe.

Wie fürchte ich mich,
wenn sie aus Frankfurt kommen,
ihren Tabak mitbringen,
meine Frau betrachten
und zärtlich von Büchern sprechen.

Furcht, Pfeifenraucher
werden mich fragen,
was Goethe wo sagte,
wie das, was er meinte,
heut und in Zukunft verstanden sein will.

Ich aber, wenn ich nun meine Furcht verlöre,
wenn ich mein großes Buch,
das da neunhundert Seiten zählt
und den großen Brand beschreibt,
vor ihren Pfeifen aufschlüge?

Furcht, fängt mein Buch an,
bestimmte Herrn Goethe,
als er mit Vorsatz und Lunte
Weimars Theater in Flammen
aufgehen ließ —

wie ja schon Nero auch Shakespeare
Brandstifter waren und Dichter.

■ Günter Grass

Goethe

or a Warning to the National Theater at Mannheim

I fear people
who smell of English pipe tobacco.
Their points don't point,
but instead are broadcast
when I'm already asleep.

I'm so afraid
when they come from Frankfurt,
bring their tobacco along,
look my wife over
and talk caressingly about books.

Fear, that pipe smokers
will ask me
what Goethe said where
how what he meant should be
understood today or tomorrow.

But I, if I were to lose my fear,
if I in front of their pipes
opened my large book
which numbers nine hundred pages
and describes the great fire?

Fear, my book claims,
guided Mr. Goethe
when with premeditation and a fuse
he made Weimar's Theater
go up in flames—

like Nero and Shakespeare before us
also arsonists and poets.

Peter Rühmkorf

Mit unsern geretteten Hälsen

Mit unsern geretteten Hälsen,
Immer noch nicht gelyncht,
Ziehn wir von Babel nach Belsen
Krank und karbolgetüncht.

Fraßen des Daseins Schlempe,
Zelebrierten in gleitender Zeit
Unter des Hutes Krempe
Das Hirn, seine Heiligkeit.

Tätowiert mit des Lebens Lauge.
Doch von erstaunlichem Bestand
Das Weiße in unserm Auge,
Das Warme in unserer Hand.

Wir haben gelärmt und gelitten.
Wir schrieben Pamphlete mit Tau und mit Teer —
Worte schöpfen, Worte verschütten,
In ewiger Wiederkehr.

Lied der Benn-Epigonen

Die schönsten Verse der Menschen
— nun finden Sie schon einen Reim! —
sind die Gottfried Bennschen:
Hirn, lernäischer Leim —
Selbst in der Sowjetzone
Rosen, Rinde und Stamm.
Gleite, Epigone,
ins süße Benn-Engramm.

Peter Rühmkorf

With Our Saved Necks

With our saved necks from the rabble
Of a hostile lynching mob,
We roam from Belsen to Babel
Carbolic rinsed, our heads throb.

Once we slopped life's swill
Celebrating at times in vain
What's under our hatbill
That sacred relic, the brain.

Tattooed with the world's lye.
But still we manage to stand,
The whites glint in our eyes,
The warmth sweats in our hand.

We've suffered and we've clamored
With dew and fluff penned petitions—
In turn, words lost, words hammered,
In eternally spun repetitions.

Song of the Benn Epigones

The most beautiful verses of men
—now see if you find a rhyme!—
are those by Gottfried Benn:
Brain and learned birdlime—
Even on the Soviet side
Roses, bark, tribal band.
Oh epigone, glide
into the sweet Benn-engram.

Wenn es einst der Sänger
mit dem Cro-Magnon trieb,
heute ist er Verdränger
mittels Lustprinzip.
Wieder in Schattenreichen
den Moiren unter den Rock;
nicht mehr mit Rattenscheichen
zum völkischen Doppelbock.

Tränen und Flieder-Möwen —
Die Muschel zu, das Tor!
Schwert aus dem Achtersteven
spielt sich die Tiefe vor.
Philosophia per anum,
in die Reseden zum Schluß — :
So gefällt dein Arcanum
Restauratoribus.

Außer der Liebe nichts

Flüchtig gelagert in dieses mein Gartengeviert,
wo mir der Abend noch nicht aus dem Auge will,
schön ist's,
hier noch sagen zu können: schön,
wie sich der Himmel verzieht und die Liebe zu Kopf steigt,
all nach soviel Unsinn und Irrfahrt
an ein seßhaftes Herz zu schlagen, du spürst
einen Messerstich tief in den ledernen Brust
DIE FREUDE.

Wo nun dieser mein Witz das Land nicht verändert,
mein Mund auf der Stelle spricht,
— hebt sich die Hand und senkt sich für garnichts das Lid —
doch solang ich noch atmund-rauchund-besteh,

Though for the Cro-Magnon sector
he once played the minstrel,
now he is our Hector
by means of the pleasure principle.
Again in the shadow's region,
moiré under his coat's veneer,
no more with the rat-sheik legions
to the Aryan bock beer.

Tear and lilac-gull bevy—
The mussel shut, the door!
Out from the stern post heavy
the depth plays itself to the fore.
Philosophia per anum   ˙
into the mignonette finally—:
Thus pleases your arcanum,
Old reactionary.

Other Than Love—Nothing

Fleetingly settled down in this garden rectangle of mine,
where the evening still refuses to leave my eye,
beautiful it is
still to be able to say: beautiful,
as the sky slowly covers itself and love rises into one's head,
after all that nonsense and straying
to beat against a sedentary heart, you feel
a knife stab deep in your leathery chest:
JOY.

Though this wit of mine does not change the land,
though my mouth dribbles in place
—the hand raises, the lid lowers, for nothing at all—
as long as still I breatheand-smokeand-exist,

solang mich mein Kummer noch rührt
und mein Glück mich noch angeht,
will ich
was uns die Aura am Glimmen hält,
mit langer Zunge loben!

Unnütz in Anmut: Dich,
wo die Nacht schon ihr Tuch wirft
über dein ungebildetes Fleisch, es kehren
alle Dinge sich ihre endliche Seite zu,
und aus ergiebigem Dunkel rinnt
finstere Fröhlichkeit . . .
Ich aber nenne diesseits und jenseits der Stirn
außer der Liebe nichts,
was mich hält und mir beikommt.

as long as my grief still touches,
my happiness still stirs me,
I will,
to what for us keeps the aura aglow,
with long tongue, give praise!

Useless in grace: You,
when night casts its cloth
over your uneducated flesh, and all things
turn to each other their final side,
and from the teeming dark there runs
sinister cheerfulness . . .
I on the other hand name inside and outside the head
other than love nothing
that will hold me and goad me.

1965–1975

Poetry as Dialogue or Soliloquy

And how we burned once in our youth . . .

■ Ilse Aichinger

Breitbrunn

Es neigen sich
die Tage der Kindheit
den späten Tagen zu.
Und fragst du nach der Heimat,
so sagen alle, die blieben:
Das Gras ist gewachsen.
Aber nichts davon,
daß die gewundenen Wege
die Hügel hinab
aufstanden und seufzten.
Ehe sie sterben,
ziehen die Pfarrer
in andere Dörfer.

■ Adolf Endler

Als der Krieg zu Ende war:

Da war ein Nest blutroten Schwalbenflaums,
da war ein Nest, gebaut aus nackten Knöchlein
der kleinen Schwalben, die in diesem Nest,
gebaut aus ihren Knöchlein, hausen wollten,
sehr warm im Nest aus ihrem Flaum blutrot.

Ilse Aichinger

Breitbrunn Village

The days of childhood
incline
toward the late days.
And if you ask about your hometown
all who stayed on say:
The grass grew.
But nothing about
how the winding paths
down the hills
rose and sighed.
Before they die
the pastors move
to other villages.

Adolf Endler

When the war was over:

There was a nest of blood red swallow down,
there was a nest, built with the naked bones
of little swallows that wanted to live
in this nest built with their little bones,
so warm in the nest of their down blood red.

Ilse Tielsch

Ich gehe durch die alte Schule

Die Fenster sind zerbrochen.
Wind schlägt die Türen zu.
Der Direktor
hat sich das Leben genommen.

Alle Schränke stehen offen.
Schiefer und Eisenblüte.
Klassenbuch und Rotstift.
Einsam glänzt
ein böhmischer Granat.

Direktion.
Der Schulwart hat nicht abgeschlossen.
Zeugnisformulare liegen bereit.
Ich tauche die Feder in rote Tinte,
streiche ein Leben durch
und schreibe mit schöner Schrift
darunter

Nicht genügend.

Sonja Schüler

Weimar–Buchenwald

Die Spur Goethes ist nicht mehr zu finden
auf den Krähenwegen.
Durch die Gedanken mühe ich mich, über
die grauen Steine. Die Ohren schmerzen
vom Hall der Schritte. Die Sekunden —

Ilse Tielsch

I Walk Through the Old School

The windows are broken.
Wind slams the doors.
The director
took his own life.

All the lockers are open.
Slate and hematite.
Class register and red pencil.
In solitary splendor
a Bohemian garnet.

Principal's office.
The caretaker didn't lock it.
Report forms are lying about.
I dip the pen into red ink,
cross out a life
and in my best calligraphy write
under it

Not satisfactory.

Sonja Schüler

Weimar–Buchenwald

No trace of Goethe can now be found
on the paths of the crows.
I struggle through the thoughts, over
the gray stones. My ears ache
from the echo of the steps. The seconds—

wie lang können sie sein, wie viele Tode
starb ein Mensch, um zu leben.
Unendliche Blicke ins Tal blieben im rostigen Draht.

Schwer und eisig liegt
wie ein toter Blaufuchs der Horizont. Aber
ein Lied haben sie gesungen, die
das Grauen niedertraten auf dem Marsch,
in unser Gedächtnis gebrannt. Das ist
nicht zu begraben.

Wir gehen die Krähenwege. Wir, die wir uns
Bibliotheken erschließen und gelben Sand auf die Wege streuen.
In unser Gedächtnis, das ist nicht zu begraben,
kehren Gesichter, die habe ich vorher nicht gekannt.

Für W.

Ich bin ganz zart zu dir, wenn du nicht bei mir bist.
Und grob genug, wenn deine Heiterkeit mich brennt.
Wie lange braucht man jeden Tag, bis man sich kennt.
Ein Wort verschweigt uns oft, was in ihm ist.

Wir werden nicht zu träge sein, uns immer neu zu finden,
wenn Jahr um Jahr in unsre Stirnen dringt.
Hab keine Angst, daß meine Stimme anders klingt,
wenn hundert Müdigkeiten dir den Herbst verkünden.

■ **Erich Fried**

Einbürgerung

Weiße Hände
rotes Haar
blaue Augen

how long they can be, how many deaths
did one man die in order to live.
Infinite glances into the valley got caught in the rusty wire.

Heavy and icy, like a dead blue fox,
lies the horizon. But
a song have they sung who
stomped down the horror on the march,
burned it into our memory. That is
not to be buried.

We walk on the paths of the crows. We who
slowly reap the libraries and put yellow sand on the footpaths.
Into our memory, not to be buried,
some faces return which we never used to know.

For W.

I'm very tender with you when you're not with me.
And rude enough when your old cheerfulness offends.
How long it takes us every day to know each other.
A word will often hide what it intends.

No sloth will stop us as we find ourselves anew,
when years have etched our brows in sundry ways.
Be not afraid, my voice will sound no different
when weariness preludes your autumn days.

■ **Erich Fried**

Naturalization in Vietnam

White hands
red hair
blue eyes

Weiße Steine
rotes Blut
blaue Lippen

Weiße Knochen
roter Sand
blauer Himmel

Das Land liegt sieben Fußtritte
und einen Schuß weit

seine südliche Hälfte
heißt Demokratie

In ihrer Hauptstadt Sodom
regiert ein Soldat der *Mein Kampf* lernt

Die Mönche sind buddhistisch
oder katholisch

Die buddhistischen Mönche
werden oft Rote genannt

In Wirklichkeit sind sie gelb
aber nicht wenn sie brennen

Der Stamm Nung spricht chinesisch
und bringt schweigende Menschen zum Sprechen

Das wußte schon Tschiang Kai-Schek
das wußten auch die Franzosen

Die Zungenlöser der Nung
erhalten jetzt fünf Dollar täglich

Nicht aus Washington nur von Soldaten
auf eigene Rechnung

White stones
red blood
blue lips

White bones
red sand
blue sky

The country lies seven kicks
and a shot away

its southern half
is called Democracy

In its capitol Sodom
a soldier reigns who studies *Mein Kampf*

The monks are Buddhist
or Catholic

The Buddhist monks
are often called Reds

Actually they are yellow
but not when they burn

The Nung tribe speaks Chinese
and makes silent people talk

Chiang Kai-Shek knew that long ago
the French also knew it

The Nung who loosen tongues
now receive five dollars a day

Not from Washington just from soldiers
out of their own pockets

Die New York Times nennt die Verhöre
Orientalische Fragespiele

Gefangene Partisanen werden getauft
sie erhalten alle den Namen Patrice Lumumba

Fleisch wird zubereitet
auf zweierlei Art

Entweder langsam mit Napalm
oder schnell mit Benzin

Letzteres gilt als barbarisch
ersteres nicht

Geschlachtet wird vorher
bei keiner der beiden Methoden

Das Land ist leicht zu erreichen
auch für größere Expeditionen

Die Fremdenführer
werden Ephialtes genannt

Man fährt durch die Bucht der Schweine
ohne Umweg zu den Bordellen

Die Mädchen sind zierlich
ihre Särge sind leicht zu tragen

Die Toten werden verbrannt
wie die Lebenden

Wenn man die Augen zumacht
und völlig stillsitzt

kann man von weitem sehen
was in dem Land geschieht

The New York Times calls the interrogations
Oriental Question Games

Captured partisans are baptized
they all get the name Patrice Lumumba

Meat is prepared
in two ways

Either slowly with Napalm
or quickly with gasoline

The latter is considered barbaric
the former is not

Butchering is not done first
with either of the two methods

The country is easy to reach
even for larger expeditions

The guides for foreigners
are called Ephialtes

You go through the Pigs' Bay
with no detour to the brothels

The girls are petite
their coffins are light to carry

The dead are burned
just like the living

If you close your eyes
and sit very still

you can see from a distance
what is happening in this country

Günter Kunert

Fernöstliche Legende

Der eine so klein, der andere
so groß: Mr. Goliath, Berufsgigant, die Keule
taktischer Luftstaffeln geschwungen
wider den David im grünen Harnisch der Dschungel,
sicher des Sieges
über die winzige Schleuder,
und während den Himmel er triumphal bedeckt,
ist unter den Völkern der Erde
sein mächtiges Bild
schon zerschmettert.

Bedauerlicher Hitler

1

Bedauerlicher Hitler,
gejagt von Plänen ohne Maß,
zu Fuß dabei in seinem Reich von Front zu Front,
zu den Armeen,
die kaum verlassen, schon gefallen sind.

2

Autobahnen Panzerwagen Bomben gar
schafft er selber, indem er dort Zement aufschüttet,
da eine Panzerplatte walzt und hier
den Sprengstoff einwiegt, wobei
ihn höchstens eine Tasse Brühe stärkt.

Günter Kunert

Legend from the Far East

The one so small, the other
so large: Mr. Goliath, professional giant, the club
of tactical air squadrons swung
against David in the green armor of the jungle,
sure of victory
over the tiny slingshot,
and while he triumphantly hides the heavens from view,
among the peoples of the earth
his powerful image
is already shattered.

Pitiable Hitler

1

Pitiable Hitler,
chased by plans without bounds
always there, on foot, from front to front in his Reich
to the armies
that scarcely has he left, have fallen.

2

Autobahns tanks bombs even
he makes himself, pouring cement,
rolling out tank metal there, adding
explosives here, strengthened
by nary a cup of broth.

3

Auch ständig ohne Schlaf, denn die Gemälde
und Gedichte, die ihn als ihn feiern,
fertigt er zu später Nachtstund
einsam selber.

4

In den Menschenschlächtereien
krepierte keiner, würfe nicht er
mit eigener Hand das Todesgas auf jene, die seiner
erbarmungslos geharrt.
Während er die Leichen, Millionen um Millionen Stück,
vor die Verbrennungsöfen schleppt, bleibt
ihm kaum Rast
von dem belegten Brötchen abzubeißen, das,
halbvertrocknet, er bei sich führt,
der Führer.

5

O trübes Schicksal des gewalttätig Gewaltigen,
daß er alles, was er tat, allein getan, schlachten
seinen Leichnam aus
Wurm und Plutarch junior, Platz zu schaffen
für und für
immer wieder neue alte selbe gleiche
Kopien ohne Original.

3

And constantly without sleep because the paintings
and poems that celebrate him as himself
he manufactures personally late at night
alone.

4

In the human slaughterhouses
no one would croak if he did not throw
the death gas with his own hand at those who
await him pitilessly.
While he drags the bodies, millions upon millions
to the crematory ovens, he hardly
has a moment's rest
to take a bite of the sandwich that,
half-stale, he brings with him,
the Führer.

5

Oh sad fate of the violently mighty,
since everything he did he did alone,
the worms and Plutarch junior
cannibalize his corpse to make room
forever for,
again and again, the new old same identical
copies without the original.

Yaak Karsunke

Kilroy war hier

als ich 11 war stand
„Kilroy is here"
auf den geborstenen mauern
auf gestürzten säulen
auf kneipentischen in klos
die amis schrieben
es überall hin

als ich 11 war trugen
meine schwestern rote röcke
den weißen kreis mit dem vierfach
gebrochenen kreuz
hatte meine mutter selber
abgetrennt & verbrannt
jetzt war Kilroy hier

als ich 11 war war
der krieg aus & „Hitler kaputt"
wie die häuser die fenster die juden
& deutschland (was war das?)
dafür war Kilroy gekommen
brachte uns basketball bei
& kaugummi & cocacola

als ich 11 war lehrte
mich Kilroy worte wie fairneß
& demokratie
parolen wie nie wieder krieg
brachte mir jitterbug bei
& selbst an Shakespeare-sonetten
noch den brooklyn-akzent

als ich 11 war waren
das drei goldene worte
„Kilroy is here"

■ Yaak Karsunke

Kilroy was here

when i was 11
"Kilroy is here"
was written on busted walls
on toppled columns
on bar room tables in johns
the yanks wrote it
everywhere

when i was 11
my sisters wore red skirts
the white circle with the four times
broken cross
had been taken off
by my mother & burned
Kilroy was here now

when i was 11 the war
was over & "Hitler kaput"
so were the houses the windows the jews
& germany (what was that?)
that's why Kilroy had come
taught us about basketball
& chewing gum & coca cola

when i was 11 Kilroy
taught me words like fairness
& democracy
slogans like no more war
taught me the jitterbug
& even with Shakespeare sonnets
the brooklyn accent

when i was 11
those were three golden words
"Kilroy is here"

fast so schön wie die drei
der french revolution
von der er erzählte
freiheit & gleichheit & brüderlichkeit

als ich 11 war hatten
meine eltern
mich falsch erzogen
Kilroy gab sich die mühe
erklärte mir menschenrechte
& uno-charta
erzog mich um

als ich 11 war
war Kilroy der beste
freund den ich hatte
sein haus stand mir offen
in seinem keller
hörte ich jazz & Strawinsky
& keine sirenen

: viel von dem blieb zurück
— jahre später —
als Kilroy sein flugzeug bestieg
es mit napalm belud & verschwand
jetzt steht auf pagoden
& den rauchschwarzen resten von dörfern
„Kilroy is here"

— wir
sind geschiedene leute

almost as good as the three
from the french revolution
that he told us about
freedom & equality & fraternity

when i was 11
my parents had
raised me wrong
Kilroy tried hard
explained the rights of men to me
& the u.n. charter
reeducated me

when i was 11 Kilroy
was the best
friend i had
his house was open to me
in his clubs
i heard jazz & Stravinsky
& no sirens

:much of that was still with me
—years later—
when Kilroy climbed into his plane
loaded it with napalm & disappeared
now it's written on pagodas
& the smoke black remains of villages
"Kilroy is here"

it's over
between us

mann   &   frau
in der welt des deutschen

der blut	die blüte
der bruck	die brücke
der buhn	die bühne
der burd	die bürde
der bust	die büste
der flot	die flöte
der full	die fülle
der holl	die hölle
der hull	die hülle
der hutt	die hütte
der kruck	die krücke
der kuhl	die kühle
der kust	die küste
der luck	die lücke
der muck	die mücke
der muh	die mühe
der muhl	die mühle
der mutz	die mütze
der pfutz	die pfütze
der raud	die räude
der rug	die rüge
der sag	die säge
der sund	die sünde
der tuck	die tücke
der tut	die tüte
der wust	die wüste

Ernst Jandl

man   &   woman
in the world of the german

the best	the bust
the botch	the bitch
the bread	the brood
the coarse	the curse
the crass	the cross
the crutch	the crotch
the deed	the dead
the dredge	the drudge
the firm	the form
the hull	the hell
the hun	the hen
the lord	the lard
the luck	the lack
the lust	the last
the pants	the pints
the pen	the pin
the ploy	the play
the raise	the rose
the rope	the rape
the slap	the slip
the sun	the sin
the sweat	the sweet
the tent	the tint
the trail	the trial
the truck	the trick
the war	the wear

Franz Mon

wo: wenn es wo war
wer: wenn es wer war
wann: wenn es wann war
was: wenn es was war
wie: wenn es wie war

war wo es wenn wie
war wie es wenn was
war was es wenn wann
war wann es wenn war
war wer es wenn wo

es war wo wenns wer war
es war wer wenns wann war
es war wann wenns was war
es war was wenns wie war
es war wie wenns wo war

Friedrich Achleitner

a
so

so
a

m
hm

hm
hm

Franz Mon

where: if it was where
who: if it was who
when: if it was when
what: if it was what
how: if it was how

was where it if how
was how it if what
was what it if when
was when it if who
was who it if where

it was where if it was who
it was who if it was when
it was when if it was what
it was what if it was how
it was how if it was where

Friedrich Achleitner

uh
hu

hu
uh

m
hm

hm
hm

a
ha

so
so

Gerhard Rühm

leib	leib	leib	leib
leib	leib	leib	leib
leib	leib	leib	leib
leib	leib	leib	leib
leib	leib	leib	leib
leib	leib	leib	leib
leib	leib	leib	leib
leib	leib	leibleib	

Eugen Gomringer

vielleicht baum
baum vielleicht

vielleicht vogel
vogel vielleicht

vielleicht frühling
frühling vielleicht

vielleicht worte
worte vielleicht

ah
ha

yeah
yeah

■ Gerhard Rühm

body   body   body   body
body   body   body   body
body   body   body   body
body   body   body   body
body   body   body   body
body   body   body   body
body   body   body   body
body   body   bodybody

■ Eugen Gomringer

perhaps tree
tree perhaps

perhaps bird
bird perhaps

perhaps spring
spring perhaps

perhaps words
words perhaps

■ Christa Reinig

Endlich

endlich entschloß sich niemand
und niemand klopfte
und niemand sprang auf
und niemand öffnete
und da stand niemand
und niemand trat ein
und niemand sprach: willkomm
und niemand antwortete: endlich

■ Günter Eich

Bewerbung

Einige Kenntnis
in Wildbachverbauung,
mit Krankenkassenbescheiden
für Weberknechte vertraut,
unerschrocken
vor elektrischem Strom,
kann auch mit Tieren umgehen,
gewandt in Handelskorrespondenz,
besonders gottlob mandschurisch,
tocharisch und in
Stenografie von unflätigen
Uhurufen, eine
Allround-Begabung,
geeignet
für leitenden Posten
in submarinem Betrieb.

Christa Reinig

At Last

at last no one decided
and no one knocked
and no one jumped up
and no one opened
and there stood no one
and no one entered
and no one said: welcome
and no one answered: at last

Günter Eich

Application

Some knowledge
of how to regulate mountain streams,
familiar with insurance claims
for daddy longlegs,
undaunted
by electric current,
can also handle animals,
skilled in business correspondence,
especially thank God in Manchurian,
Tocharian and in
the stenography of lewd
owl cries, an
all-around talent,
suited
for executive position
in a submarine plant.

Ingeborg Bachmann

Keine Delikatessen

Nichts mehr gefällt mir.

Soll ich
eine Metapher ausstaffieren
mit einer Mandelblüte?
die Syntax kreuzigen
auf einen Lichteffekt?
Wer wird sich den Schädel zerbrechen
über so überflüssige Dinge —

Ich habe ein Einsehn gelernt
mit den Worten,
die da sind
(für die unterste Klasse)

Hunger
      Schande
           Tränen
und
                Finsternis.

Mit dem ungereinigten Schluchzen,
mit der Verzweiflung
(und ich verzweifle noch vor Verzweiflung)
über das viele Elend,
den Krankenstand, die Lebenskosten,
werde ich auskommen.

Ich vernachlässige nicht die Schrift,
sondern mich.
Die andern wissen sich
weißgott
mit den Worten zu helfen.
Ich bin nicht mein Assistent.

Ingeborg Bachmann

No Delicacies

Nothing pleases me any more.

Am I
to deck out a metaphor
with an almond blossom?
crucify the syntax
on a lighting effect?
Who would rack his brains
about such superfluous things—

I have acquired an insight
with the words
that are there
(for the lowest class)

hunger
      disgrace
           tears
and
                darkness.

Unrefined sobbing,
despair
(and I despair yet of despair)
about misery everywhere,
sickness, the cost of living—
that will do for me.

I will not neglect the text,
but myself.
The others understand
god knows
how to help themselves with words.
I am not my assistant.

Soll ich
einen Gedanken gefangennehmen,
abführen in eine erleuchtete Satzzelle?
Aug und Ohr verköstigen
mit Worthappen erster Güte?
erforschen die Libido eines Vokals,
ermitteln die Liebhaberwerte unserer Konsonanten?

Muß ich
mit dem verhagelten Kopf,
mit dem Schreibkrampf in dieser Hand,
unter dreihundertnächtigem Druck
einreißen das Papier,
wegfegen die angezettelten Wortopern,
vernichtend so: ich du und er sie es

wir ihr?

(Soll doch. Sollen die andern.)

Mein Teil, es soll verloren gehen.

■ Rolf Dieter Brinkmann

Einen jener klassischen

schwarzen Tangos in Köln, Ende des
Monats August, da der Sommer schon

ganz verstaubt ist, kurz nach Laden
Schluß aus der offenen Tür einer

dunklen Wirtschaft, die einem
Griechen gehört, hören, ist beinahe

Should I
take a thought prisoner,
lead it off to a sentence's lit cell?
Feed eye and ear
with premium word morsels?
research the libido of a vowel,
determine the connoisseur value of our consonants?

Must I
with hail damaged head
with writer's cramp in this hand,
under the pressure of three hundred nights
rend the paper,
sweep away the word operas written on scraps,
thus destroying: I you and he she it

we all of you?

(should really. The others should . . .)

My portion, let it be lost.

■ Rolf Dieter Brinkmann

To hear one of those classic

black tangos in Cologne, at the end of
the month of August, when the summer is

already all covered with dust, just after shops
close from the open door of a

dark restaurant that belongs to
a Greek, is almost

ein Wunder: für einen Moment eine
Überraschung, für einen Moment

Aufatmen, für einen Moment
eine Pause in dieser Straße,

die niemand liebt und atemlos
macht, beim Hindurchgehen. Ich

schrieb das schnell auf, bevor
der Moment in der verfluchten

dunstigen Abgestorbenheit Kölns
wieder erlosch.

Die Orangensaftmaschine

dreht sich & Es ist gut, daß der Barmann
zuerst auf die nackten Stellen eines
Mädchens schaut, das ein Glas kalten

Tees trinkt. „Ist hier sehr heiß,
nicht?" sagt er, eine Frage, die
den Raum etwas dekoriert,

was sonst? Sie hat einen kräftigen
Körper und, als sie den Arm
ausstreckt, das Glas auf

die Glasplatte zurückstellt,
einen schwitzenden, haarigen
Fleck unterm Arm, was den Raum

einen Moment lang verändert, die
Gedanken nicht. Und jeder sieht, daß
ihr's Spaß macht, sich zu bewegen

a miracle: for a minute a
surprise, for a minute

a fresh breath, for a minute
a pause on this street

that no one loves and makes you
breathless when you walk through. I

jotted it all down, before
that minute faded again

in the damn steamy deadness
of Cologne.

The Orange Juice Machine

turns & good thing that the bartender
first looks at the naked parts of a
girl who's drinking a glass of cold

tea. "It's hot around here,
isn't it?" he says, a question that
decorates the room a little,

what else? She has a strong
body and when she stretches out
her arm and puts the glass

back on the glass tray,
a sweaty, hairy
patch under the arm, which

for a minute alters the room, not
the thoughts. And everyone sees that
it amuses her to move

auf diese Art, was den Barmann
auf Trab bringt nach einer langen
Pause, in der nur der Ventilator

zu hören gewesen ist wie
immer, oder meistens, um
diese Tageszeit.

Gedicht

Zerstörte Landschaft mit
Konservendosen, die Hauseingänge
leer, was ist darin? Hier kam ich

mit dem Zug nachmittags an,
zwei Töpfe an der Reisetasche
festgebunden. Jetzt bin ich aus

den Träumen raus, die über eine
Kreuzung wehn. Und Staub,
zerstückelte Pavane, aus totem

Neon, Zeitungen und Schienen
dieser Tag, was krieg ich jetzt,
einen Tag älter, tiefer und tot?

Wer hat gesagt, daß sowas Leben
ist? Ich gehe in ein
anderes Blau.

in this way, which gets
the bartender moving after a long
pause during which only the fan

could be heard as
always, or usually, at
this time of day.

Poem

Devastated landscape with
tin cans, the doors to houses
empty, what's inside? I arrived

here on the train in the afternoon,
two jars tied tight
to my suitcase. Now I am

beyond the dreams that flutter
over a crossroads. And dust,
disintegrated pavane, of dead

neon, newspapers, and rails
this day, what do I get now,
one day older, deeper and dead?

Who said that this is
life? I'm going into
another blues.

Jürgen Becker

Eine Zeit in Berlin

Zwischen den Autobussen
                  (aber
es ist ein Foto von drei Autobussen,
eine Haltestelle der BVG)
                      steht
ein Mädchen
                 (und
es ist das Foto von einem Mädchen,
das zwischen den Autobussen steht
an einer Haltestelle der BVG),
                    und
es ist ein grobkörniger Tag
                 (ein
graues Foto)
          in den sechziger Jahren,
über die wir jetzt sprechen, über
etwas
       (du sprachst von der Resignation;
ich sprach von der Neuen Einsicht)
                     auf
einem Foto,
         das in der Zukunft
zwischen den Fotos
          aus anderen Zeiten
an meiner Wand hängt.

Coney Island

— also, dann essen; zum Essen, unten
im Haus, ruft meine Frau, und
ich will
      (warum? wir sehen noch)

Jürgen Becker

A Time in Berlin

Between the autobuses
         (but
it is a photo of three autobuses,
a Berlin Transit stop)
            stands
a girl
    (and
it is the photo of a girl
standing between autobuses
at a Berlin Transit stop),
            and
it is a grainy day
       (a
gray photo)
     in the sixties
which we're talking about now, about
something
      (you talked about resignation;
I talked about the new insight)
             in
a photo
    that in the future
will hang among the photos
            from other times
on my wall.

Coney Island

—ok, so let's eat; down in the house
my wife calls me, and
I want
      (why? we'll see)

auf meine aufgewärmten Spaghetti
Tomaten-Ketchup
: aber von „Heinz".

Mittag. Und müde. Und Unterbrechung,
denn ich saß ja
(Impuls der Erinnerung)
gerade an einem Gedicht.
Nun weiter.
Aber ich weiß nicht.
Aber ich weiß, ich
wollte Ketchup von „Heinz": Erinnerung
an Coney Island, wo
(unterbrochenes
Gedicht) die alten, sehr alten Leute
sitzen, im eisigen Märzwind, mit
Sonnenbrillen und in den Hüllen
der New York Times
— so ungefähr,
und dann noch einige Zeilen über
die Sehnsucht, über den eisigen, sonnigen
Nachmittag mit Blicken
(aus dem Exil)
über die Krümmung des Meers,
weil
(Erzähltes) dahinten,
hinter
der Krümmung,
Erinnerung und Europa
— Zeilen
über Erinnerung;
und über die Emigration?

Nachmittag. Ich weiß nicht. Geschmack
von Ketchup, „Heinz".
— also, essen;
kein Gedicht über Coney Island, später, im Mai.

on my reheated spaghetti
tomato ketchup
: but only "Heinz."

Noon. And tired. And interruption,
because I was just
(impulse of memory)
working on a poem.
Now go on.
But I don't know.
But I know, I
wanted "Heinz" ketchup: memory
of Coney Island where
(interrupted
poem) the old, really old people
sit in the icy March wind, with
sun glasses and wrapped up
in the New York Times
—something like that,
and then a few lines about
the longing, about the icy, sunny
afternoon with looks
(from exile)
over the curve of the sea,
because
(narrated) behind that,
behind
the curve,
memory and Europe
—lines
about memory;
and about emigration?
Afternoon. I don't know. Taste
of ketchup, "Heinz."
—ok, let's eat;
no poem about Coney Island, later, in May.

Elisabeth Borchers

Die große Chance

Abends entspannen uns eilfertige Bilder,
die Story der Gerechtigkeit,
das Epos zu dritt.
Da geht mit dem Killer
das Unrecht des Tages.
Da wird Sehnsucht gelehrt und gestillt.
Da sind wir nach Maß.
Wenn alles vorbei ist
und die Schöne am verwilderten Grab
des Vaters ihr Haupt neigt,
gehen wir schlafen.
Der nächste Morgen
kommt
blütenrein.

Jährlich, im Sommer

Die heiteren Hügel,
die ernst bewaldeten Berge,
seit Generationen
bellt abends der Hund im Tal,
und die Quelle fließt.
Nicht erkennbar der Austausch
von Vögeln.
Die Ruine ist stabil.
Goethe war hier, Die Stätte,
die ein guter Mensch betrat, etc.
Auf den Bänken mit schöner Aussicht,
ökonomisch verteilt,
Urlauber.
Nichts kommt, nichts geht,
alles ist.

Elisabeth Borchers

The Big Chance

In the evening avid pictures relax us,
the story of justice,
the epic triangle.
There with the killer
goes the injustice of the day.
There longing is learned and quenched.
There we are quite up to par.
When everything is over
and the beautiful heroine bends her head
at the overgrown grave of the father,
we go to bed.
The next morning
arrives
lily white.

Annually, in Summer

The cheerful hills,
the seriously wooded mountains,
for generations
the dog has barked evenings in the valley
and the spring has flowed.
Not recognizable the exchange
of birds.
The ruin is solid.
Goethe was here, The Place
that a good man set foot in, etc.
On the benches with the beautiful lookout,
economically distributed,
vacationers.
Nothing comes, nothing goes,
everything is.

Nur hier, diese rapide Veränderung,
die einzige
in einer verläßlichen Landschaft.

■ Nicolas Born

Selbstbildnis

Oft für kompakt gehalten
für eine runde Sache
die geläufig zu leben versteht —
doch einsam frühstücke ich
nach Träumen
in denen nichts geschieht.
Ich mein Ärgernis
mit Haarausfall und wunden Füßen
einssechsundachtzig und Beamtensohn
bin mir unabkömmlich
unveräußerlich kenne ich
meinen Wert eine Spur zu genau
und mach Liebe wie Gedichte nebenbei.
Mein Gesicht verkommen
vorteilhaft im Schummerlicht
und bei ernsten Gesprächen.
Ich Zigarettenraucher halb schon Asche
Kaffetrinker mit den älteren Damen
die mir halfen
wegen meiner sympathischen Fresse und
die Rücksichtslosigkeit mit der
ich höflich bin.

Only here, this rapid transformation,
the only one
in a reliable landscape.

■   Nicolas Born

Self-Portrait

Often regarded as compact
a round thing
that really knows how to live—
but I breakfast alone
after dreams
in which nothing happens.
I my annoyance
with hair loss and sore feet
six feet one and the son of a civil servant
am indispensable to myself
undeniably I know
my worth too well by a shade
and make love and poems on the side.
My face somewhat seedy
seen to best advantage at twilight
and during serious conversations.
I cigarette smoker already half ash
drinker of coffee with older ladies
who helped me
on account of my appealing mug and
the recklessness with which
I am polite.

Drei Wünsche

Sind Tatsachen nicht quälend und langweilig?
Ist es nicht besser drei Wünsche zu haben
unter der Bedingung daß sie allen erfüllt werden?
Ich wünsche ein Leben ohne große Pausen
in denen die Wände nach Projektilen abgesucht werden
ein Leben das nicht heruntergeblättert wird von Kassierern.
Ich wünsche Briefe zu schreiben in denen ich ganz enthalten bin — .
Ich wünsche ein Buch in das ihr alle vorn hineingehen und hinten
    herauskommen könnt.
Und ich möchte nicht vergessen daß es schöner ist
dich zu lieben als dich nicht zu lieben.

■ Helga Novak

Ballade von der Türkin Nigar

1

Zuerst dienen sie den Vätern
und lassen sich verkaufen
dann gehorchen sie ihren Männern
die ihnen den Mund verbieten
zum dritten gängelt sie ein Chef —
da ist kein Davonlaufen
als viertes werden sie beherrscht
von der Staatsmacht und frommen Riten
bis eine Frau wie Nigar
vom Leder zieht daß es knallt —
(was ich hier von ihrem
sehr kurzen Leben berichte
ist wirklich passiert
und keine Fantasie-Geschichte)
— und sie erdrosselt wird
von einer uferlosen Befehlsgewalt

Three Wishes

Aren't facts troublesome and boring?
Isn't it better to have three wishes
with the condition that everyone has his granted?
I wish for a life without long pauses
in which the walls are searched for projectiles
a life that is not doled out by cashiers.
I wish to write letters that contain me completely—.
I wish for a book you can all enter in the front
    and exit in the rear.
And I do not want to forget that it is nicer
to love you than not to love you.

■ Helga Novak

Ballad of the Turkish Woman Nigar

1

First they serve the fathers
and let themselves be sold
then they obey their husbands
who forbid them to open their mouths
third a boss toddles them—
there's no running away
then fourth they are ruled
by state power and pious rites
until a woman like Nigar
chafes at the bit so things explode—
(what I here report
about her very short life
really happened
and is not a made-up story)
—and she is strangled
by an unrestrained dictate of force

2

die Türkin Nigar
in einem Dorf geboren bei Afyon
vom Vater regelmäßig
übers trockne Stoppelfeld
gejagt   bis sie bei Dürre
bei Schnee und bei Sturm
barfüßig ging denn Schuhe
kosteten zuviel Geld
diese Nigar wurde mit zehn
für einen Wagen Eselfutter
an Veli verkauft
mit dreizehn war sie Mutter
ohne einen blassen Schimmer
wie man sich als Frau überhaupt verhält

3

als Nigar von ihrem Sohn
heimlich lesen lernte
hat Veli — ihr Mann —
gleich Widerstand gerochen
und zwischen der Melonen-
und der Getreideernte
ihr zur Strafe das linke
Schienbein gebrochen
erst heulte die kranke
Nigar Wasser und Rotz
dann lernte sie auch noch
schreiben zum Trotz
anstatt wortlos ihre
Möhren und Linsen zu kochen

4

der Sohn ist verdurstet
während des Ramadan

2

the Turkish woman Nigar
born in a village near Afyon
regularly chased
by her father
over dry stubble fields   until in drought
in snow and in storm
she went barefoot because shoes
cost too much money
at ten this Nigar was sold
for a wagon load of donkey feed
to Veli
was a mother at thirteen
without the faintest inkling
of how a woman acts

3

when Nigar secretly learned
to read from her son
Veli—her husband—
promptly smelled resistance
and between the melon
and grain harvest
broke her left
shin as punishment
first the sick Nigar
howled water and snot
then out of spite
she also learned how to write
instead of without a word
cooking her lentils and carrots

4

the son died of thirst
during Ramadan

und Nigar   deutlich
von Schwindsucht geschüttelt
kommt zwei Jahre später
mit Veli in Frankfurt an
unterdessen ihr Mann
überall um Arbeit bettelt
wird ihr im Grüneburgpark
zwischen Kinderkarren
— dort wo ihre heimischen
Liebeslieder knarren —
vorübergehend die Ecke
eines kahlen Zimmers vermittelt

5

noch lange bevor Nigar
und Veli am Fließband stehen
werden sie zur Gesundheits-
behörde kommandiert
Nigar wollte auf keinen Fall
hinter den Röntgenschirm gehen
und hat die Ausländerpolizei
einfach angeschmiert —
daß keine Schwester
kein Arzt ihre Lunge erblickt
wurde mit Nigars Paß
eine Bekannte hingeschickt
die hat ihr ein tadelloses
und gestempeltes Attest präsentiert

6

ein Monat später hat Nigar
mit andern ein leeres Haus
besetzt   der Eigentümer
stellt vergebens Ultimaten
noch während sie schreien:
wir gehen nicht raus!

and Nigar   clearly
shaken by consumption
arrives two years later
in Frankfurt with Veli
while her husband
begs everywhere for work
there in Grüneburg Park
between baby buggies
—where her native
love songs croon—
the corner of a bare room
is temporarily put at her disposal

5

long before Nigar
and Veli stand in the assembly line
they are commanded to appear before
the health officials
Nigar did not want by any means
to go behind the x-ray screen
and simply cheated
the police in charge of aliens
so that in the end
no nurse no doctor saw her lungs
Nigar's passport was sent
with a friend
who proffered
a flawless and stamped bill of health

6

a month later Nigar
with others occupied
a vacant house   the owner
gives ultimatums in vain
even while they scream:
we won't get out!

verteilt Nigar Stuhlbeine
Küchenmesser und Spaten
denn Bullen umstehen das Haus
mit erhobenen Stöcken:
los Weiber drauf!
und seis in Unterröcken!
jagt sie davon
verprügelt sie in Raten!

7

Nigar schlägt zu und sticht
einem Wachtmeister in die Flosse
neugierige Passanten
die hier ein Schauspiel wittern
treibt sie und trampelt sie
rücksichtslos in die Gosse
pausenlos hört man in ihrer Nähe
Visiere zersplittern:
tagtäglich schuften wir
für dieses eingeborne Gefrett
dafür gönnen sie uns kein Dach
überm Kopf kein Bett!
jetzt hat Nigar beides
und zwar kostenlos hinter Gittern

8

zwei Türkinnen auf demselben Flur
die eine schlägt Krach
Ausländer sind alle gleich
und namenlos im Knast
daher wird einfach die falsche
in den Bunker gebracht
plötzlich geweckt wird Nigar
von drei Wärtern geschaßt:
die werden wir die Hammelbeine
schon noch langziehn!

Nigar distributes chair legs
kitchen knives and shovels
since the pigs surround the house
with lifted clubs:
charge women!
even if in petticoats!
chase them off
thrash them good!

7

Nigar pounds away and stabs
a policeman in the paw
curious passersby
who smell a drama here
she drives and tramples
ruthlessly into the gutter
incessantly you hear near her
visors splintering
everyday we work like mad
for this German millstone round our necks
and for that they begrudge us a roof
over our heads no bed!
now Nigar has both
and even for free behind bars

8

two Turkish women in the same corridor
the one causes an uproar
foreigners are all the same
and nameless in jail
that's why the wrong one was simply
brought into the special cell
suddenly awoken, Nigar got the
third degree from three guards:
we'll stretch
those mutton legs of yours yet!

an die Pritsche gefesselt
hat sie wieder Blut gespien
hat geschluckt und gewürgt
und ist gegen Morgen abgekratzt

■ H. C. Artmann

landschaft 5

da läßt die köchin alles fallen topf und teller gehn
in scherben die suppe rollt auf den dielen fett zischt

über linoleum hinweg napoleon sinnt unter seinem hut
wild tobt die schlacht von austerlitz vorbei wehn fahnen

dragoner stürzen aus den zuckermörsern husaren purzeln
von den küchentischen vorbei vorbei die jungen aare ha

wie da die feger wischen ha wie da das steingut schnarrt
es ist ein weißes dampfen überm feld der held napoleon

fegt durch die helle küche grenadiere her o öffnet mir
des windes weite fenster den bruch zur pyramide türmt die

köchin hoch noch ist ein kohl im haus der edle wirsing
zieht die konsequenz wie einen säbel schwingt die deutsche

faust zum gegenstoß es scheppern die kanonen en avant mes
braves gaillards die köchin stöhnt ein vöglein zirpt bereits

im blätterhaus ein tränlein netzt der köchin schöne breite
brust am bache steht napoleon er linst er watet rüber drüber

verrat ein schrei wer war es o das schmucke teure porzellan
es ist ein wahrer jammer ihr hohen götter stillet meine klage

chained to the plank bed
she spit blood again
swallowed and choked
and towards dawn popped off

■ H. C. Artmann

landscape 5

then the woman cooking dropped everything bowl and plate go
to pieces the soup spills on the floor fat sizzles

across linoleum napoleon broods in his hat
the battle austerlitz rages wildly past flags wave

dragoons charge from the sugar mortar hussars tumble
from the kitchen tables past past the young eagles ha

how the scullions wipe ha how the stoneware rattles
there's a white steam above the field the hero napoleon

sweeps through the bright kitchen grenadiers forward oh open
the wide wind's window for me the breach to the pyramid the

cook piles high yet a cabbage is still in the house the noble savoy
draws the consequences like a saber brandishes the german

fist for a counterthrust the cannons clatter en avant mes
braves gaillards the cook groans a little bird chirps already

in the arbor a tear moistens the cook's beautiful broad bosom napoleon
stands beside the stream he looks through a spyglass he wades over over there

treason a scream who was it oh the expensive pretty porcelain
it's a real shame you gods on high oh soothe my pain

■ Kurt Marti

wir müssen platz machen

wir müssen platz machen
     hat er gesagt
platz für die jungen
es sind zu viele menschen
es ist zu wenig platz auf der welt
     hat er gesagt
und jetzt
hat er platz gemacht
seine wohnung wird frei
sein parkplatz steht zur verfügung
bald fährt ein anderer seinen wagen
er steigt in kein tram mehr
fremde sitzen am mittagstisch seiner wirtschaft
die rente kann zinstragend angelegt werden
ein neuer kunde findet beim zahnarzt zulaß
wir müssen platz machen
     hat er gesagt
es ist zu wenig platz auf der welt

■ Wolf Biermann

Acht Argumente für die Beibehaltung des Namens „Stalinallee" für die Stalinallee

Es steht in Berlin ein Straße
Die steht auch in Leningrad
Die steht genauso in mancher
Andern großen Stadt

Kurt Marti

we have to make space

we have to make space
    he said
space for the young
there are too many people
there's not enough space in the world
    he said
and now
he's made space
his apartment is vacant
his parking space is available
soon someone else will drive his car
he doesn't ride the tram any more
strangers sit at the lunch table in his usual restaurant
the pension fund can be accumulated with interest
a new patient will be accepted at the dentist's
we have to make space
    he said
there's not enough space in the world

Wolf Biermann

Eight Arguments for Retaining the Name "Stalin Avenue" for the Stalin Avenue

There is a street in Berlin
The same in Leningrad too
In other cities you've been
You'll find another few

Und darum heißt sie auch STALINALLEE
Mensch, Junge, versteh
Und die Zeit ist passé!

Und Henselmann kriegte Haue
Damit er die Straße baut
Und weil er sie dann gebaut hat
Hat man ihn wieder verhaut

Auch darum heißt das Ding STALINALLEE
Mensch, Junge, versteh
Und die Zeit ist passé!

Und als am 17. Juni
Manch Maurerbrigadier
Mit Flaschen schwer bewaffnet schrie
Da floß nicht nur das Bier

Ja, darum heißt sie auch STALINALLEE
Mensch, Junge, versteh
Und die Zeit ist passé!

Und weil auf dieser Straße
Am Abend um halb Zehn
Schon Grabesstille lastet
Die Bäume schlangestehn

Auch darum heißt sie ja STALINALLEE
Mensch, Junge, versteh
Und die Zeit ist passé!

Es hat nach dem großen Parteitag
Manch einer ins Hemde geschissn
Und hat bei Nacht und Nebel
Ein Denkmal abgerissn

Ja, darum heißt sie d o c h STALINALLEE

Die weißen Kacheln fallen
Uns auf den Kopf ja nur

And so it's called Stalin Avenue
Boy, I wish you knew:
And that time is through!

And Henselmann was thrashed
So he would build the street
And since he did it fast
They trashed him again as a treat

That's also why it's called Stalin Avenue
Boy, I wish you knew:
And that time is through!

And on June seventeen
Many a work brigadier
Got armed, forgot his routine
What flowed was not just beer

Yes, that's why it's Stalin Avenue
Boy, I wish you knew:
And that time is through!

And since by 9:30 at night
The street is quiet too
A grave that's shut up tight
The trees lined up in a queue

That's also why it's called Stalin Avenue
Boy, I wish you knew:
And that time is through!

After the big party congress
Many shat in their pants
And in the fog and darkness
Tore down some monuments

Yes, that's why it's still called Stalin Avenue

White bricks come crashing down
But only on our friends

Die Häuser stehen ewig!
(in Baureparatur!!)

    Auch darum heißt das Ding STALINALLEE
    Mensch, Junge, versteh
    Und die Zeit ist passé!

Karl Marx, der große Denker
Was hat er denn getan
Daß man sein' guten Namen
Schreibt an die Kacheln dran?!

    Das Ding heißt doch nicht KARL-MARX-ALLEE
    Mensch, Junge, versteh:
    STALINALLEE!

Wir wolln im Sozialismus
Die schönsten Straßen baun
Wo Menschen glücklich wohnen
Die auch dem Nachbarn traun
                . . . könn'n!

    dann baun wir uns 'ne KARL-MARX-ALLEE!
    dann baun wir uns 'ne ENGELS-ALLEE!
    dann baun wir uns 'ne BEBEL-ALLEE!
    dann baun wir uns 'ne LIEBKNECHT-ALLEE!
    dann baun wir uns 'ne LUXEMBURG-ALLEE!

    dann baun wir uns 'ne LENIN-ALLEE!
    dann baun wir uns 'ne TROTZKI-ALLEE!

    dann baun wir uns 'ne THÄLMANN-ALLEE!
    dann baun wir uns 'ne PIECK-ALLEE
    dann baun wir uns 'ne . . .
        (verflucht, da fehlt doch noch einer!)
        BIERMANN-Straße

Mensche, Junge, versteh
Und die Zeit ist passé!
Die alte Zeit ~~ist~~ passé!   *war*

The houses still stand tall!
(Repair work never ends!!)

> That's why it's called Stalin Avenue
> Boy, I wish you knew:
> And that time is through!

Karl Marx that great thinker
What did he do after all
To have his honest name
Written on this or that wall?!

> But it's not called Karl Marx Avenue
> Boy, I wish you knew:
> STALIN AVENUE!

In our Socialist state we want
To build the nicest streets
Where a man can live happily
Can trust the neighbor he meets

> > > > > > . . . we hope!

> so then let's build a Karl Marx Avenue!
> so then let's build an Engels Avenue!
> so then let's build a Bebel Avenue!
> so then let's build a Liebknecht Avenue!
> so then let's build a Luxemburg Avenue!

> so then let's build a Lenin Avenue!
> so then let's build a Trotsky Avenue!

> so then let's build a Thalmann Avenue!
> so then let's build a Pieck Avenue!
> so then let's build a . . .
> > (damn it, there's one missing!)
> > Biermann Street

> Boy, I wish you knew:
> And that time is through!
> That old time ~~is~~ through!   *was*

■ Reiner Kunze

Gegenwart

Was ich verwahre hinter schloß und siegel?

Keine konspiration nicht einmal
pornografie

Vergangenheit, tochter

Sie zu kennen kann
die zukunft kosten

Selbstmord

Die letzte aller türen

Doch nie hat man
an alle schon geklopft

■ Hanns Cibulka

Losgesprochen

Abschußrampen, Akademien,
wo die Bakterien den Sandkasten ersetzen,
was soll der Engel
mit dem Flammenschwert vorm Paradies?
Künstliche Sonnen
explodieren
über der Haut unserer Erde,

Reiner Kunze

The Present

What do I keep behind lock and seal?

No conspiracy not even
pornography

The past, daughter

To know it can
cost the future

Suicide

The last of all doors

But one has never
knocked on all the others

Hanns Cibulka

Acquitted

Launching ramps, academies,
where bacteria replace sandboxes,
what does that angel mean
with his sword of flames before paradise?
Artificial suns
explode
over the skin of our earth,

ein Quantenhagel
schlägt
auf deinen Körper ein,
der Stein beginnt zu schreien,
empörte Inseln
tauchen in den Ozean zurück.

Losgesprochen
hat dich die Natur,
die Wälder sind ohne Sprache
und auch die Flüsse
geben dir keine Antwort
du bist mündig geworden,
du kannst

dein eigenes Bild
in der Asche zertreten,
im Staub der Erde
den Rosenstock
pflanzen.

■ Karl Mickel

Petzower Sommer

Latten, zu Zunder gedörrt, Zaun unter zögernden Schritten:
Lautlos zerfällt er, es knirscht zwischen Sohle und Holz.
Hier war die Kette, jetzt Rost. Glühender Sand! und es legt der
Wind das Emailleschild frei: Vorsicht! Bissiger Hund.
Das Astwerk im Winde gespannt, früchteschleudernde Bögen.
Unter geborstenem Baum greift im Liegen der Mund
Kirschen, von Kirschfleisch gefleckt flattert die Bluse der Freundin
Über uns, Hohlform der Luft, Fahne, Trophäe des Siegs.
Stimmen, von weither geweht. Schlurfende Schritte, ein Bauer
Knurrt zwischen Pfeife und Zahn: Stehlt soviel ihr nur könnt.

a quantum hail
pummels
your body,
the stone begins to scream
outraged islands
dive back into the ocean.

Acquitted
you were, by nature,
the woods are without speech
and also the rivers
give you no reply,
you have come of age,
you can

stomp out your own image
in the ash,
in the dust of the earth
plant
a rosebush.

■ Karl Mickel

Petzow Summer

Laths parched to tinder, fence under hesitating steps:
Silently it crumbles, a crunching between sole and wood.
Here was the chain, now rust. Glowing sand! and the wind
Uncovers an enamel sign: Beware of dog!
The branches spread in the wind, fruit slinging arches.
Under a split tree while you lie your mouth grabs
Cherries, flecked with cherry flesh the blouse of the girl friend
Over us, hollow shape of the air, flag, trophy of victory.
Voices blown from afar, shuffling steps, a farmer
Grumbles between his pipe and teeth: steal as much as you can.

Paul Wiens

Stoffwechsel

Hieronymus Bosch

Ich öffne das buch. Ich betrete ein haus.
Dort wird einer geboren: ich. Aber
ich öffne ein fenster und klettre hinaus.
Auf der strasse am kandelaber
hängt einer, schwarzhäutig, streckt
seine zunge heraus: ich. Indessen
verlass ich die stadt. Im kornfeld neckt
einer nackt eine nackte: ich. Sie fressen
eines das andre — abendmahl. Doch
ich steh schon am kreuzweg. Dort stritten
zwei. Nun hat der eine ein rotes loch
im bauch und schreit: ich. Der andere, mitten
im dom auf der säule, entmannt sich: ich.
Ich senke den blick. Unter mir schimmert
die weltzentrale. Dort schläft einer: ich.
Einer bedient dort den knopf und wimmert:
ich. Ich wende mich ab, ich steig in den zug.
Wir rollen durch nächte und spielen
schach: ich gegen mich. Draussen im funkenflug
glüht einer: ich. Falle, ohne zu zielen,
finde das weisse blatt: mich. Brenne aus.
Springe frisch aus dem feuer, gesalbt und erkoren:
ein buch wird geöffnet, betreten ein haus,
dort einer geboren . . . Ich, ich, ich, ich . . .

Paul Wiens

Metabolism

Hieronymus Bosch

I open the book. I enter a house.
Someone is being born there: me. But
i open a window and climb out.
In the street from a chandelier
someone is hanging, black skinned, sticks
his tongue out: me. Meanwhile
i leave the city. In a rye field one naked person
teases another: me. They eat
one another—supper. But
i already stand at the crossroads. There two
were arguing. Now the one has a red hole
in his stomach and screams: me. The other, in the middle
of the cathedral atop a column, castrates himself: me.
I lower my eyes. Beneath me shimmers
the center of the earth. Somebody sleeps there: me.
Someone presses the button there and whimpers:
me. I turn away, i step onto the train.
We roll through nights and play
chess: i versus me. Out there, among the sparks,
someone is aglow: me. Fall, without aiming,
find the white sheet of paper: me. Burn out.
Jump fresh out of the fire, anointed and chosen:
a book is opened, a house entered,
someone is being born there . . . I, i, i, i . . .

Peter Huchel

Exil

Am Abend nahen die Freunde,
die Schatten der Hügel.
Sie treten langsam über die Schwelle,
verdunkeln das Salz,
verdunkeln das Brot
und führen Gespräche mit meinem Schweigen.

Draußen im Ahorn
regt sich der Wind:
Meine Schwester, das Regenwasser
in kalkiger Mulde,
gefangen
blickt sie den Wolken nach.

Geh mit dem Wind,
sagen die Schatten.
Der Sommer legt dir
die eiserne Sichel aufs Herz.
Geh fort, bevor im Ahornblatt
das Stigma des Herbstes brennt.

Sei getreu, sagt der Stein.
Die dämmernde Frühe
hebt an, wo Licht und Laub
ineinander wohnen
und das Gesicht
in einer Flamme vergeht.

Auf den Tod von V.W.

Sie vergaß die Asche
auf den gekrümmten Tasten des Klaviers,
das flackernde Licht in den Fenstern.

Peter Huchel

Exile

In the evening, friends draw near,
the hills' shadows.
Slowly they step over the threshold,
darken the salt,
darken the bread
and converse with my silence.

Outside, in the maple,
the wind stirs:
my sister, the rain water
in the limy hollow,
imprisoned
she looks after the clouds.

Go with the wind,
the shadows say.
The summer lays
its iron sickle on your heart.
Go away, before the stigma of autumn
burns in the maple leaf.

Be constant, says the stone.
The early dawn
is rising, when light and leaves
live in one another
and your face
vanishes in a flame.

On the Death of Virginia Woolf

She forgot the ashes
on the warped piano keys,
the flickering light in the windows.

Mit einem Teich begann es,
dann kam der steinige Weg,
der umgitterte Brunnen, von Beifuß bewachsen,
die löchrige Tränke unter der Ulme,
wo einst die Pferde standen.

Dann kam die Nacht,
die wie ein fallendes Wasser war.
Manchmal, für Stunden,
ein Vogelgeist,
halb Bussard, halb Schwan,
hart über dem Schilf,
aus dem ein Schneesturm heult.

■ **Eva Strittmatter**

Bilanz

Wir alle haben viel verloren.
Täusche dich nicht: auch ich und du.
Weltoffen wurden wir geboren.
Jetzt halten wir die Türen zu
Vor dem und jenem. Zwischen Schränken
Voll Kunststoffzeug und Staubkaffee
Lügen wir, um uns nicht zu kränken.
Und draußen fällt der erste Schnee . . .
Wir fragen kalt, die wir einst kannten:
Was machst denn du, und was macht der?
Und wie wir in der Jugend brannten . . .
Jetzt glühn wir anders. So nie mehr.

It began with a pond,
then came the stony path,
the trellised well, overgrown with artemisia,
the pitted watering place under the elm
where the horses once stood.

Then came the night
that was like a falling water.
Sometimes, for hours,
a bird spirit
half hawk, half swan,
just above the reeds
from which a blizzard howled.

■ Eva Strittmatter

Balance Sheet

And all of us have lost a lot.
Don't fool yourself: both me and you.
Born open to the world, now not.
We hold the doors shut tightly to
This one or that. Our lies extend,
Between the cupboards of synthetics
And instant coffee—just don't offend.
Outside the first snow falls poetic . . .
Those we once knew we coldly sleuth:
What do you do, and what he, then?
And how we burned once in our youth . . .
Now we burn otherwise. So not again.

Sarah Kirsch

Ich wollte meinen König töten

Ich wollte meinen König töten
Und wieder frei sein. Das Armband
Das er mir gab, den einen schönen Namen
Legte ich ab und warf die Worte
Weg die ich gemacht hatte: Vergleiche
Für seine Augen die Stimme die Zunge
Ich baute leergetrunkene Flaschen auf
Füllte Explosives ein — das sollte ihn
Für immer verjagen. Damit
Die Rebellion vollständig würde
Verschloß ich die Tür, ging
Unter Menschen, verbrüderte mich
In verschiedenen Häusern — doch
Die Freiheit wollte nicht groß werden
Das Ding Seele dies bourgeoise Stück
Verharrte nicht nur, wurde milder
Tanzte wenn ich den Kopf
An gegen Mauern rannte. Ich ging
Den Gerüchten nach im Land die
Gegen ihn sprachen, sammelte
Drei Bände Verfehlungen eine Mappe
Ungerechtigkeiten, selbst Lügen
Führte ich auf. Ganz zuletzt
Wollte ich ihn einfach verraten
Ich suchte ihn, den Plan zu vollenden
Küßte den andern, daß meinem
König nichts widerführe

■ Sarah Kirsch

I Wanted to Kill My King

I wanted to kill my king
And be free again. The bracelet
He gave me, that one beautiful name,
I took off and threw away the words
I had made: similes
For his eyes his voice his tongue
I arranged emptied bottles and
Filled them with explosives—that was
To drive him away for good. So that
The rebellion would be complete
I locked the door, went out
Among people, fraternized in
Various houses—still,
Freedom refused to grow large
The soul, that bourgeois thing,
Not only persisted, it grew milder,
Danced when I ran my head
Against the walls. I pursued
rumors in the country that
Spoke against him, collected
Three volumes of misdeeds, a folder
Of injustices, even lies
I registered. At the very end
I simply wanted to betray him
I sought him out to complete the plan
Kissed another, so that nothing
would happen to my king

1975–1990

From New Subjectivity to a "New World Order"

History makes a wide curve around us, but it comes back again.

■ Sarah Kirsch

Death Valley

1

Hier ist nicht Disney-Land. Alice
Steht am Anfang der Wüste, setzt ihren Fuß
Ins geologische Freiluftmuseum
Lernt in den folgenden Stunden
Erosion an großen Modellen.
Angefressene Hügel gutartige Haufen Erde
Ahmten Termitenbaue griechische Tempel
Mühelos nach Pompeji
Folgt ihr der Freund in zerspaltene Canyons
Die schöngefalteten Kaskaden
Stürzender Bäche aus Sand
Luden müde verdurstete Seelen
Trügerisch ein das Gestirn
Krachte durch Kuppeln gläserner Luft.

2

Im totenblassen Totenreich
In wüster kreisender Sonne
Treffen wir furchtbare Äcker an, Land
Der größten Kolchose der Welt.
Das Saatgut ist rein, des Himmels Kind
Hat die Disteln von altersher
Geduldig gewaltsam zu Kugeln verdreht.

In diesem ehrlichen Landstrich ohne den Zuspruch der Bäume
Erschrocken und fröhlich, schlingernde Seelen
Tauchen wir nach strahlenden Steinen Schiefertafeln
Eingekratztes zaubrisches Zeug Shoshonengemurmel
Salzseen Brennspiegel werfen die Bilder
Uns in den Kopf vergessene Szenerien
Auf dem Waschbrett des Winds.

■ Sarah Kirsch

Death Valley

1

This is not Disney Land. Alice
Stands at the edge of the desert, sets foot
In the geological open-air museum
Learns in the following hours
Erosion from large-scale models.
Gnawed hills benign piles of earth
Mimicked termite mounds Greek temples
Effortlessly from Pompeii
The friend follows her into cleaved canyons
The beautifully creased cascades
Of tumbling streams of sand
Invited weary parched souls
Deceptively the stars
Crashed through domes of glassy air.

2

In the deathly pale kingdom of death
In the bleak, circling sun
We come to ominous acres, land
Of the world's largest kolkhoz.
The seedcorn is pure, heaven's child
Has since eternity twisted the thistles
Patiently, powerfully into balls.

In this frank tract of land without consolation of trees
Frightened and joyful, swaying souls
We dive for shining stones, slates
Etched magic token of Shoshone murmuring
Salt lakes burning mirrors reflect the images
Of forgotten sceneries in our minds
On this the wind's washboard.

Die knisternden windgedrechselten Kugeln
Zerreißen sich, greifen uns gnadenlos an
Sie durchdringen die Kleider die Schuhe, sie wollen
Bis unter die Haut, jagen uns ins Auto zurück
Und ruhen nicht während wir fahren. Wir sehen
Ihre Komplizen die Raben über des Teufels Kohlplantagen.

3

Des Freundes wehendes wildaufgestelltes Haar
Macht einen hellen Schein in der Wüste. Er späht
Nach wirbelndem Sand verborgenen Kratern er sucht
Einen englischen Weg mir vor die Füße.

4

Luft-Orgeln sirrende Steine
Riefen die Winde meilenweit her
Gierig stürzten sie sich in die Arbeit
Dem grauen dem schwarzen so rotem Gras
Letztes Leben ausblasen, ununterbrochen
Berge und Täler vertauschen
Das niedergegangene Bergwerk
Endgültig schleifen, die Spiegel
Schimmernder Borax-Seen
Auslöschen Splitter verstreun.

Wir flogen schnell dahin fanden
Nichts in den Dünen und Gott
Jagt als Sheriff hinter uns her.

5

Hinter Schienen als wäre es gestern geliefert
In dieser elenden Fremde dem Jammertal o wir glaubten
Ohne Vernunft und des Teufels zu sein
Stand plötzlich ein glitzerndes Opernhaus.

The crackling wind-lathed balls
Split apart, grab us mercilessly
They penetrate clothes, shoes, they try
Even to bore under our skin, chase us back to the car
And do not rest when we drive. We see
Their accomplices the ravens over the devil's cabbage fields.

3

The friend's fluttering wildly bristled hair
Has a bright shine in the desert. He spies out
Whirling sand hidden craters he looks for
An angelic path before my feet.

4

Air-organs hissing stones
Summoned the winds from miles away
Greedily they set to work
Blowing the last life out of the gray
The black so red grass, without cease
Exchanging mountains and valleys
Finally razing
The abandoned mine, extinguishing
The mirrors of shimmering Borax lakes
Strewing splinters.

We flew along quickly found
Nothing among the dunes and God
Chasing after us as the sheriff.

5

Across the train tracks as if delivered yesterday
In this desolate foreign place this vale of sorrow O we believed
We had lost our minds and belonged to the devil
Stood suddenly a glittering opera house.

Die Besucher waren im Innern des Saales
Gleich auf die Wände gemalt, oben
Der König die Königin Halskrausen Schönheit
Auf den Balkonen, der Veilchenstrauß
Fällt schwebend die jüngere Schwester
Liebkost eine Katze und Scheitel und Locken
Der Trichter der Tuba das Flattern der Bögen
Französische Herren Zigeuner viel Volk überhaupt
In Ränge und Gänge verteilt. Die Klosterfräulein
Sitzen versteckt, aufgerissene Augen
Sehen Küsse und heimlich getauschte Briefe
Niemand weiß was hier wirklich geschieht
Alice schlägt die Gaukelei
Mit fliegenden Fingern im Baedeker nach
Die Oper ist aufgeführt und ihr Ende steht fest
Wir sind gekommen und werden gehen
Die abwesende schwarze Garderobenfrau
Reicht uns den Mantel, die Autopapiere.

6

Und später in Deutschland
Hat sie den Blick hinter die Spiegel
Vergessen, würde sie wieder
Ihr hübsches kleines Leben führen
Mit Kind und Blumentöpfen
Der Postbote bringt Briefe die froh
Die langweilig sind
Der Schreibtisch hat Schubladen
Für Steine getrocknete Blätter
Kraut und Teufelskohl
Bunt durcheinander. Und das Gefühl
Großer Vergänglichkeit
Gelänge in die Pralinenschachtel
Vom ersten Flug übern Atlantik.

The visitors in the hall's interior
Were painted right on the wall, above
The king the queen, ruffs, beauty
In the balcony, the violet nosegay
Falls hovering the younger sister
Fondles a cat and head and curls
The tuba's funnel the fluttering bows
French gentlemen gypsies in fact many people
Divided according to level and aisle. The nuns
Sit hidden, with wide-open eyes
See kisses and secretly exchanged letters
No one knows what is really going on here
Alice checks the ruse
With flying fingers in Baedeker
The opera has been performed and its end is certain
We have come and will go
The blank-faced black checkroom woman
Hands us the coat, the papers for the car.

6

And later in Germany
She has forgotten the look behind
The mirrors, she would again lead
Her nice small life
With child and potted plants
The mailman brings letters that are
Happy, boring
The desk has drawers
For stones dried leaves
Wild flowers and devil's weed
All jumbled together. And that sense
Of immense mortality
Would fit in the candy box
From the first flight over the Atlantic.

Katzenleben

Aber die Dichter lieben die Katzen
Die nicht kontrollierbaren sanften
Freien die den Novemberregen
Auf seidenen Sesseln oder in Lumpen
Verschlafen verträumen stumm
Antwort geben sich schütteln und
Weiterleben hinter dem Jägerzaun
Wenn die besessenen Nachbarn
Immer noch Autonummern notieren
Der Überwachte in seinen vier Wänden
Längst die Grenzen hinter sich ließ.

■ Helga Novak

Ach, ich stand an der Quelle

endlich angekommen
habe ich zu trinken vergessen
von Ruten eingekesselt
überdacht von Knallbeeren
habe ich in der feuchten
Wölbung aus Stein gesessen
warum
wollte ich unbedingt alleine gehen
du hast noch gesagt —
ich komme mit zur Quelle

brütend in der Kälte
aus Wasser und Moos
spüre ich
unter eines sonnigen Tages Helle
den Tod ringsum
und denke — es ist alles zu Ende
und ich bin dich los

Cat Life

But poets love cats
The uncontrollable gentle
Free ones who sleep dream away
The November rains
On silken chairs or in rags
Mutely reply shudder and
Live on behind the hunter's blind
When the obsessed neighbors
Are still noting the license numbers of cars
When the person spied on within his four walls
Has long ago left the borders behind him.

■ **Helga Novak**

Oh, I stood by the spring

finally arrived
I forgot to drink
encircled by twigs
under a witch hazel roof
I sat in the damp
hollow of stone
why
did I absolutely want to go by myself
you still said—
I'll come along to the spring

brooding in the cold
of water and moss
I sense
beneath the brightness of a sunny day
death all around
and think—it is all over
and I am rid of you

nachdem ich raus war aus der Hölle
bin ich in einen Fuchsbau gesunken
der war unter den dornigen
Ranken gar nicht zu sehn
ach ich stand an der Quelle
und habe nicht getrunken

Brief an Medea

Medea du Schöne dreh dich nicht um
vierzig Talente hat er dafür erhalten
von der Stadt Korinth
der Lohnschreiber der
daß er dir den Kindermord unterjubelt
ich rede von Euripides verstehst du
seitdem jagen sie dich durch unsere Literaturen
als Mörderin Furie Ungeheuer
dabei hätte ich dich gut verstanden
wer nichts am Bein hat
kann besser laufen
aber ich sehe einfach nicht ein
daß eine schuldbeladene Gemeinde
ihre blutigen Hände an deinen Röcken abwischt
keine Angst wir machen
das noch publik
daß die Korinther selber deine zehn Gören gesteinigt haben
(wie sie schon immer mit Zahlen umgegangen sind)
und das mitten in Heras Tempel
Gewalt von oben hat keine Scham
na ja die Männer die Stadträte
machen hier so lustig weiter
wie früher und zu hellenischen Zeiten
(Sklaven haben wir übrigens auch)
bloß die Frauen kriegen neuerdings
Kinder auf Teufel komm raus
anstatt bei Verstand zu bleiben
(darin sind sie dir ähnlich)
andererseits haben wir
uns schon einigermaßen aufgerappelt
was ich dir noch erzählen wollte: die Callas ist tot

after I was out of that hell
I sank into a fox den
that was under the thorny runners
not to be seen
oh I stood by the spring
and did not drink

Letter to Medea

Medea you beauty don't turn around
forty talents he was given
from the city of Corinth
the old hack
for fixing that infanticide on you
I speak of Euripides you understand
ever since then they have chased you through our literatures
as a murderer fury monster
but I could have understood you well
nothing tied to your legs
makes running easier
what I don't see is why
a community heavy with guilt
wipes its bloody hands on your skirts
but don't worry
we'll make it public yet
that the Corinthians themselves stoned your ten kids
(the way they're always so free with numbers)
and what's more right in Hera's temple
violence from above knows no shame
and of course those men the city council
carry on merrily
as before and in Hellenic times
(we also have slaves by the way)
only the women of late
are having kids as quick as the devil
instead of keeping their heads
(in that respect they are like you)
on the other hand we have
worked our way up somewhat
and before I forget it: Callas is dead

■ Rolf Dieter Brinkmann

Nach Shakespeare

Die Winterhand fällt ab
und liegt im Garten, wo nun
ein hölzernes Gerüst errichtet
ist. Die dunklen Sommer

fallen wie die Hand.
Du frierst im Kopf.
Der Herbst mit seinen
toten Fischen auf dem

Grund der Flüsse ist
wie die Bude mit der alten
Frau, die sitzt und liest
die Tageszeitung, bis jemand

kommt und eine von den kalten
Frikadellen kauft, die in der
fettbespritzten Glasvitrine
liegen. Der Passant zahlt,

ißt, wirft den Knochen
nach dem unsichtbaren Engel.

Und Frühling kommt, verstreut
die Autolichter durch

blechernes Laub am Abend,
der mit den hölzernen Gerüsten
niedersinkt am Fluß.

■ Rolf Dieter Brinkmann

After Shakespeare

The hand of winter falls away
and lies in the garden where now
a wooden framework is
set up. The dark summers

fall like the hand.
You freeze in your head.
The fall with its
dead fishes at the

bottom of the rivers is
like the booth with the old
woman who sits and reads
the daily paper until someone

comes and buys some of the
fish and chips that
lie in the fat splattered
glass vitrine. The passerby pays,

eats, tosses the bone
to an invisible angel.

And spring comes, scatters
the headlights through

tinny foliage at evening
which sinks with the wooden scaffolding
down near the river.

■ Guntram Vesper

Frohburg, von Manhattan aus

Im Hotel Edison hinter dem Broadway
in Höhe Times Square
mit den dreitausend Riegeln an den dreitausend
dunkelrosa gestrichenen Zimmertüren
mit der hohen halbdunklen Bahnhofshalle als Foyer
voller kräftiger Wachleute am Tag und nachts
mit den beiden Eingängen zur 46. und 47. Straße
vorn stehen ab Nachmittag schlanke
hochmütige Nutten
hinten liegt schon am Morgen
im Theatereingang ein Mann
der für die Frauen die bei Howard Johnson
an den Fenstertischen frühstücken
seine Hose aufknöpft
in dieser anderen
in einer ganz ganz anderen Welt
liegen wir lange nach Mitternacht auf dem Bett
in einem kleinen Zimmer im 16. Stock
geblendet durch die Lichtreklame von Sony
gefesselt vom Geheimnis des Riesenschildes
am Haus gegenüber King Kong
for Christmas
umtost von Polizeisirenen aus dem
Fernseher und von der 8. Avenue wir halten
einander bei der Hand rauchen
gucken immer an die Decke und
sie erzählt mir
von den endlosen trostlosen Straßen in Brooklyn
vom Getto im Norden Spritzen Messern
großen Vermögen und ich
ich erzähle von einer anderen
ganz anderen Welt nämlich
von Frohburg der armen Kleinstadt in Sachsen
von der Töpfervorstadt die

■ Guntram Vesper

Frohburg as Seen from Manhattan

Hotel Edison behind Broadway
Up near Times Square
three thousand bolts on three thousand
doors all painted a dark pink
with a high semi-dark railroad station of a foyer
full of strong guards both daytime and nights
with the two entrances on 46th and 47th Street
in front of it starting at noon stand slim
arrogant whores
behind it the theater entrance
in the morning already a man lies there
who for the benefit of the women
having breakfast at Howard Johnson's window tables
unbuttons his pants
in this different
this truly and entirely different world
we lie on our bed long after midnight
in a small room on the 16th floor
blinded by Sony's neon signs
captivated by the secrets of the gigantic poster
on the house opposite King Kong
for Christmas
deafened by police sirens from the
TV set and from 8th Avenue we hold
each other's hands smoke
stare at the ceiling and
she tells me
about endless hopeless streets in Brooklyn
about the ghetto in the North needles knives
huge fortunes and I
tell about a different
a quite different world namely
about Frohburg a poor little town in Saxony
about the outskirts where they made pots

bei Eisgang immer unter Wasser stand
der verfallenden Webergasse
dem teils grasbewachsenen teils
braungelb gepflasterten Kirchplatz mit
den herrlichen weitkronigen Bäumen
von den kleinen sicheren Verhältnissen in denen ich
wie selbstverständlich groß geworden bin
ein Raubmord und eine Brandstiftung waren
in dreihundert Jahren die größten Katastrophen die man
dort miterlebte wirklich mitansah
jeder hatte einen Namen einer kannte
der anderen zählte auf ihn rechnete mit ihm das
war meine Kindheit
die Menschen in dieser Gegend sind freundlich und
redselig die Hügel
sind sanft und
die Bäche klar
und die Burgen verfallen und die Dörfer
waren wohlhabend und doch
habe ich als Kind viel geweint viel mehr
als in dieser anderen
ganz anderen Welt wie merkwürdig

■ Karin Kiwus

Im Alten Land

Lange bin ich nicht mehr
wie früher im Dezember
im Alten Land
die Feldwege entlanggekommen an Backsteingehöften
hinter braunen Kanälen hinter niedrigen
splitternden Zäunen und runden Rhododendronbüschen

Die ziehende Wärme aus den Fenstern
nach außen geöffnete Flügel verhakt

where they always had floods at the thaw
about the crumbling Weaver's Lane
the church square, half covered with grass
half with brown-yellow cobbles
with its gorgeous broad-crowned trees
about the cramped safe conditions in which I
grew up as if they were a matter of course
a robbery and killing or some arson were
in three hundred years the greatest catastrophes
people encountered there actually saw them
everyone had a name, everyone knew
everyone else counted and relied on him that
was my childhood
the people in that region are friendly and
talkative the hills
are gentle and
the brooks clear
the fortress crumbling and the villages
were prosperous and yet
as a child I cried a lot much more
than in this different
quite different world how odd

■ Karin Kiwus

In the Old Country

Not for a long time have I gone
as always in December
in the Old Country
along the fields past the brick farmsteads
behind the brown canals behind low
splintering fences and round rhododendron bushes

The warm draft from the windows
shutter opened outward latched

im Wind die milchigen Gardinen
weich gerafft über dem Efeu im Topf
den Alpenveilchen und den Begonien

Die gelben Äpfel an unbelaubten Bäumen
die Wäscheleinen in den Gärten
das Brombeergestrüpp und der zertretene Kohl
das graue Gerümpel vor dem Schuppen
und scharrende Tiere am Verschlag

Die nackte Luft zwischen den Deichen
der blanke Ausblick über die Ebenen
scharf wie eine Kaltnadelradierung
weitwinklig bis zum Meer
die flache Sonne klirrend unter den Fußsohlen
und die Hände fühllos fremd wie Prothesen

Und lange bin ich nicht mehr
wie früher im Dezember
nachhaus
zurückgekehrt unter die Lampe
mit sieben Segelschiffen auf dem Schirm
an den gedeckten Tisch mit Rosenporzellan
Silberkannenkaffee und duftenden Putten aus Marzipan
mit aufgeschnittenem Klaben in der Schale
und der Frauenhand
sanft neben der Tasse
und innig auf meinem Arm
wie jung ich war und eng
als ich sie abgewehrt habe
achtlos und verlegen

Die Nachmittage waren voll
selbstverständlicher Versprechen
der Himmel schneehell
wie eine Märzbecherwiese
und die Zukunft dahinter
ein sicherer Schimmer über dem Tau
so leicht und groß und griffbereit

the milky curtains in the wind
gathered up softly over ivy in the pot
the cyclamen and begonia

The yellow apples on the bare trees
the clotheslines in the gardens
the blackberry bushes and the trampled cabbage
the gray junk in front of the shed
and pawing animals in the stalls

The raw air between the dikes
the smooth vista over the plains
sharp as a drypoint etching
with broad angles to the sea
the shallow sun clattering under the soles of my feet
and hands numbly alien as prostheses

And not for a long time
as always in December
have I returned
home beneath the lamp
with seven sailboats on its shade
to the table set with rose porcelain
silverpot coffee and fragrant putti of marzipan
with raisin cake cut open in its wrapping
and the woman's hand
gentle beside the cup
and tenderly on my arm
how young I was and narrow
when I rebuffed her
heedless and embarrassed

The afternoons were full
of unquestioned promises
the skies snow bright
like a meadow of snowdrops
and the future beyond that
a lasting shimmer over the dew
so light and large and ready to be taken

Entfremdende Arbeit

Es macht mir wirklich nichts aus
   dir in der Küche zu helfen
      aber manchmal vermisse ich jetzt
      diese zögernden halbwachen Momente
im Türrahmen gelehnt und dir zugesehen
      wie du ein Frühstück eingesammelt hast
         mit deinem ganzen Körper

Du hast immer den Tee
      Häufchen für Häufchen abgemessen
         in der Mulde deiner linken Hand
und mit den Zähnen
      eine Packung Schnittkäse aufgerissen
die Tür des Kühlschranks hast du
      mit dem Schenkel zugedrückt
und sperrige Eierpappen eingestampft
      mit deinen Holzpantinen

Du hast immer mit dem Ellenbogen
      Kochtöpfe von der Herdplatte geschoben
und andere aufgesetzt die mit beiden Händen
      kaum noch zu halten waren

Du hast immer diese Pfannenschippe
   in der einen Hand gehabt
      und einen Keks in der anderen
und ein rutschendes Geschirrtuch über der Schulter
      wenn irgend etwas Flüssiges zu Boden ging
und du mit bloßen Zehen
      einen Lappen hervorgezerrt und gewischt hast
         als wäre ein Hobel unter deinem Fuß

Und wie ein verschlafener Posaunenengel
   hast du immer leicht entrückt
      in die kochende Milch geblasen
und die 5-Minuten-Eier heiß
      in die Brusttasche deines Bademantels gesteckt

Alienating Work

I really don't mind at all
   helping you in the kitchen
      but sometimes now I miss
   those hesitating half-awake moments
leaning in the door frame and watching you
  as you put together a breakfast
      with your entire body

You always measured the tea
   pile by little pile
      in the hollow of your left hand
and with your teeth
   would tear open the sliced cheese wrapper
the door of the refrigerator you
   used to shut with your thigh
and those bulky egg cartons
   you stomped down with your clogs

With your elbows you always
   used to shove pots off the burners
and put on others that could
   barely be held on to with both hands

You always had that spatula
   in one hand
      and a cookie in the other
and a slipping dish towel over your shoulder
   when something liquid hit the floor
and you with your bare toes
   dragged out a rag and wiped
      as if you had a grater under your foot

Like a sleepy cherub
   and always slightly transfigured
      you would trumpet into the boiling milk
and the five minute eggs you stuck
   hot in the breast pocket of your bathrobe

Es ist immer so besänftigend gewesen
zu spüren wie du voller Zuversicht
alles anpacken konntest am Morgen
selbstvergessen in einer Beweglichkeit
bei der ich mich einig fühlte mit dir
auf den ersten Blick

Wenn ich jetzt neben dir stehe in der Küche
und auf meine Art
aufmerksam hantiere mit den Dingen
habe ich dich nie mehr vor Augen
und seit wir tatsächlich miteinander anfangen
habe ich aufgehört zu erleben
wie es wirklich ist
wenn du und ich einen Tag beginnen

Ich bin dir näher gekommen vielleicht
aber du bist jetzt immer
eine halbe Stunde
weiter weg

Hommes à femme

Wenn eine kleine unscheinbare Frau
lange kluge und ein wenig
lispelnde Reden hält
über Don Juan und Casanova
dann stehen so Männer auf
und zischen Herrgottnochmal
was soll das überhaupt
die ist doch viel zu fipsig dafür

It was always so soothing
    to feel how you full of confidence
        could tackle anything in the morning
unselfconscious with an agility
    which made me feel at one with you
        at first sight

When I now stand next to you in the kitchen
    and in my own way
        carefully handle those things
 I no longer have you before my eyes
and now that we in fact begin together
 I have ceased to experience
        what it is really like
    when you and I start a day

I've gotten closer to you perhaps
    but you're now always
        half an hour
            further away

Hommes à femme

When a small inconspicuous woman
delivers long, clever, and slightly
lisping speeches
about Don Juan and Casanova
then these men just get up
and hiss forchristsake and
what's the point of it all—
she's too much of a shrimp anyhow

Fragile

Wenn ich jetzt sage
ich liebe dich
übergebe ich nur
vorsichtig das Geschenk
zu einem Fest das wir beide
noch nie gefeiert haben

Und wenn du gleich
wieder allein
deinen Geburtstag
vor Augen hast
und dieses Päckchen
ungeduldig an dich reißt
dann nimmst du schon
die scheppernden Scherben darin
gar nicht mehr wahr

■ Hans Magnus Enzensberger

Andenken

Also was die siebziger Jahre betrifft,
Kann ich mich kurz fassen.
Die Auskunft war immer besetzt.
Die wundersame Brotvermehrung
beschränkte sich auf Düsseldorf und Umgebung.
Die furchtbare Nachricht lief über den Ticker,
wurde zur Kenntnis genommen und archiviert.

Fragile

When I now say
I love you
I only cautiously
hand over the present
for a feast that the two of us
have never celebrated together

And when you
right away
can think of nothing but
your own birthday
and impatiently snatch
this small parcel then
you no longer even notice
the broken pieces
rattling inside

■ ## Hans Magnus Enzensberger

Souvenir

Well, as far as the seventies go,
I can keep it brief.
The operator was always busy.
The miracle of the loaves
was limited to Düsseldorf and surroundings.
The awful news ran over the ticker,
was duly noted and then archived.

Widerstandslos, im großen und ganzen,
haben sie sich selber verschluckt,
die siebziger Jahre,
ohne Gewähr für Nachgeborene,
Türken und Arbeitslose.
Daß irgendwer ihrer mit Nachsicht gedächte,
wäre zuviel verlangt.

■ Eva Strittmatter

Nachts

Ich fürchte den Tod.
Ich gebe es zu.
Ich fühlmichbedroht.
Auch du und du,
Ihr habt Angst wie ich
Vor dem Krebs und vorm Krieg.
Das behält man für sich
Und glaubt an den Sieg
Der Vernunft und der Wissenschaft.
Gott geb uns allnächtlich zum Glauben
Die Kraft.

Vor einem Herbst

Im Herbst soll einer auf mich warten.
Er soll so warten, daß ich kommen muß.
In einem gelben alten Garten.
Kurz vor dem Winter. Kurz vorm Schluß
Von allem. In der Weile,
Die zwischen Schnee und Regen bleibt.
Da suche ich die eine Zeile,
Die man vielleicht im Leben schreibt.

Without a fight for the most part
they choked themselves down,
the seventies,
with no guarantee for Brecht's "next generation,"
Turks and the unemployed.
That anyone would think of them with indulgence
would be too much to ask.

■ Eva Strittmatter

At Night

I'm afraid to die.
I admit it's true.
I feelsothreatenedby.
And you and you
You're all afraid like me
Of cancer and war.
We know it privately
And believe in victory for
Reason and science.
Grant us the power each night
For faith and reliance.

Before One Fall

In fall someone must wait for me.
He shall wait so that I must come past.
In an old and yellow garden will be.
Just before winter. Just before the last
Of everything. In the time
That's left between rain and snow again.
There I will seek that single line
That one perhaps in life can hope to pen.

■ Elisabeth Borchers

Das Begräbnis in Bollschweil

Wenn jemand gestorben ist,
den wir gut kannten,
prüfe ich unser Gedächtnis.
Es taugt nichts,
stelle ich fest.
Es ist nicht haltbar.
Wir sind bald verloren.

Wir nehmen den Berg wahr mit erstem Schnee
und den Nebel im Feld
und finden das passend und schön.
Undere Bedürfnisse sind einfach und stark,
wir frieren, haben Hunger und Durst
und einen nächsten Termin.

Zwischen uns die kleinen langsamen Gespenster.

■ Jürgen Theobaldy

Schnee im Büro

Eine gewisse Sehnsucht nach Palmen. Hier
ist es kalt, aber nicht nur. Deine Küsse
am Morgen sind wenig, später sitze ich
acht Stunden hier im Büro. Auch du
bist eingesperrt, und wir dürfen nicht
miteinander telefonieren. Den Hörer abnehmen
und lauschen? Telefon, warum schlägt
dein Puls nur für andere? Jemand fragt:
„Wie gehts?", wartet die Antwort nicht ab

Elisabeth Borchers

The Funeral in Bollschweil

When someone has died
whom we knew well,
I test our memory.
It is good for nothing,
I find.
It is not permanent.
Soon we are lost.

We take the mountain in with the first snow
and the fog in the field
and find that fitting and beautiful.
Our needs are basic and strong,
we freeze, have hunger and thirst
and another appointment.

Between us the small, slow ghosts.

Jürgen Theobaldy

Snow at the Office

A certain longing for palm trees. Here
it is cold, but not just that. Your kisses
in the morning are little, later I sit
for eight hours here at the office. You also
are imprisoned, and we may not
telephone each other. Pick up the receiver
and listen? Telephone, why does your pulse
beat only for others? Someone asks:
"How's it going?" doesn't wait for the answer

und ist aus dem Zimmer.
Was kann Liebe bewegen? Ich berechne
Preise und werde berechnet. All die Ersatzteile,
die Kesselglieder, Ölbrenner, sie gehen
durch meinen Kopf als Zahlen, weiter nichts.
Und ich gehe durch jemand hindurch
als Zahl. Aber am Abend komme ich zu dir
mit allem, was ich bin. Lese von
Wissenschaftlern: auch die Liebe ist
ein Produktionsverhältnis. Und wo sind
die Palmen? Die Palmen zeigen sich am Strand
einer Ansichtskarte, wir liegen auf dem Rücken
und betrachten sie. Am Morgen kehren wir
ins Büro zurück, jeder an seinen Platz.
Er hat eine Nummer, wie das Telefon.

■ Rolf Haufs

Unsere alten Träume

Eines Tages ist es nicht mehr wichtig. Das Haar
Wird weiß. Die Hände fühlen sich hart an. Die Haut
Läßt sich ziehen, ohne daß es weh tut.
Was wirst du tun heute abend. Einen
Schnaps trinken. Deine Zigarettenration schnell hinter dich
Bringen. Reden wir von dem, was noch kommt.
Oder von unseren alten Träumen, für die wir
Zu wenig getan haben. Von unserem
Zu zaghaften Widerstand. Davon, daß wir
Verführbar waren. Zu oft sprachen wir
Über den Zustand unserer Straßen zu oft über
Geschwindigkeiten sportliche Übungen über
Aufgesteckte Fahnen, die uns sagten, woher
Der Wind kam. Was sollen wir tun.
Jetzt. In unserer Lage. Steigen wir nicht

and is out of the room.
What can love affect? I calculate
prices and am calculated. All the replacement parts,
the boiler components, oil burners, they pass
through my head as numbers, nothing else.
And I pass through someone
as a number. But in the evening I come to you
with everything that I am. Read of
scientists: love, too, is
a production factor. And where are
the palms? The palms appear on the beach
of a picture postcard, we lie on our backs
and contemplate it. In the morning we go
back to the office, each to his own place.
It has a number, like the telephone.

Rolf Haufs

Our Old Dreams

Someday it is no longer important. Your hair
Turns white. Your hands feel hard. Your skin
Can be pulled without hurting.
What will you do this evening. Drink
A schnapps. Go through your ration of cigarettes
Quickly. Let's talk about what's still to come.
Or about our old dreams about which
We did too little. About our too
faint-hearted resistance. About how
We could be led astray. Too often we talked
About the condition of our roads too often about
Speed limits sports about
Unfurled flags that told us from which direction
The wind was blowing. What are we to do.
Now. In our situation. Let's not climb

Hinauf bis auf die höchsten Gebirge, wo es
Zu leben schwer wird. Wo sind
Die Gedanken, die uns doch allein
Weiterbringen.

■ Rainer Malkowski

Mitten in einen Vers

Mitten in einen Vers
aber die Vergeblichkeit menschlicher Beziehungen
klingelt das Telefon.
Sollen wir kommen? fragen die Freunde.
Ja, rufe ich erleichtert, ja!
Und der Vers bleibt auf dem Schreibtisch liegen,
wo er eine Weile verstaubt.

■ Alfred Kolleritsch

Todesstück

Was stehenblieb und seither ist,
wie es gewesen war: im Füreinander,
die grüne Flasche, Gewürze, Brot,
die Gläser, das geselchte Fleisch,
finstergrün das Öl.

Die Frau ist tot. Ich sehe den Tod.
Alles im Raum ist dieser Tod,
die abgetretene Schwelle ist der Tod.
Durchs Fenster: Licht. Durchs Fensterlose
verschlüpfte sich die Frau (vor ihrer Rast).
Und wer den Raum betritt, betritt den Tod.

Up to the top of the highest mountain range where it
Will be hard to live. Where are
Those ideas which are all that
Will make us progress.

■ Rainer Malkowski

Into the Middle of a Verse

Into the middle of a verse
about the vanity of human relationships
the telephone rings.
Can we come over? the friends ask.
Yes, I shout relieved, yes!
And the verse is left lying on my desk
where it collects dust for a while.

■ Alfred Kolleritsch

Death Piece

What was left standing and now remains
just as it was: for one another—
the green bottle, spices, bread,
the glasses, the smoked meat,
forest green, the oil.

The woman is dead. I see that death.
Everything in the room is her death,
the worn threshold is her death.
Through the window: light. Through something windowless
the woman slipped away (before her rest).
Whoever enters the room, enters death.

Der Garten überwächst. Was ihr gehörte,
ist verarmt, an sich geworden,
ohne ihre Hand ein Rest,
kein Blick darin, ein Erbstück,
schamlos anheimgefallen.
Das Glücksgefühl der Neuen war ihre Last.

Die Fliegen halten noch die Treue.
Ihr Sausen kreist die leere Stelle ein,
der Ort stürzt ein, Hinterbliebenes
schiebt sich vom Licht zum Schatten,
mehr Erde nimmt dem Himmel,
was sie an ihn gerichtet hat.

■   ## Wolf Wondratschek

All You Need Is Love

Jeder kennt das.

Die Sonne scheint,
ein Auto hupt und Kinder
streiten sich um
einen Ball.

Einer rast gegen den Baum,
einer schluckt Tabletten,
einer geht wie Hemingway
auf Nummer sicher.

Vielleicht gibt es Gründe,
vielleicht auch nicht.
Vielleicht wird es tatsächlich eines Tages
zu kompliziert,
über das Leben nachzudenken,
dazusitzen und über das Leben nachzudenken

Weeds overgrow the garden. What was once hers
is now impoverished, is just itself,
without her hand: a leftover,
no insight, an heirloom,
shamelessly given away.
The happiness of newcomers was her burden.

The flies still remain loyal.
Their humming encircles the empty spot,
the place collapses, what is left
now shifts from light to shade,
more earth takes from the sky
what it directed toward it.

■ Wolf Wondratschek

All You Need Is Love

Everybody knows about it.

The sun is shining,
a car honks and children
argue about
a ball.

One slams into a tree,
one takes pills,
one, like Hemingway,
picks the sure bet.

Maybe there are reasons,
maybe there aren't.
Maybe one day it will really be
too complicated
to think about life
to sit there and think about life

und anschließend tanzen zu gehn,
die Fragen vergessen,
auf Antworten verzichten,
die Schmerzen ertragen.

LACHT NICHT,
jeder kennt das.

Daß einer nicht mehr leben will, versteh ich;
daß einer sterben will, auch klar.
Aber tot sein?

Gestern sprang wieder einer aus dem Fenster,
einer in meinem Alter. Ich weiß nicht, wer er war
und was er dachte und fühlte und warum
es sein mußte.

Aber ich kann's ihm nachfühlen,
ein Sturz und die größte Lebensfreude
und dann ein Aufprall.
In der Zeitung stand eine Notiz,
sein Name und seine Freundin wird ihn
jetzt wahrscheinlich eine Weile wirklich lieben,
mehr als je zuvor.

Es ist stumpfsinnig,
darüber nachzudenken,
und jeder weiß, es ist
sinnlos.

Und das ist manchmal gerade
das Schönste an allem.

and then go dancing,
forget the questions,
give up on the answers,
bear the pain.

DON'T LAUGH,
everybody knows about it.

If someone doesn't want to live anymore, I can understand it;
if someone wants to die, OK.
But to be dead?

Yesterday someone jumped out of a window again,
a guy my age. I don't know who he was
and what he thought and felt and why
it had to be.

But I can identify with him,
a leap and the greatest joy in life
and then the impact.
There was a note in the paper,
his name, and probably his girl friend will
now really love him for a while,
more than ever before.

It is idiotic
to think about it,
and everybody knows it
makes no sense.

And sometimes that's precisely
the beauty of it.

■ Ulla Hahn

Wartende

Sie sitzt an einem Tisch für zwei Personen
allein mit diesem wachen starren Blick
schaut sie umher als hätt sie was verloren
und hält sich fest an einem Buch: Ihr Strick

der sie herauszieht aus den Augenpaaren
die nach ihr züngeln mitleidlos und spitz
wie Wellen über ihr zusammenschlagen
sie niederdrücken auf den Plastiksitz

der unter ihren Schenkeln klebt. Sie schwenkt
ihr Glas das Eis schmilzt klirrend schneller
sie selbst wird immer kleiner und versänk

gern als Erfindung in ihr Buch
das sie nun zuschlägt. Eh sie auftaucht
zahlt und geht. Es ist genug.

Verbesserte Auflage

Nur noch wenige Schritte dann
wird sie ihm wieder gehören hören
beschwören sein Lied das ohne sie
ihm versiegt. Hals Nase Ohren
die Augen die Haare den Mund
und so weiter wie
will er sie preisen allein
zu ihrem ewigen Ruhm.
Als eine Stimme anhebt.
Orpheus hört:
die zum Lauschen Bestellte fällt
singend ihm in den Rücken.

■ Ulla Hahn

Woman Waiting

She sits beside a table set for two
alone intently stares as if in hope
of finding what she's lost into the blue
and in her hand holds fast a book: the rope

to pull her out from all the pairs of eyes
that dart her way so sharp and pitiless
like pounding waves that rush and mount and rise
and washing down upon her push and press

until her thighs stick where she sits. Her drink
is swiveled to speed up the melting ice
while she herself grows smaller, tries to shrink

would gladly disappear, a mere device
to rim the novel that she shuts. Before
she surfaces then pays and goes. No more.

Improved Version

Just a few steps more then
she will again belong to him listen to
conjure up his song which without her
trickles away. Neck nose ears
the eyes the hair the mouth
and so on how
he wants to praise her alone
to her eternal fame.
When a voice ascends.
Orpheus listens:
the one supposed to listen
attacks him from the rear singing.

Da
dreht er sich um und
da
gleitet aus seinen verwirrten Händen
die Leier. Die Euridike aufhebt
und im Hinausgehn schlägt in noch
leise verhaltenen Tönen. Hals Nase Ohren
die Augen die Haare den Mund
und so weiter wie
will sie ihn preisen allein
zu seinem ewigen Ruhm.
Ob Orpheus ihr folgte
lassen die Quellen
im Trüben.

■ Ursula Krechel

Der Anfang des Wochenendes

Während ich im Supermarkt einer Frau
die Vorderräder des Einkaufswagens
auf die Fersen schiebe, fahre ich auch
meinen Kopf spazieren.
Im Wald der Konservendosen suche ich Blaubeeren
und die Erinnerung an die kleine Lust
auf einen trockenen, dünnen Fichtenast zu treten.
Während du daheim die Kühlschranktür zuschnappen läßt
wieder das kindliche Gefühl
das ich auch beim Aufwachen habe
wenn mich im Traum jemand geschlagen hat.
Freitagnachmittags läppert sich das Glück zusammen
aus prallen Einkaufstüten, aus Flaschen
Kisten, Kartons. Komm!
Wir setzen uns im Flur auf den Teppich
und fliegen mit unseren Hoffnungen davon.

Then
he turns around and
then
from his confused hands the lyre
slips, Eurydice picks it up
and while leaving strums in still
quiet restrained tones. Neck nose ears
the eyes the hair the mouth
and so on how
she wants to praise him alone
to his eternal fame.
As to whether Orpheus followed her
the sources
are vague.

■ Ursula Krechel

Start of the Weekend

While in the supermarket I shove
the front wheels of a shopping cart
against the heels of a woman, I also let
my mind stroll.
In the forest of preserve jars I look for blueberries
and the memory of the small pleasure
stepping on a dry, thin fir branch.
While at home you let the refrigerator door snap shut
again that childlike feeling
that I have upon waking
when someone has hit me in a dream.
Friday afternoons good fortune accumulates
from taut shopping bags, bottles
crates, cartons. Come!
Let's sit down on the rug in the entry
and fly off with our hopes.

Erster Februar

Was von einem Winternachmittag bleibt:
die spiegelnde Nässe auf den Straßenbahnschienen
blaue Kacheln in einem offenstehenden Haus
in dem pfeifende Arbeiter Wände einreißen
eine Wolke aus Staub über den Gehweg gefegt
eine Fuhre Schutt
ich fotokopierte fremde Gedichte
jetzt sind sie mein bewegliches Eigentum.

Was auch bleibt: die Zeit sitzt im Nacken
und wärmt die Schultern unverhofft.
Ein rosiges Licht über den Bankentürmen
und Spatzen schwätzen an den Pfützen.
Genügt, was nicht genügt, was bleibt?

■ **Friederike Roth**

Ehe

Die Frau beschimpft ihn
und er sieht nur so aus dem Fenster.

Einmal war sie
ein schönes stilles Mädchen
schwarzweißes Wachsfräulein
mit feinen Armen, Händchen
die hielten ihn, den Kenner, fest.

Jetzt ist ein eigenes Fest in ihren Augen
Erinnerungen von weit her:
   Großmutters Truhen geöffnet.
   Der Himmel
   lag auf den Hügeln vor der Tür.
   Und dahinein das Mädchen

First of February

What remains of a winter afternoon:
the dampness reflecting on the street car rails
blue tiles in a house standing open
where whistling workers tear down the walls
a cloud of dust sweeps over the sidewalk
a cartload of rubble
I photocopy others' poems
now they are my portable property.

What also remains: time sits at my nape
and warms my shoulders unexpectedly.
A rosy light over the bank towers
and sparrows gossip by the puddles.
Is it enough, what isn't enough, what remains?

■ Friederike Roth

Marriage

The woman calls him names
and he just looks out of the window.

Once upon a time she was
a beautiful quiet girl
black and white wax figurine
with fine arms, little hands
that held him, a connoisseur, tight.

Now there is a different feast in her eyes
remembrances from afar:
  Grandmother's trunks opened.
  Heaven
  lay across the hills in front of the door.
  And in all this the girl

das einmal Brombeerpflücken ging.
Und sie war dieses Mädchen.
Was für ein Glück hätt' können sein
wenn ein's gewesen wär.
Fort und fort
ein enthauptetes Leben
das wer verschuldet haben soll.

Er weiß von nichts.
So nimmt er's eben an
und seine Augen werden immer kleiner.

Fast Nacht um ihn.
Darin ist ausgestellt
feinsäuberlich der Herd, der Tisch, das Bett
gänzlich vermummt die Frau
und ohne Eingeweide
wie er selbst.

Er schließt die Augen.
In ihren liegen fremde Tränchen eh.

Vielleicht

wird greller Sonnenschein vielleicht
über unseren Gräbern liegen
und ein Himmel
ein Himmel sag ich Dir
sich darüberwölben.

Die dann dastehn (wahrscheinlich)
sonst aber über kühle Fliesen gehn
die Augen ganz und gar begehrlich
in eine schöne Weite gerichtet
künftige Jahrhunderte einzuläuten

who once had gone picking blackberries.
And she was this girl.
What happiness there could have been
if there had been any.
On and on
a decapitated life
that someone is said to be guilty of.

He knows of nothing.
And he accepts it all
his eyes grow smaller all the time.

Almost night around him.
And in it, neatly on display,
the hearth, the table, and the bed
completely muffled: the woman
and without entrails
just like he himself.

He shuts his eyes.
In hers there are some alien little tears.

Perhaps

harsh sunshine will perhaps
lie over our graves
and a heaven
a heaven I tell you
arch itself above.

Those who then stand there (probably)
who otherwise walk over cool flagstones
their eyes quite covetously
set on a beautiful expanse
to ring in future centuries

die ihre Wohnzimmergeheimnisse emsig vergolden
über den Schwiegersohn schimpfen wahrhaftig
ein Saufloch, herrjeh,
eine Uhr bauen
hoch in Samen geschossen

die geschüttelt werden vom Kindbettfieber
von Hochzeitstorte und Leichenschmaus zehren
(fahre hin du teure, treue Seele
mit Tränen gesät)

setzen gegen den dicken Tod
eine ferne Regsamkeit fort.

■ Hannelies Taschau

Aids en VOGUE

Gingen wir
eben noch halb enthüllt
gehen wir
wieder halb verhüllt
tragen wir die pudrigen
Farben wiederentdeckter
Keuschheit
Bereits in den Wintermoden
war es erkennbar
im Sommer setzte es sich fort
Lieben wir
wieder lieber
nicht
gefährlicher als
leicht lieber
nicht gefährlicher
lieber wieder nicht

who eagerly gild their living room secrets
complain about the son-in-law really
a lush, my God,
build a clock
go to pot

who will be shaken by childbed fever
feed on wedding cakes and wakes
(go forth you dear, true soul
sowed with tears)

resume against stout death
a distant bustle.

■ Hannelies Taschau

AIDS en VOGUE

Though just then
we walked half disrobed
now we walk
half robed again
wearing the powdery
shades of rediscovered
chastity
Winter fashions already
hinted at it
in the summer it continued
We love again
rather to love
not
more risky than
easy rather
not more risky
again rather not

Brigitte Struzyk

Die Tochter des Sisyphos berichtet dem Vater

Ach Väterchen, du bist ein Waisenknabe
Du hattest noch ein Ziel vor den Augen
Bergauf, bergab der gleiche Stein
Ein Unternehmen voller Übersicht
                Und ich?
Konfus ist diese Welt der tausend Dinge
Ich kann nicht wissen, was mir heute auf den Kopf fällt
                welches Rohr bricht
Was ist ein hochgewälzter Stein
Hält man ihn gegen einen Berg von Wäsche?

Julian Schutting

Abschied

Abschied, glaubst du, auf wenige Tage,
und so kann ich die kleine Abschiedsumarmung
wie eine auf wenige Tage umarmen
und bloß geträumt den Abschied nehmen,
der es trotzdem gewesen sein wird
ohne Auferstehung nach drei Tagen

Abschied, glaubst du auf drei vier Tage,
und die Stiegen ein letztes Mal hinuntersteigend
möchte auch meine Abschiedsbetäubung
an die Unsterblichkeit abzutötender Liebe glauben —
nicht zurückschauen über den Abschied hinweg
in das entleerte Herz,
damit du mir nicht wiederkommst,
bevor ich nie mehr komme,

Brigitte Struzyk

The Daughter of Sisyphus Reports to Her Father

O Daddy, you are an orphan boy
You still had your eyes set on a goal
Uphill, downhill the same stone
An enterprise with clear outline.
                    And me?
Confusing is this world of a thousand things
I cannot know what will fall down on my head today
                    What pipe will break
What is a stone rolled up
If one is holding it against a mountain of laundry?

Julian Schutting

Farewell

Farewell, you believe, for a few days
and so I can embrace the small farewell embrace
as if for a few days
and merely say a dreamt farewell
that even so will have been one
without resurrection after three days

Farewell, you believe, for three four days,
and descending the stairs a last time
my farewell numbness also wants to believe
in the immortality of love to be mortified—
do not look back beyond the farewell
into the emptied heart,
so that you do not come again to me,
before I come no more,

zurückschauen einmal noch,
zu schwer das leere Herz, es ohne Rast von dir zu tragen,
und ich winke zurück,
einmal und noch ein Mal und ein letztes Mal
ehe du auf immer zurücktrittst
aus dem mir und meinem Heimgang
ins Nie-wieder Winken

aber dann im Schatten der Bäume
ins noch nicht ganz beendete Leben zurück,
mich einzuschleichen in das Zimmer,
in welchem von mir ein leerer Koffer übriggeblieben ist,

leise und schnell die Stiegen hinauf,
als wollte ich nach drei schnell vergangenen Tagen
dich mit meiner Rückkehr ins Leben überraschen,
wie ein träumender Dieb
die Stiegen hinunter in die Befreiung:

schmerzfrei schläft noch der Schmerz,
aber er rührt sich schon,
als ich über das Gitter hinweg dich wie einen Schatten
ein allerletztes Mal durch dein Zimmer gehen sehe,
vielleicht auf meine letzten Grüße zu

Abschied, weiß nun auch ich,
nicht auf Tage und Wochen —
Modergeruch bleibt in dem Koffer zurück,
und immer noch ein Brief, der mich bei dir weiß,
damit du mit einem Strich
mich aus deinem Haus und Herzen wirfst
und meinem früheren Leben vor die Tür setzt

look back once more,
too heavy the empty heart, to carry it without rest from you,
and I wave back,
once and once again and a last time,
before you withdraw forever
from me and my going home
into never-wave-again

but then in the shadow of the trees
back into not yet wholly finished life
to sneak myself into the room
where an empty suitcase of mine remains,
quiet and quickly up the stairs,
as if after three quickly passed days
I wanted to surprise you with my return to life,
like a dreaming thief
descending the steps to deliverance:

painless the pain still sleeps,
but it rouses itself already
when I see beyond the screen like a shadow you
one final time going through your room
perhaps toward my last greetings

Farewell, now I know too,
not for days and weeks—
mustiness remains behind in the suitcase
and still another letter that places me with you
so that you with one stroke
throw me out of your house and heart
placing me in front of the door of my earlier life

■ Christa Reinig

Februar

24 FREITAG

    Manchmal
    ist mir das schwule hemd
    näher
    als der feministische rock

25 SAMSTAG

    Und außer diesem apfel
    ist Eva schuld daran
    daß Kain ausflippte
    und Abel nichts geworden ist

September

7 DONNERSTAG

    Meine frau sichtet
    meine gesammelten werke
    Unsere gedichte sind schöner
    sagt sie

Christa Reinig

February

February 24, Friday

> At times
> the gay shirt
> is closer to me
> than the feminist coat

February 25, Saturday

> And quite apart from that apple
> it's clearly Eve's fault
> that Cain flipped out
> and Abel never made it big

September

September 7, Thursday

> My woman sifts through
> my collected works
> *Our poems are more beautiful*
> she says

■ Hilde Domin

Mauern sortierend

Mauern sortierend

Kataloge von Blumenzwiebeln
Stoffmuster
Muster
von Mauern.

Die chinesische Mauer
aus Porzellan.
Mauern von Avila
ihre Tore
die kleinen Hufe der Getreideesel.

Die türelosen Mauern
für Hektor
und die Paßlosen.
Gartenmauern.
Mauern aus Menschenfleisch.

Mutter
Mauer
zwischen Geschwistern
jeder auf seiner Seite
Berlin

Unsichtbare Mauer
steiler
härter
länger

die Mauer aus Rücken

■ Hilde Domin

Sorting Walls

Sorting walls

Catalogues of flower bulbs
textile patterns
patterns
of walls.

The Chinese wall
of porcelain.
Walls of Avila
her gates
the small hoofs of the grain donkeys.

The doorless walls
for Hector
and the passportless.
Garden walls.
Walls of human flesh.

Mother
wall
between siblings
each on his own side
Berlin

Invisible wall
steeper
harder
longer

the wall of backs

Peter-Paul Zahl

über das reisen in die verbannung

vermögen habe ich keines und auch keines zu erwarten.
Johann Georg Elser

I

laotse *gürtete den schuh*
als er gegangen wurde
seine begleiter:
ein ochs und ein knabe

II

brecht ließ die virginia
kalt werden zwischen den lippen
als er gegangen wurde
ihn begleiteten hier und da
sein sohn die frauen
auch freunde und immer
das rollbild vom zweifler

III

ich dagegen reise komfortabel
und nie allein
wenn ich gegangen werde
hin und her
reise in hand- auch in fußschellen
im hubschrauber oder per bus
im konvoi
für meine sicherheit
sorgen die schützer
des staates mit funk
spezialausbildung und mpi's

Peter-Paul Zahl

on traveling into exile

wealth I neither have nor expect.
Johann Georg Elser

I

lao tse fastened his shoe
when they made him leave
his companions:
an ox and a boy

II

brecht let his cigar
go cold between his lips
when he was made to leave
here and there accompanied him
his son the women
also friends and always
the rolled pictures of the doubter

III

i on the other hand travel comfortably
and never alone
when I am made to leave
back and forth
travel in hand- also in leg-irons
by helicopter or bus
in convoy
for my safety
the guards
of the state provide with radio
special training and submachine guns

IV

noch nie
war der dichter
so wertvoll
wie heute

■ Michael Buselmeier

Kunst

Ich schreibe aus Schüchternheit
lieber wäre ich Guerillero
Chirurg, Begleiter von Filmstars
würde gern Wagners Tristan singen
Halten wir gerade den Atem an
oder holen wir Luft
für die Kämpfe der achtziger Jahre?
Die letzten Erfahrungen
ein genaueres Hinsehen
auf Wirkliches
Da ist meine politische Gruppe
meine alte Fremdheit
Angst vor Berührung, vorsichtig
bewege ich mich durch das Uni-Gebäude
wo man mich rausgeworfen hat
ohne besonderen Aufwand
hoffentlich redet mich keiner an
während ich die Aushänge
und die Wandzeitungen lese
Im Buchladen klappe ich die Neuerscheinungen
der Reihe nach auf und zu
Theo rennt hinter mir her
„Hast du mein langes Gedicht eingesteckt?
ich habe keinen Durchschlag davon"

IV

never
was the poet
as valuable
as today

Michael Buselmeier

Art

I write out of shyness
I'd rather be a guerrilla
surgeon, escort of film stars
would like to sing Wagner's Tristan
Are we stopping a breath
or getting our wind
for the battles of the eighties?
The most recent experiences
a closer look
at real things
There is my political group
my old estrangement
fear of contact, cautiously
I move through the university building
where they tossed me out
without much ado
I hope nobody talks to me
while I read the notices
and the flyers tacked up on the walls
In the bookstore I open the covers of new releases
one after the other and shut them
Theo runs along behind me
"Did you hang on to my long poem?
I don't have a copy of it"

Zu Hause öffne ich das Fenster
klopfe den Staub
aus Clemens Brentanos Gesammelten Werken
„Alle Menschen, welche ihr Brot
nicht im Schweiß ihres Angesichts verdienen
müssen sich einigermaßen schämen"
Das Gleichgewicht verlieren
ist keine Kunst
Bei starkem Regen steuere ich
meine Tochter auf dem Fahrrad
durch den abendlichen Großstadtverkehr.

„Auf, auf, Lenau!"

Februarfrost. Ein gewisses Freudeklopfen
    am eigenen Unglück, der diabolische Zug
      in Niembschs Gesicht. Mordbrenner Dichter,
ach Lotte. „Werd ihr entsagen."

Auf die Gasse gehetzt. Viel Violine gespielt.
    Geschrieben manches Gedicht, dies Fetzchen
      Überschuß, Geschichte, ins Ofeneisen gebissen.
Der Staatsknüppel Zensur.

Mich frierts ins Herz hinein, der Schnee im Hirn
    kracht. Aber sie merken nichts, auf der Suche stets
      nach Abwechslung und lehrreichen Krankheitsfällen.
„Daß einmal Ruhe drinnen sei."

Im Mondschein ein Mistkarren: Acht Polen,
    verlorene Helden, zusammengekauert,
      in Lumpen gehüllt, knarrend über das Pflaster
der Krämergasse.

Sterbt ab, Wälder; greif nur herunter, tiefer,
    du Eis der Gletscher. Auf nach Amerika
      mit dem Fledermausnest unterm Brustgefieder.
Niagara, Niagara!

At home I open the window
beat the dust
from Clemens Brentano's Collected Works
"All those who do not earn their bread
by the sweat of their brows
must feel shame to a certain degree"
To lose equilibrium
is no big deal
In heavy rain I steer
my daughter on the bicycle
through the evening rush hour traffic.

"Up, Up, Lenau!"

February frost. A certain joyful throbbing
        about his own misfortune, the diabolical trait
        in Niembsch's face. Incendiary poet,
O Lotte. "Shall renounce her."

Chased into the street. Played violin a lot,
        Written quite a few poems, this little scrap
        of excess, history, bit into the stove iron.
That state cudgel of censorship.

It freezes me to the heart, the snow in the brain
        crunches. But they notice nothing, always in search
        of diversion and instructive medical cases.
"So at last there be quiet within."

In the moonlight a manure cart: eight Poles,
        lost heroes, crowded together,
        covered in rags, creaking over the pavement
of Kramer Lane.

Die out, forests, just reach down here, lower
        you ice of the glaciers. Off to America
        with the bat nest under the breast feathers.
Niagara, Niagara!

Die Neue Welt der Poesie: Das Totengesicht übergezogen
        Am Ohio Wortfetzen von den Fingerkuppen gerupft,
        Sehnsuchtverse auf die Heidelberger Ruine.
Der Skorbut und die Gicht.

Wieder im fremden Daheim: Die verfluchte Geige
        des göttlichen Guarnerius; steirische Ländler
        und wilde Luftsprünge. Ein Winseln, das plötzlich
verstummt. „Wenns Wahnsinn wäre!"

Das Kreuz. Steif, in Schweißtücher gehüllt. Niebschs
        Schädel zuckt hin und her. „Auf, auf, Lenau!" Der Riß
        durchs Gesicht. Zwangsjacke. Im Waschbecken
verkohlte Gedichte.

■　Gabriele Wohmann

Das könnte ich sein

Sechzehnuhrzwanzig, wirds bald
Noch nichts gesagt, kein Wort
Wirds bald, es wird bald dunkel
Da draußen kann es schneien
Im Sitzungsraum das Sprechen
Gelingt mir nicht, ich stelle
Zur Probe immerhin
Vier Teller auf, vier Tassen
Damit ich die nicht bin
Mit Sachverstand, begabt
Für Stummsein, Unterlassen.
Der Samstag wäre günstig
Wirds bald, ich lade ein
Ich spreche bald, Geduld
Noch zehn Minuten, dann
Dann aber! Lautgebilde
Mein Mund kann sich bewegen

The New World of Poetry: the death face pulled over.
    By the Ohio snatches of words plucked from the finger tips
    verses of longing for the Heidelberg ruin.
Scurvy and gout.

Once again at home abroad: The damned fiddle
    of the divine Guarnieri; Styrian ländler
    and wild leaps into the air. A whimpering that suddenly
dies. "If it were insanity!"

The cross. Stiff, wrapped in sweat sheets. Niembsch's
    skull jerks back and forth. "Up, up, Lenau!" The rift
    through the face. Straight jacket. In the wash basin
charred poems.

■ Gabriele Wohmann

That Could Be Me

Four twenty p.m., get going
Nothing said yet, not a word
Get going it will soon be dark
Outside it could snow
In the meeting room I'm unable
To talk, I give it
A try just the same
four plate settings four cups
So that I'm not the one
With expertise, talented
In being quiet, abstaining.
Saturday would be good
Get going I'll invite
I'll talk soon, be patient
Another ten minutes, then
But then! Phonetic forms
My mouth can move

Bei mir zu Haus, beim Kaffee
Mit Gästen, mit Kollegen
Bald fällt am Tagungsort
Mein Einspruch, bald, kein Wort
Ich weiß; erschüttert, redlich
Sehe ich aus, bald wird
Mein Ausdruck deinem ähnlich
Was hier geschieht, verstehen
Wir beide, Mutter, nicht
Schlecht hören, schlechtes Sehen —
Wirds bald, wer demnächst spricht
Das könnte ich sein, bald
Es schneit vielleicht, das hindert
Die Gäste anzukommen
Angrenzend kranker Wald
Jetzt wird es siebzehn Uhr
Jetzt muß ich aber sprechen
Ich will nicht, daß der Preis
An X geht, nicht an Z
Will nicht den Kaffee kochen
Ich will nicht länger bleiben
Will nicht das Tischlein decken
Für Gäste, von Kollegen
Wegstreben, draußen treiben
Schneeflocken über Wald, verstecken
Will ich mich, will zum Bahnhof
Mich regt das auf, das Leben
„Ich nehme nicht mehr teil":
Am Kaffeetisch, bei Jurys
Will ich zum Sitzungsabschluß
Wirds bald — durch mich, verfrüht,
Für heute von mir geben.

At my place, over coffee
With guests, with colleagues
Soon my objection falls
At the meeting place, soon, not a word
I know; shaken, I look
Sincere, soon my expression
Will become like yours
What is happening here, we
Both, mother, don't understand
Listening wrong, seeing wrong—
Better get going whoever speaks soon
That could be me, soon
It might snow, that will keep
The guests from arriving
Bordering on the diseased forest
Now it's five o'clock
But now I really must speak
I don't want the prize
To go to X and not to Z
Don't want to make the coffee
Don't want to stay any longer
Don't want to set the table
For guests, from colleagues
Struggle away, outside snowflakes
Drift over forest, I want
To hide myself, go to the station
It irritates me, life
"I am no longer part of it":
At the coffee table, on juries
I want to get to the meeting's end
Get going—through me, too soon,
And just for once give something of myself.

Peter Schütt

Göttliche Fügung

Spielschulden nötigten
1740 den König von Sachsen,
das Herzogtum Lauenburg
samt seinen 18000 Seelen
an den dänischen König
zu verkaufen: eine Extrazeitung
teilte den Untertanen
die göttliche Fügung mit.

Heute früh erfuhren
die 2200 Beschäftigten
der Firma Heidenreich und Harbeck
in Hamburg, daß der Besitzer
sie aufgrund von Zahlungsschwierigkeiten
samt Betriebsanlagen und Aktienkapital
an den Gildemeister-Konzern
verkauft hat: eine außerordentliche
Betriebsversammlung machte
die Verkauften mit der Entscheidung
des Firmeninhabers bekannt.

Den Preis haben die Heidenreicher
zu zahlen: 600 von ihnen werden entlassen.
Da hatten die Lauenburger es besser:
sie bekamen vom Dänenkönig
einen Park und ein Vierteljahr
Steuernachlaß geschenkt.

Peter Schütt

Divinely Ordained

In 1740 gambling debts
forced the King of Saxony
to sell the Duchy of Lauenburg
with its 18,000 souls
to the King of Denmark:
a newspaper extra
informed the subjects
of the divinely ordained turn.

This morning the
2,200 employees
of Heidenreich & Harbeck
in Hamburg found out that the owner
due to cash flow problems
had sold them
complete with plant and shares
to the Gildenmeister corporation:
a specially called meeting
informed the sold
of the owner's decision.

The Heidenreichers had to
foot the bill: 600 of them were laid off.
Those Lauenburgers were really better off:
from the Danish king they received
a park and a quarter's
tax remission

■ Christoph Meckel

u.A.w.g.

Davon ausgehend
daß die Materie erhalten bleibt, und nicht verwechselt wird mit Utopie oder
    Lyrik
weiter davon ausgehend
daß der Dreckige Jakob und sein Neinsein nicht verwechselt wird mit Mister
    Rockefeller und seinen Geschäften
ferner davon ausgehend
daß der Tod Fleisch frißt und nicht verwechselt wird mit einem Genickschuß
alles in allem davon ausgehend
daß der Mensch die Krone der Schöpfung ist und nicht verwechselt wird mit
    Schwein, Laus oder Affe —
Licht der Welt! Um Antwort wird gebeten.

■ Adolf Endler

Immer wieder was Neues

Erst gestern die irre Geschichte mit dem BIG BANG
(Das hätte man sich ja eigentlich denken können
Daß so was wie unser Universum per UR-KNALL entsteht)
Jetzt wieder (als wäre das nichts) die Benachrichtigung
Über die kürzliche Umpolung unserer Pole
(Vom END-KNALL falls noch Zeit bleibt gerne ein anderes Mal)
Vor kaum achthunderttausend Jahren und etwas
Soll das passiert sein Ach immer wieder was Neues
Nein wirklich Elke ich halte es fast nicht mehr aus

Christoph Meckel

R.S.V.P.

Assuming
that matter is conserved, and is not to be confused
   with utopia or poetry
and assuming
that the average Joe and his nonexistence is not to be
   confused with Mister Rockefeller and his deals
further assuming
that death devours flesh and is not to be confused with
   a shot in the back of the head
all things considered assuming
that man is the crown of creation and not
   to be confused with swine, louse, or ape—
Light of the world! Response requested.

Adolf Endler

Always Something New

Just yesterday the crazy story about the BIG BANG
(True, we really could have guessed
That something like our universe started with a primal bang)
Now again (as if that were nothing) the news
About the recent polar reversal of our poles
(More on the FINAL BANG another time if time remains)
Scarcely eighthundredthousand and something years ago
This supposedly happened Oh always something new
No seriously Elke I can hardly take it any more

Oskar Pastior

doch rasch flockt

latex oder fugen-kompost der gum-
miartig aus dem löffel schwitz

der zu löffeln sich andient und
steht steht schon im berge zu tau

früh einem haut- und weichensystem
da noch im gegenzuge selbiges ist

eingeselcht vor interdependenz
— und sagen „hörnung" dazu wo's

eher „organ-mus" wär oder „mel-
tau-photon" — gequetscht zum

tango mit „alpha" und „beta"
einem zur verfügung steigenden

neu wie hoch — stimmt es sei und
heiße deutsch „quirl-aus-dem-balg"

der zu beweisendes schlingt in
klumpen aus „reiß-fuß-spreiz"

über nominalen darren „etruskisch
labbermahl" das nie hören will

doch rasch flockt — kautschukartig
ist eben ein „kleister aus patex"

Oskar Pastior

but quickly flakes

latex or fugue-compost which rub-
berlike sweats from the spoon

who to spoon subservients himself and
stands already trail on the ward-

up we're to a skin and soft switching system
since the self-same is still in the countertrain

smoke cured with interdependence
—and call it 'feverel' when

really it should be 'organ pap' or 'mil-
dew photon'—squashed to

the tango with alpha and beta
to rise to the disposal of

new as high—true be it and
be called german 'whisk from the bellows'

who gorges what is to be proved in
clumps of 'rib-foot-spread'

over nominal desiccants 'etruscan
slurping meal' that never wants to hear

but quickly flakes—rubberlike
simply is a 'glue from mastic'

Kito Lorenc

DIE STIMME GIBT EMPFEHLUNGEN ZUM ÜBERLEBEN BEI ATOMKRIEG
Wenn Büchsenmilch abgeworfen wird verglüht sie
unterwegs aber man kann einen Frosch nehmen wenn er schläft
Er schlief
Man zieht ihm die Oberlippe über die Unterlippe
Ich zog
Macht einen queren Schnitt in seinen Hals
Ich schnitt
Steckt einen Schlauch oder Halm hinein, trinkt
und überträgt sich so sein Blut
Ich trank
So ein Frosch gibt pro Stunde vier Liter Blut ab
während man neben ihm liegt so die Stimme
Ich sprudelte:
Wir lassen uns in unserem Engagement
für den Frieden von neimandem
übertreffen

Erika Burkart

Homo faber

Von Jahr zu Jahr schärfer die Angst,
sieht man irgendwo einen Mann
stehn im Gelände. Was plant er?
Einen Ankauf? Einen Verkauf?
Will er Häuser baun,
eine Schnellstrasse legen,
will er den Bach betonieren
den Feldweg sanieren
und trockenlegen den Teich?

Kito Lorenc

THE VOICE GIVES RECOMMENDATIONS for surviving in case of atomic war
When canned milk is dropped it will burn up
en route, but you can catch a frog if he's sleeping
He was sleeping
You pull his upper lip over the lower lip
I pulled
Make a cut across his neck
I cut
Insert a tube or straw, drink
and thus transfer his blood
I drank
This kind of frog yields four liters of blood per hour
while you lie beside him according to the voice
I bubbled:
In our commitment to peace
we let no one
outdo us

Erika Burkart

Homo Faber

Sharper year by year that fear
when somewhere you see a man
standing in the countryside. What is he up to?
A buy? A sale?
Does he want to build houses,
lay out a highway,
does he want to concrete the creek,
reconstruct the country lane
and drain the pond?

Sucht er ein Terrain,
um Modellflugzeuge zu starten,
seinen Hund zu dressieren?
Wittert er Bodenschätze? Zieht er
das schöne Feld in Betracht
für eine Mülldeponie?

Plant er vielleicht einen Wanderweg,
macht er ein Fotobuch „Heile Landschaft"?
Oder hält er gar Ausschau
nach einem Ufo?

Gesetzt, er schaute sich einfach ein Gras an,
die blühende Rispe, den blanken Halm,
müsst ich ihn melden beim Posten,
falls er nicht selbst sich bekennt
als Narren, der nichts sucht,
der seines Wegs geht und anhielt,
weil ihm eine Mücke ins Aug flog.

■ Margarete Hannsmann

Heimaterde

Ymos, Schleifstaub-Dauerauftrag, 56,1 m^3
Äthylacetat Cylol
chlorierte Kohlenwasserstoffe
Siemens, 236 Fässer Härtesalze Reinigungsmittel
Glanzstoff, 34,9 m^3 Toluol u. Äthomin
Salpetersäure Alu- u. Cu-Beize
Buderus, 7 m^3 Ätznatron
Marienhütte, 1275 t Formsand
EMDA, 14 t Schwefelsäure
cyanidhaltige Härtesalze
Altöle Ölschlämme Galvanikschlämme
Akkumulatorensäuren

Is he looking for a site
to start his model airplanes,
to train his dog?
Is he sniffing out mineral deposits? Or
considering the beautiful field
for a garbage dump?

Is he perhaps planning a nature trail,
is he making a picture book called "Pristine Landscape"?
Or, worse yet, is he on the lookout
for a UFO?

Suppose he was simply looking at a blade of grass,
the flowering panicle, the clean stalk,
I would have to report him to the police,
unless he himself confessed to be
just some fool, looking for nothing,
just walking along here and who stopped
because a gnat landed in his eye.

■ Margarete Hannsmann

Sweet Native Soil

Ymos Co, grinding dust standing order, 56.1 m^3
ethyl acetate cylol
chlorinated hydrocarbons
Siemens, 236 barrels of hardening salts detergents
polishing agent, 34.9 m^3 toluol + ethyl amine
nitric acid alu + cu paints
Buderus, 7 m^3 caustic soda
Marienhütte, 1275 t molding sand
EMDA, 14 t sulfuric acid
cyanous hardening salts
waste oils oil sludge galvanization residues
accumulator acids

polychlorierte Biphenyle
schwermetallhaltige Klärschlämme
Dünnsäuren Filterkuchen Haushaltsmüll
Arzneien Farbreste Batterien
jahraus jahrein 500 Millionen Tonnen

Seid fruchtbar und mehrt euch und bevölkert die Erde
und macht sie euch untertan und herrscht
über die Fische im Meer und die Vögel am Himmel
und über alles Getier das sich auf Erden tummelt
sagte der HERR zu Adam

■ Brigitte Oleschinski

Weglos

Immer führen die Reifenspuren, solchen Brachpfaden nach,
im zirpenden Mittag zu den Rastplätzen zerknüllter Tauben-
flügel, zwischen Scherben und Blech, an dem noch die
Dichtungen kleben wie ausgeblasene Finger.

Reglos ballt sich die Stunde unter der Hitze, durchflochten
von Ziegelgesträuch. Rundum nur das Nicken der Grannen,
über das auf und ab flimmernde Käfer hasten.

Einmal war hier eine Kuh vergraben. Eingenäht
in den Rippenkorb fand sich ein Sack. In
diesem Sack ein Gesicht.

polychlorinated biphenyls
purification wastes with heavy metals
diluted acids filtration cakes household garbage
medicines dye remnants batteries
year in year out 500 million tons

Be fruitful and multiply and fill the earth
and subdue it and have dominion
over the fish of the sea and over the birds of the heavens
and over every living thing that moveth upon the earth
thus spoke the LORD unto Adam

■ Brigitte Oleschinski

No Path

Always the tire tracks lead, along such fallow paths,
at chirping noon to the resting places of crumpled dove-
wings, between potsherds and tin, where the
poems still cling like blown out fingers.

Motionless the hour doubles itself into a ball under the heat, intertwined
with brick shrub. All around the nodding of the awn,
over which back and forth glimmering beetles hasten.

Once a cow was buried here. Sewn
into its rib cage was a sack. In
this sack a face.

Volker Braun

Die Mauer

1

Zwischen den seltsamen Städten, die den gleichen
Namen haben, zwischen vielem Beton
Eisen, Draht, Rauch, den Schüssen
Der Motore: in des seltsamen Lands
Wundermal steht aus all dem
Ein Bau, zwischen den Wundern
Auffallend, im erstaunlichen Land
Ausland. Gewöhnt
An hängende Brücken und Stahltürme
Und was noch an die Grenze geht
Von Material und Maschinen, faßt
Der Blick doch nicht
Das hier.

Zwischen all den Rätseln: das ist
Fast ihre Lösung. Schrecklich
Hält sie, steinerne Grenze
Auf, was keine Grenze
Kennt: den Krieg. Und sie hält
Im friedlichen Land, denn es muß stark sein
Nicht arm, die abhaun zu den Wölfen
Die Lämmer. Vor den Kopf
Stößt sie, das gehn soll wohin es will, nicht
In die Massengräber, das
Volk der Denker.

Aber das mich so hält, das halbe
Land, das sich geändert hat mit mir, jetzt
Ist es sichrer, aber
Ändre ichs noch? Von dem Panzer
Gedeckt, freut sichs
Seiner Ruhe, fast ruhig? Schwer
Aus den Gewehren fallen die Schüsse:

■ Volker Braun

The Wall

1

Between the peculiar cities that bear the same
Name, among much cement
Iron, wire, smoke, the shots
Of motors: at the merging point
Of all the wonders of this peculiar land there stands out
A construction, striking among the wonders
In this astonishing country,
Foreign country. Accustomed
To suspension bridges and steel towers
And whatever else runs to the border
By way of material and machines, the eye
Still does not comprehend
This here.

Among all the riddles: that is
Almost their solution. Terrible
It holds back, stone border,
What knows no bounds:
War. And it holds
In the peaceful land, for it must be strong
Not poor, those who flee to the wolves:
The lambs. This is a slap
In the face of those who should go where they want, not
To mass graves, the
"People of the thinkers."

But what holds me so strongly, the half
Country that has changed with me, now
It is more secure, but
Am I still going to change it? Protected
By the tanks, does it enjoy
Its peace almost peacefully? Heavy
From guns fall the shots:

Auf die, die es anders besser
Halten könnte. *Die Mauern stehn*
Sprachlos und kalt, im Winde
Klirren die Fahnen.

2

Die hinter den Zeitungen
Anbelln den Beton und, besengt
Von der Sendern, sich aus dem Staub machen
Der Baustellen oder am Stacheldraht
Unter Brüdern harfen und
Unter den Kirchen scharrn Tunnel: die
Blinden Hühner finden sich
Vor Kimme und Korn. Unerfindlich
Aber ist ihnen, was diese Städte
Trennt. Weil das nicht
Aus Beton vor der Stirn pappt.
Uns trennt keine Mauer

Das ist Dreck aus Beton, schafft
Das dann weg, mit Schneidbrennern
Reißt das klein, mit Brecheisen
Legts ins Gras: wenn sie nicht mehr
Abhaun mit ihrer Haut zum Markt
Zerhaut den Verhau. Wenn machtlos sind
Die noch Grenzen ändern wollen
Zerbrecht die Grenze. Der letzte Panzer
Zerdrückt sie und sie ihn.
Daß sie weg ist.

Jetzt laßt das da.

3

Aber
Ich sag: es steht durch die Stadt

On those whom it might hold better
In other ways. The walls stand
Speechless and cold in the wind
The flags whip.

2

Those behind the newspapers
Bark at the cement and, scorched
By the broadcasts, run away from the dust
Of construction sites or along the barbed-wire
Piously sing among brothers and
Beneath churches scrape tunnels: those
Blind hens find themselves
Dead center in gun sights. Incomprehensible,
However, for them is that which divides
These cities. Because it is not
Made of cement staring them right in the face.
It's not a wall that divides us.

That is filth made of cement, take
That away then, with blow torches
Tear it to pieces, with crowbars
Put it into the grass: when they no longer
Flee with their skins to sell at the market
Chop up the barricades. When those
Who still want to change borders are powerless
Smash the border. The last tank
Crushes it and vice versa.
So that it will be gone.

Now let that be.

3

But
I say: there stands throughout the city,

Unstattlich, der Baukunst langer Unbau
Streicht das schwarz
Die Brandmauer (scheißt drauf)
Denn es ist nicht
Unsre Schande: zeigt sie.
Macht nicht in einem August
Einen Garten daraus, wälzt den Dreck nicht
Zu Beeten breit, mit Lilien über den Minen
Pflanzt Nesseln, nicht Nelken
Vermehrt nicht, zwischen den seltsamen
Städten die Rätsel, krachend
Schmückt das Land nicht
Mit seiner Not. Und
Laßt nich das Gras wachsen
Über den offenen Schande: es ist
Nicht unsre, zeigt sie.

■ ## Thomas Brasch

Selbstkritik 3

Der Plan Die Trauung Das Mandat Der Stacheldraht
Das blöde Grinsen der Behörde Das ist nicht der Staat
Längst schon bist du der Staat Dein eigenes Gericht
Geschrei nur noch im Schädel Und ein Vers Der bricht

Liebeserklärung

Anders als der Staat das will (dieser jener jeder)
leben wir (du ich) unzufrieden in der kleinsten Zelle
die er uns bereitstellt und Familie nennt Anders
als der Staat das braucht lieben wir einander hastig
und betrügen eins das andere wie
der Staat das tut mit uns sagen wir einander Worte

Unimposing, architecture's long non-construction
Paint it black
The firewall (shit on it)
Because it is not
Our shame: show it.
Do not make a garden of it during
Some August, do not turn the dirt over
In wide beds, with lilies over the mines
Plant nettles, not carnations
Do not increase, between the peculiar
Cities, the riddles, roaring
Do not adorn the land
With its misery. And
Do not let the grass grow
Over the open shame: it is
Not ours, show it.

■ Thomas Brasch

Self-criticism 3

The plan The wedding The barbed wire The mandate
The stupid grin of officials That is not the state
You have long been the state Your own highest courts
Screams inside your skull now And a verse That contorts

Declaration of Love

Differently from what the state intends (this one that one every one)
we live (you I) discontented in the tiniest cell
that it puts at our disposal and calls a family unit Differently
from what the state needs we love each other hastily
and deceive the one the other the way
the state does with us say words to each other

unverständlich eins dem anderen wie Gesetze die der Staat
(dieser jener jeder) ausruft Anders
als der Staat das gern sieht leben wir (du ich) nicht in Frieden
miteinander und befriedigen einander ungleichzeitig
wenn wir zueinander fallen in der Abend-Dämmerung der Geldzeit Anders
als der Staat das tut (dieser jener) spielen wir
in jeder Nacht das Spiel
Vereinigung Wieder und Wieder
hastig aufgerüstet schwer behängt mit Waffen
wie der Staat der uns doch ganz anders will wehrlos nämlich aber
der uns lehrt Mißtraun blankes So
lieben wie einander weggeduckt unterm Blick wie
unter ausgeschriebner Fahndung Feinde (dieses jenes jedes) Staats
aber ähnlich ihm in der kleinsten Zelle angefressen schon
Krebs die Krankheit ist der Staat
(meiner nicht nicht deiner) anders als ers will
sterben wir ihm weg
aus seinem
großen kalten Bett

■ Wolfgang Hilbig

abwesenheit

wie lang noch wird unsere abwesenheit geduldet
keiner bemerkt wie schwarz wir angefüllt sind
wie wir in uns selbst verkrochen sind
in unsere schwärze

nein wir werden nicht vermißt
wir haben stark zerbrochne hände steife nacken —
das ist der stolz der zerstörten und tote dinge
schaun auf uns zu tod gelangweilte dinge — es ist
eine zerstörung wie sie nie gewesen ist

incomprehensible one to the other like the laws that the state
(this one that one every one) proclaims Differently
from what the state likes to see we (you I) do not live in peace
with each other and satisfy each other not simultaneously
when we fall at each other in the evening twilight of the money age Differently
from how the state does it (this one that one) each night
we play the game of
union over and over
hastily armed heavily decked with weapons
like the state which wants us to be different namely defenseless but
which teaches us mistrust bare so
we love each other dropping out of its sight as if
wanted fugitives enemies of (this one that one every) state
but like it gnawed upon in the tiniest cell
cancer that illness is the state
(not mine not yours) differently than it wants it
we die out from under it
out of its
large cold bed

■ Wolfgang Hilbig

absence

how much longer will our absence be tolerated
no one notices how we are filled up with black
how we have crawled inside ourselves
into our blackness

no we are not missed
we have severely broken hands stiff necks—
that is the pride of things dead and destroyed
looking upon us, things bored to death—there is
destruction such has never been before

und wir werden nicht vermißt unsere worte sind
gefrorene fetzen und fallen in den geringen schnee
wo bäume stehn prangend weiß im reif — ja und
reif zum zerbrechen

alles das letzte ist uns zerstört unsere hände
zuletzt zerbrochen unsere worte zerbrochen: komm doch
geh weg bleib hier — eine restlos zerbrochne sprache
einander vermengt und völlig egal in allem
und der wir nachlaufen und unserer abwesenheit

nachlaufen so wie uns am abend
verjagte hunde nachlaufen mit kranken
unbegreiflichen augen.

■ Barbara Köhler

Selbstportrait

ICH STELLE MICH VOR vollendete tatsachen (die mauer im
rücken halbdunkel im kopf die hand zwischen den
schenkeln nach welt schreien): undurchsichtig was ich
gelegentlich durchschaue als tarnung einer gewissen ab-
neigung TRANSPARENT zu sein um nicht zu verschwinden
tauche ich unter agent provocateur in der dritten person
ICH IST DAS SPIEGELBILD MEINES SPIEGELBILDS: ER SIE ES
die unvollendete gegenwart als zeitform jeglicher revolte
gegen das gesagtsein nach den gesetzen deutscher gram-
matik gefoltert vom schweigen rede ich um mein leben
bringe mich wort für wort um kopf und kragen müßten
mal wieder gewaschen werden — DAS SIEHT MIR ÄHN-
LICH . . .

and we are not missed our words are
frozen scraps and fall in the meager snow
where trees stand ripe with white hoar-frost—yes and
ripe to break to pieces

all the last things are destroyed for us our hands
at last broken our words broken: just come
go away stay here—a completely broken language
mixed together and all the same in every way
and which we chase after and our absence

chase after just like at evening
dogs driven away chase after us with sick
uncomprehending eyes.

■ Barbara Köhler

Self-portrait

I PLACE MYSELF BEFORE faits accomplis (the wall in
my back semi-dark in my head my hand between my
thighs screaming for some world): opaque what I
sometimes see through as camouflage for a certain dis-
inclination to be TRANSPARENT in order not to disappear
I go underground agent provocateur in the third person
THE I IS THE REFLECTION OF MY REFLECTION: HE SHE IT
the incomplete present as tense form of any revolt
against having been said according to the rules of german gram-
mar tortured by silence I talk for dear life
risking myself word by word head and collar should
be washed again—that's just like me . . .

■ Richard Wagner

Geschichte

Der Wind raucht.
Der Schornstein weht
aus dem Museum herüber.
Die alten Geschichten
kommen wieder.
Die Spinnen springen
von Wand zu Wand.

Ich habe es gewußt, sagt der,
der es gewußt hat.
Ich kann nichts dafür.
Die Geschichte macht
einen großen Bogen um uns,
aber sie kommt wieder.
Wir hüten uns vor uns,
aber es nützt nichts.

Wir halten uns Pässe ins Gesicht,
Paßwörter.
Pflegeleichte Erfindungen,
die wir ständig machen.
Es nützt nichts.
Der es weiß,
schweigt und
macht weiter.

Der Himmel wölbt sich
über dem Auge.
Das Auge wühlt
in alten Geschichten.

Ein Video — Clip, schwarz — weiß,
übersetzt sie in die Gegenwart.

■ Richard Wagner

History

The wind smokes.
The smokestack blows
out over from the museum.
The old stories
come back again.
The spiders jump
from wall to wall.

I knew it, says one
who knew it.
It's not my fault.
History makes
a wide curve around us,
but it comes back again.
We protect ourselves from ourselves
but it's all for naught.

We hold up passports to our faces,
passwords.
Permapress discoveries
that we constantly make.
It's all for naught.
Whoever knows it
says nothing and
carries on.

The sky arches itself
over the eye.
The eye wallows
in old stories.

A video-clip, black-white,
translates them into the present.

Wir sind Zuschauer,
die verstehen,
die nicht verstehen,
was sie verstehen.
Wir sind Zuschauer,
wache, heitere Zuschauer.
Wir haben Eintrittskarten.
Wir haben Angst.

■ Elke Erb

Sklavensprache

Die Hände, die gestreichelt haben, kann man ruhig ab-
hacken.
Das ändert nichts, denn sie würden das Streicheln nicht
lassen, und es führt zu nichts Gutem.
Man kann sie aber auch fesseln, und die Person, der sie
gehören, folgt ihnen nach bis in die finsterste Zelle.

Groß und Klein
Das Einzelne und das Allgemeine

Bliebe ich nicht bei dem Kleinen, Einzelnen,
bekäme ich das Große nicht in Sicht.
Ich erlebe es ja hier,
wie es vor meinen Augen entsteht.
Als ob ein Gebirgsmassiv sich
dem Auge nach dem Maß des Fußes,
der zu dem Auge gehört,
aufbaut, unüberblickbar. Die Sicht
entsteht an irgendeiner Kehre, nicht
stets beim Tippeln. Bewege ich mich

We are observers,
who understand,
who do not understand
what they understand.
We are observers,
alert, cheerful observers.
We have admission tickets.
We have fear.

■ Elke Erb

Slave Language

Hands that have caressed—one can simply chop them
off.
That will change nothing because they would not
stop caressing and that leads to no good.
But one can also shackle them, and the person they belong to
will follow after them right into the darkest cell.

Large and Small
The Particular and the General

If I didn't stay with the small, the particular,
I would never bring the large into view.
I experience it right here,
how it materializes before my eyes.
As if a mountain range were to
construct itself by the standard of the foot
that belongs to that eye,
unsurveyable. The view
opens up at some hairpin curve or other, not
always while trudging along. When I move

in Erörterungen, bei denen ich nicht
das eindruckhafte Gefühl
eines Aufenthalts bei Kleinem
habe, liegt
das Große unbeachtet
und unverändert (zur vorgestellten
Sicht) in der Gefahr, verkannt zu werden.
Und nicht gut auffindbar.
Der Blick auf das Große, das ja dann
eher das Allgemeine ist als das Große,
zeigt es außerhalb des Aufenthalts bei Kleinem
als das Komplizierte!

Du und die Kartoffel oder
Wer ausscheidet, stirbt

A&B gehen über die Felder.
   B&C reden über die KARTOFFEL.
      C&D sind bei der Dorfkneipe angelangt.
         D&E essen in der Dorfkneipe eine Kleinigkeit.
            E&F trinken jeder drei Korn, drei Bier.
         F&G zahlen und gehn.
           G&H laufen im Mondschein nach
Hause.   H(ase) & I(gel) schließen
Freundschaft unterwegs.   I&J nehmen zu Hause noch
einen Happen zu sich.   J&K schalten das Fern-
sehen ein, um auf den Wetterbericht zu warten.
                  K&L sehen das
Programm bis zu Ende an.   L&M sagen sich:
„Morgen ist auch noch ein Tag."   M&N putzen
sich die Zähne.   N&O
gehn ins Bett.
O&P unterhalten sich vor dem Einschlafen über ihren
Nachbarn Detlev Lilien, welcher einen Fiat fährt und seiner
Frau den Golf läßt, und über die KARTOFFEL.
   P&Qu (Quendel) träumen von der Seefahrt.
      Qu&R schlafen ohne Störungen sechs Stunden durch.

in commentary without having
the impression and feeling
of a sojourn with the small
the large
lies unnoticed
and unchanged (from the imagined
view) in danger of being misapprehended.
And not easily found.
The look at the large, which then
is the general rather than the large,
shows it to be, when outside a sojourn with the small,
simply the complicated!

You and the Potato or
Drop Out and You're Dead

A&B walk across the fields.
   B&C talk about the POTATO.
      C&D have reached the village tavern.
         D&E eat a bite in the village tavern.
            E&F each drink three ryes and beers.
         F&G pay and go.
           G&H run home in the
moonlight.   H(edgehog)&(rabb)I(t) make
friends underway.   I&J have another
snack at home.   J&K turn the tele-
vision on to wait for the weather report.
                  K&L watch the
program to the end.   L&M say to themselves:
"Tomorrow is another day."   M&N brush
their teeth.   N&O
go to bed.
O&P before falling asleep talk about their
neighbor Detlev Lilien who drives a Fiat and lets
his wife have the Rabbit, and about the POTATO.
   P&Qu(Queen Anne's lace) dream about seafaring.
      Qu&R sleep six hours long without interruption.

R&S wachen gleichzeitig auf.

S&T lieben sich.

T&U schlafen erschöpft wieder ein.

U&V erwachen und lieben sich,

weil Samstag ist, erst noch einmal.

V&W blicken nach der Uhr.

W&X, Xusi, gehn unter die

Dusche.

X&Y bereiten das

Frühstück vor, bravo!

Y&Z setzen sich an

den gedeckten Tisch.

Z&A frühstücken,

A wundert sich (Ausnahme!)

■ Uwe Kolbe

Für den Anfang

Ich will es hier zu Anfang gleich gestehen,
wie das Gewissen mir noch immer schlägt,
und sie, fernab, mir stets vor Augen steht,
die Heimat, die zugleich ich lauthals schmähe.

Lieb Freunde, halb im Wohl und ganz im Wehe,
wenn mir der Westfraß oft den Darm aufbläht,
liegts daran, was die Elbe mir herträgt.
Da wird die zartste Taube letztlich zähe.

Wähnt Mutter nicht mich im Schlaraffenlande?
Spricht Vater nicht Treue als Tugend an
und deutet seltsam heimlich auf die Reußen?

Ich aber suche, endets dreist im Wahne,
ein undeutsch (und drum ungeteiltes) Land,
gleich weit entfernt von Daimlerland und Preußen.

R&S wake up simultaneously.
S&T love each other.
T&U fall asleep again exhausted.
U&V wake up and make love
again because it's Saturday.
V&W look at the clock.
W&X, Xerxes, stand under the
shower.
X&Y fix
breakfast, hooray!
Y&Z sit down
at the set table.
Z&A breakfast.
A is surprised (anomaly!)

■ **Uwe Kolbe**

To start out with

Well, let me start right out now by confessing
how much my mulish conscience keeps on nagging,
and how, though far, there sharply stands before me
that homeland which I yet disparage loudly.

Dear friends, if half in weal and all in woe,
that West grub often bloats my Eastern gut,
it's all because of what the Elbe brings.
That makes the tenderest dove a stringy morsel.

To mother don't I live on milk and honey?
Does father not insist on bond as virtue?
And hint in sly ways at his loyal Russia?

But as for me, and to the point of madness,
I seek a land, un-German, undivided,
and equidistant from both Daimlerland and Prussia.

die schuldigen

sterben, leider, meist

an schnupfen
in einem großen bett
nahe beim flughafen
also

eines natürlichen todes

Male

Fünfmal
wurde mir von Vergewaltigungen
erzählt

Viermal
sah ich
Männer sich prügeln

Dreimal
mißhandelten welche ihre Hunde
unter meinen Augen

Zweimal
rannte ich zum Jugendamt
für meine Freundin

Einmal
wollte ich
der kranken Mutter an die Gurgel

Ich bin achtzehn.
Im Sozialismus aufgewachsen.
Hab keinen Krieg erlebt.

the guilty parties

die, unfortunately, most of the time

of a cold
in a big bed
close to the airport
i.e.

of natural causes

Times

Five times
people told me about
rapes

Four times
I saw
men in fistfights

Three times
some mistreated their dogs
in front of my very eyes

Two times
I ran to the youth office
for my girl friend

Once
I wanted to strangle
my sick mother

I am eighteen.
Grew up under Socialism.
Have not lived through a war.

■ Annerose Kirchner

Sonntag

Fliegende Teppichhändler tauschen
eins zu eins
Hanswürste gegen Zinnsoldaten.

Mein Verstand denkt deutsch
und probiert Maulkörbe, die es gratis gibt,
13 gehn auf ein Dutzend.

Morgen, flüstert mir
eine besoffne Stimme ins Ohr,
wandern wir aus.

■ Annerose Kirchner

Sunday

Flying carpet dealers exchange
one to one
clowns for tin soldiers.

My mind thinks German
and tries on muzzles, which are handed out free,
or go for a dime a dozen.

Tomorrow, a boozy voice
whispers in my ear,
we emigrate.

Notes to the Poems

page 41
Oder-Neisse line: Eastern border between the two Germanies, demarcated by the Oder and Neisse rivers. Until the end of the Third Reich, German territory extended beyond this line into what is the present-day Poland and (part of East Prussia) the former Soviet Union.

page 43
"Can Be No Mourning": Presumably Benn's last finished poem.

page 63
"Homecoming," *Bertolt Brecht Poems 1913–1956*, ed. John Willett and Ralph Mannheim (New York: Routledge, 1976), 392.

page 63
"When in My White Room at the Charité," *Bertolt Brecht Poems 1913–1956*, ed. John Willett and Ralph Mannheim (New York: Routledge, 1976), 451–52.

page 63
Charité: East Berlin hospital where Brecht died. Brecht's use of the verb *fehlen* (to lack) appears to echo and rephrase a sentence from Johann Wolfgang Goethe's epistolary novel *Die Leiden des jungen Werthers* (The Sorrows of Young Werther, 1774), "Wenn wir uns selbst fehlen, fehlt uns doch alles" ("If we lack ourselves, we lack everything"), part of an entry from Book I, for 22 August 1771.

page 69
Buchenwald: That is, "beech forest." Ironically, the concentration Camp Buchenwald was located near Weimar, a place associated with German culture and enlightened humanism because Herder, Schiller, Wieland, and Goethe all lived there, the latter for much of his life (1775–1832). The Weimar Republic (1919–1933) was founded there. (See also Sonja Schüler, "Weimar-Buchenwald," page 175.)

page 77
Morning star cudgels: A *Morgenstern* is both the morning star and a primitive peasant weapon, a spike-studded club. (See also Friederike Mayröcker, "Death by the Muses," page 149, a reference to humorous poet Christian Morgenstern).

page 79
"Two hands, born to give," trans. Ruth and Matthew Mead and Michael Hamburger, from *The Seeker and Other Poems* (New York: Farrar, Straus & Giroux, Inc., 1970), 27.

page 81
"Farewell," trans. Ruth and Matthew Mead and Michael Hamburger, from *The Seeker and Other Poems* (New York: Farrar, Straus & Giroux, Inc., 1970), 113.

page 113
"Only where find those words," from *O The Chimneys* by Nelly Sachs, trans. Michael Hamburger, Christopher Holme, Ruth and Matthew Mead, and Michael Roloff (New York: Farrar, Straus & Giroux, Inc., 1967), 279.

page 113
"Be as you were, be as you were": The quotation is taken from Goethe's *Der Zauberlehrling*.

page 181
Pigs' Bay: Pun on Bay of Pigs, site of the abortive April 1961 invasion, with C.I.A. support, to oust Fidel Castro from power.

page 195
"bodybody": Gerhard Rühm noted in a letter regarding this text (8 July 1998) that the proximity of words in the German text, which reads "lei<u>bleib</u>" draws the attention of the reader to letters that also form the verb *bleib* (meaning "remain," an imperative). His intention was originally that the letters just underlined be printed in red.

page 225
Stalin Avenue: Refers to a major thoroughfare in Berlin leading east from *Alexanderplatz* in what was the heart of the eastern sector of the city. Having named the street "Stalin Avenue" in 1949 to honor the Soviet dictator's seventieth birthday, the East German government secretly removed all street signs on the night of November 13, 1961, after Kruschchev declared his de-Stalinization program. The signs were replaced with ones bearing the names *Karl-Marx-Allee* and *Frankfurter Allee*.

page 227
Party congress: The Soviet Union's twenty-second Communist Party Congress in 1956 marked the beginning of de-Stalinization.

page 253
Medea/Callas: Maria Callas (1923–1977), the famous Greek soprano. In 1953 she recreated Cherubini's tragic opera *Medea* of 1797.

page 259
The Old Country: A strip of picturesque old farmland with thatched houses, west of Hamburg.

page 271
Bollschweil: Village near Freiburg im Breisgau where Kaschnitz lived on a family estate and is buried.

page 301
Theo: Poet Jürgen Theobaldy.

page 303
Niembsch: Austrian poet Nikolaus Lenau (1802–1850) was born Nikolaus Niembsch, Edler von Strehlenau. He traveled to America in 1832.

page 315
Homo Faber: "Man the Maker." Title of 1957 novel by Swiss author Max Frisch.

page 323
"... in the wind/The flags whip": Allusion to the poem "Hälfte des Lebens" by Friedrich Hölderlin, "... im Winde klirren die Fahnen."

Biographies

Friedrich Achleitner (1930–)
Born in Scholchen (Austria), Achleitner taught architecture at the Vienna Art Academy. Affiliated with the experimental Wiener Gruppe (Artmann, Bayer, Rühm, Wiener) for various collaborations and montages, he also wrote dialect poems. *hosn rosn baa* (1959).

Ilse Aichinger (1921–)
To avoid racial persecution she lived in hiding in Austria during World War II. She achieved early fame with the novel *Die grössere Hoffnung* (1948) and won many literary prizes for her poems, short prose, and radio plays. Aichinger worked for the Fischer press and was married to poet Günter Eich. *Dialoge, Erzählungen, Gedichte* (1971).

Erich Arendt (1903–1984)
A productive poet since the Expressionist Twenties and an anti-fascist activist, Arendt fought in the Spanish Civil War and only returned from his Colombian exile to the GDR in 1951. He was a translator and important mediator of Spanish and South American poetry in Germany. *Aus fünf Jahrzehnten* (1968); *Das zweifingrige Lachen* (1981).

Hans Arp (1887–1966)
Born in Strasbourg and famous as a Dada artist and sculptor, he wrote playful and sound-centered poetry in French and German. Arp spent the war years in Switzerland before moving to Meudon, near Paris. He was a prolific and influential forerunner of Concrete and other experimental kinds of poetry. *Gesammelte Gedichte* (1963; 1974).

Hans Carl Artmann (1921–)
A polyglot and widely traveled Viennese, whose often fantastic or Surrealist poetry draws on many traditions, Artmann was an early innovator within the avant-garde circles of "Art Club," "Wiener Gruppe," and "Forum Stadtpark." His writing exhibits wide formal range, from traditional to highly experimental, and often grotesque humor. The early work re-legitimized dialect poetry for many younger authors. *The Best of H. C. Artmann* (1970).

Rose Ausländer (1907–1988)
From Czernovitzy (now Rumania), where she was born into a German-speaking Jewish family, Ausländer emigrated to the United States (1921) and obtained American citizenship, but returned home in 1931 when her mother became ill. She spent the war years in the Czernovitzy ghetto, moving to the United States in 1946 to work as a secretary. The

bulk of her work appeared after 1965; her evocative poems about language and the past share affinities with those of her countryman Celan. *Gesammelte Werke*, 7 vols. (1985).

Ingeborg Bachmann (1926–1973)
A "poeta doctus" who wrote subtle and complex poetry as well as short stories, novels, radio plays, libretti, and essays, Bachmann was born in Klagenfurt (Austria) and earned her Ph.D. in Vienna with a dissertation on the critical reception of Heidegger's philosophy. She worked for Austrian and German radio networks and spent the last twenty years mainly in Rome, where she died of burns suffered in a freak accident. Bachmann wrote some of the most outstanding poetry of the 1950s, then turned to prose fiction with a strongly feminist perspective. She earned the highest honors open to German writers, including the *Gruppe 47* Prize (1953), Büchner Prize (1964), first Frankfurt chair of poetics (1959–1960), and the Austrian State Prize (1968). *Werke*, 4 vols. (1978); *Sämtliche Gedichte* (1983).

Johannes R. Becher (1891–1958)
Born in Munich, he is counted among the more important Expressionist poets. A conscientious objector during World War I, he joined the Communist party in 1919, and was later imprisoned for political activities. He fled Germany in 1933, lived in the Soviet Union 1935–1945, then returned to East Germany. As the GDR's first Minister for Culture (1954–1958) he wielded considerable influence in shaping the official literature to combine humanism with socialist realism. Notwithstanding his importance as a party functionary, his late, rhymed verse lacked the verve to inspire younger writers. *Gesammelte Werke* (1966).

Jürgen Becker (1932–)
After 1968 he lived again in Cologne, his birthplace, working as director of radio play production for *Deutschland Funk*. His avant-garde poems, with their quotidian detail, variable line length, shifts from external detail to internal emotion, and notation of acoustic and visual impulses, have a spontaneous quality reminiscent of the work of William Carlos Williams and Charles Olson. His most important poetry began to appear in the 1970s. *Gedichte 1965–1980* (1981).

Gottfried Benn (1886–1956)
With Brecht one of the most influential writers in postwar Germany, Benn's astonishing comeback began with *Statische Gedichte* (1949) and climaxed in 1951 when he was awarded the Büchner Prize and delivered his acclaimed lecture *Probleme der Lyrik*. Born in Mansfeld (now in Poland), Benn, a physician, spent most of his life in Berlin. He established himself as a major Expressionist talent with *Morgue und andere Gedichte* (1912). The only major German author to ally himself publicly with the Nazis (1933), he alienated fellow writers, then later became disillusioned with the regime and, in his own words, "emigrated into the *Wehrmacht* (military service)." Incorporating scientific terms, prose elements, and everyday language into his work, Benn introduced new

subjects and materials to German poetry. His poetic fiction, essays, and verse influenced an entire generation of younger German writers with their renewed conception of art's autonomy and the magic power of poetic language (in part with reference to Poe). *Gesammelte Werke*, 4 vols. (1977).

Wolf Biermann (1936–)

Son of a resistance fighter who died in Auschwitz, songwriter-performer Biermann, born in Hamburg, moved to the GDR in 1953. He worked as an assistant to Brecht's Berliner Ensemble, began composing in earnest after a student theater group he had founded was banned, then was himself forbidden to perform in 1963. His popularity grew as his works were circulated illegally and published in the West. In a move that precipitated vehement protest and the subsequent emigration of numerous prominent authors, the GDR prohibited his return after a concert in the West in 1976. His songs, which often take personal offense at matters of public issue in criticizing the GDR and FRG alike, show affinities to Villon, Heine, Brecht, Eisler, and others. Büchner Prize (1991). *Alle Lieder* (1991); *Alle Gedichte* (1995).

Johannes Bobrowski (1917–1965)

Having lived where German and Eastern European cultures meet (born in Tilsit, now Sovetsk, Lithuania; schooled in Königsberg), Bobrowski was stationed on the Eastern Front and became a Russian prisoner of war. His verse and prose are rooted in that landscape, passionately describing the country, its history and people. He began to write in the 1940s, but his literary career blossomed late; he supported himself as an editor. His dense, richly allusive poetic language is indebted to Klopstock, Trakl, Brecht, and Huchel. The great critical success of *Sarmantische Zeit* (1961) and *Schattenland Ströme* (1962) established him as one of the subtlest poets of his generation.

Elisabeth Borchers (1926–)

Born in northern Germany, she grew up in the Alsace, and worked as a literary editor for Suhrkamp publishers. Her writing includes poetry, prose, radio plays, children's books, and translations from the French. Borchers's verse is highly individual in its imagery and finely attuned to the resonance of language. *Gedichte* (1976).

Nicolas Born (1937–1979)

He grew up on the border between Germany and the Netherlands near Emmerich, lived in Essen (1950–1965), then Berlin and Pannenberg (Lower Saxony). Born wrote radio plays, prose, and several volumes of poetry, publishing a collected volume of verse shortly before his death, *Gedichte 1967–1978* (1978). His verse, with its spare, demotic language, offers impressions, experiences, and quotidian details.

Thomas Brasch (1945–)

Son of an exiled anti-fascist and later high-ranking GDR official, born in Westow (England), he briefly studied journalism in Leipzig. Arrested for pamphleteering against the

Soviet intervention in Czechoslovakia (1968), released in 1969, Brasch worked for a time at the Brecht archive, then moved to West Berlin in 1976. His writing, dating from the early 1970s, includes poetry (*Der schöne 27. September*, 1980) and prose. He is also a successful playwright who has translated Shakespeare into contemporary German.

Volker Braun (1939–)
Among the most popular of the poets and playwrights to emerge in the GDR in the 1960s, Braun, born in Dresden-Rochwitz, was initially denied university admittance for political reasons and educated as a machinist. He then studied philosophy in Leipzig (1960–1964), became dramaturge for the Berliner Ensemble (1965–1966), and worked for the *Deutsches Theater* in Berlin. His first volume of poetry, *Provokation für mich*, appeared in 1965. Braun's verse is rhetorically sophisticated, scrutinizing GDR society and the writer, yet he remained a committed socialist. *Gedichte* (1979).

Bertolt Brecht (1898–1956)
One of this century's leading dramatists (and the theoretician of an anti-Aristotelian theater) Brecht, an undogmatic Marxist since the late 1920s, author of prose fiction and both critical and political essays, wrote some of the finest poetry in the language. Born in Augsburg (Bavaria), he fled into exile in 1933 (Denmark, Sweden, Finland), then lived in Santa Monica, California, 1941–1947, until the House Committee on Un-American Activities drove him back to Europe. He settled in East Berlin, where he founded the Berliner Ensemble with his wife, actress Helene Weigel. Only a small fraction of Brecht's poetic output was published in his lifetime, the expansive and irreverent *Hauspostille* (1927), the more subdued *Svendborger Gedichte* (1939), and the highly condensed *Buckower Elegien* (1954). His broad range revitalized many forms that had fallen into disuse; he also provided powerful impulses for dialectical, socially committed poetry. Still somewhat overshadowed by Benn in the 1950s, Brecht's work has since had an enormous influence on younger German poets, as well as internationally. *Gesammelte Werke*, 20 vols. (1967).

Rolf Dieter Brinkmann (1940–1975)
Arguably the most original talent of his generation, his work marked by counterculture discontents, Brinkmann often lived marginally and was just ending a period of self-destructive isolation when he died in a traffic accident in London. Born in Cologne, he began writing at an early age (first published 1959). His work shows a fine sense of language, a keen eye for detail, and an adept command of radical techniques (splicing, montage). Inspired by American writers (O'Hara, Berrigan, William Carlos Williams, Creeley, W. S. Burroughs), whose work he mediated to European audiences, Brinkmann helped revolutionize German poetry by introducing pop diction and taboo subject matter. He also experimented with prose and multimedia works. *Gedichte* (1979).

Erika Burkart (1922–)
Born in Aarau (Switzerland), since the mid-1950s Burkart has authored over a dozen volumes, primarily poetry, but also a novel and some narrative prose. The tension

between an idyllic state of naive harmony with nature and the irrevocable loss of this relationship in the modern world characterize her carefully wrought verse. *Augenzeuge. Ausgewählte Gedichte* (1978).

Michael Buselmeier (1938–)
Born in Berlin, he lives in Heidelberg. The author of a novel, a radio play, essays, criticism, and political journalism, Buselmeier has published several volumes of poetry, beginning with *Nichts soll sich ändern* (1978); *Erdunter. Gedichte* (1992).

Christine Busta (1915–1987)
Working as a librarian in Vienna, where she was born, Busta began publishing poetry in 1947 and won the Trakl Prize in 1954. Best known as a poet of the 1950s, she continued writing all of her life and demonstrated the continued vitality of traditional literary forms and religious themes. *Lampe und Delphin* (1955); *Unterwegs zu älteren Feuern* (1965); *Gedichte* (1995).

Paul Celan (1920–1970)
Born to German-speaking Jewish parents in Czernovitzy (then Rumania), Celan spent half his life in Paris. Before World War II he briefly studied medicine in France (where he became acquainted with Surrealism), returning home in 1939. His mother and father were deported and died in 1942; Celan himself was in a work camp. The author of some of the finest poetry written in German, Celan has long been revered as a hermetic poet for his increasingly succinct verse with its recurrent themes (love, night, death, and the problematic of language), encoded content, dialogic construction, and allusions to Hölderlin, Rilke, Trakl, and others. Since his suicide, critics have come to appreciate the highly specific, often biographic origins of his work, particularly the grief and guilt over the Holocaust that color much of his work. His slim body of prose illuminates his conceptions of poetry; copious poetic translations from the French, English, Russian, Rumanian, and Hebrew are an important part of his poetic work. Büchner Prize (1960). *Gesammelte Werke* (1983).

Hanns Cibulka (1920–)
Born in Jägerndorf (Czechoslovakia), a soldier and prisoner in Sicily, then employed as a librarian, Cibulka has written poetry, diaries, and travel accounts. *Lichtschwalben* (1973); *Poesiealbum 181* (1982); *Losgesprochen* (1986).

Hilde Domin (1912–)
Not until 1951 did Domin begin writing; her debut as a poet came with *Nur eine Rose als Stütze* (1959). Born in Cologne, she left for Rome in 1932, moving to England and finally the Dominican Republic. She returned to Germany in 1954. Her work, often biographical and reflecting on the theme of language, shows the influence of Spanish Surrealism. She has written narrative prose, as well as poetry and influential essays and anthologies. *Gesammelte Gedichte* (1987).

Günter Eich (1907–1972)

One of the most important German poets since 1945, Eich was born in Lebus an der Oder (east of Berlin) and began work as a writer in the late 1920s. His major poetry, short prose, and prize-winning radio plays appeared after the war. *Abgelegene Gehöfte* (1948), cited as the epitome of postwar verse for its themes and minimal language, was partly written in an American prisoner of war camp. Unsentimental nature poetry and a contemplation of individual existence and its social threats characterize his work. Büchner Prize (1959). *Gesammelte Werke*, 4 vols. (1973).

Adolf Endler (1930–)

Author of numerous volumes of poetry, as well as of translations, prose, and influential literary essays, Endler, born in Düsseldorf, moved to the GDR in 1955, and attended the Becher Institute (1955–1957). Though recognized by his fellow poets, his work has been somewhat neglected in the GDR because Endler has refused to choose between the camps of Brecht and Becher followers, while also informing his verse with older lyrical traditions. He was married to poet Elke Erb. *Das Sandkorn* (1974); *Akte Endler* (1981; 1988).

Hans Magnus Enzensberger (1929–)

A restless intellect always on the forefront of new developments, Enzensberger, born in Kaufbeuren (in the Bavarian Allgau), attracted attention with his polemical early verse (*Verteidigung der Wölfe*, 1957; *Landessprache*, 1960). Since then his prolific writings (poetry, dramas, translations, political and literary essays) have distinguished him as one of Germany's most accomplished writers. To his poetry he brings a knack for scrutinizing politics and culture that earned him a reputation as a radical in the 1960s, but his verse also includes poems about nature and everyday life. A polyglot mediator of the international modern tradition (particularly Spanish and American poetry), Enzensberger is an eclectic talent with a keen sense of language, who has shaped the character of contemporary German poetry through his innovative subject matter (politics and the quotidian) and forms (collages, linguistic experiments, documentary and epic works). Büchner Prize (1963). *Die Gedichte* (1983).

Elke Erb (1939–)

Born in Scherbach (Eifel), Erb moved to the GDR in 1949 and resided in Berlin. She studied German and Slavic literature, history, and pedagogy in Halle, worked in agriculture, then became an editor. Since 1966 she has lived as a writer, publishing several volumes of poetry, short prose, essays, and translations. Her verse, written from an unabashedly personal perspective, tends to be idiosyncratic, with a predilection for experimental form. She has explored combinations of poetry and commentary, especially in *Kastanienallee* (1987). An influential anthologist (*Berührung ist nur eine Randerscheinung*, 1985), she generously promoted the work of younger avant-garde authors from the *Prenzlauer Berg* group. *Gutachten* (1975); *Trost* (1982); *Winkelzüge* (1990); *Unschuld, du Licht meiner Augen-Gedichte* (1994).

Erich Fried (1921–1988)

A child prodigy and a massively productive writer (sometimes dashing off a dozen poems in a day), Fried was born in Vienna. He fled to London (1938), held various jobs (BBC 1952–1968), and first published poetry in 1944. In addition to dozens of volumes of verse, Fried authored a novel, an opera, prose, radio plays, and translations (many of Shakespeare's plays; also Dylan Thomas and other authors). Much of his poetry is thought-provokingly political, employing ironic word plays, repetition, allusions, parody, or apparently simple language to make its points. He never hesitated to take stands on controversial issues and, hence, was himself the subject of controversy, that is, for his volume on the war in Southeast Asia, *und Vietnam und* (1966), and for his acceptance speech for the Büchner Prize in 1987. *Frühe Gedichte* (1986); *Gesammelte Werke* (1993); *Gedichte* (1995; 1996); *Einbruch der Wirklichkeit. Verstreute Gedichte 1927–1988* (1996).

Franz Fühmann (1922–1984)

An author whose works are rich in mythical elements, Fühmann struggled throughout his life with the dilemma posed by the need to confront the successive histories of Nazism, Stalinism, and GDR socialism. Born in Rochlitz/Rokytnice (Czechoslovakia), he lived in Berlin after his release from a Soviet prisoner of war camp in 1949, writing poems, translations, narrative prose, and children's books. *Die Richtung der Märchen* (1962), noted for its fresh use of fairy tale material, belies the quandaries that troubled Fühmann. A sensitive critic, he played a crucial role in recognizing the merits of the second generation of GDR writers, notably Sarah Kirsch.

Eugen Gomringer (1925–)

His poem "das schweigen" ("silence," from *konstellationen*, 1953) is one of the most frequently cited examples of "Concrete Poetry." Born in Cachuela Esperanza (Bolivia), Gomringer studied economics and art history in Bern and Rome (1946–1950), and worked as secretary to the painter Max Bill in Ulm (1954–1958). He brought a strong visual and architectural sensibility to his work, which dates in large part from the 1950s and 1960s. He became an important promoter of the Concrete movement, the editor of various anthologies, and author of seminal manifestos.

Günter Grass (1927–)

Overnight he rose to international fame with *The Tin Drum* (*Die Blechtrommel*, 1959), made into an award-winning film (1979), the first of three novels set in his birthplace Danzig (now Gdansk, Poland). Grass is one of today's leading novelists, known, too, in the FRG for his political activism (he campaigned for Willy Brandt). He also works in verse, drama, and is a trained sculptor and graphic artist. Grass has won numerous literary awards (Büchner Prize, 1965), and received honorary doctorates in the United States (Kenyon College; Harvard University). As in his fiction, Grass often adopts a picaresque voice in his poetry to comment on contemporary life. His poems, which are sometimes integrated into his fiction, as in *The Flounder* (*Der Butt*, 1977), complement his prose, providing a vehicle for playful experimentation. *Gesammelte Gedichte* (1971); *Werke*, 10 vols. (1987).

Michael Guttenbrunner (1919–)

A resident of Vienna, but originally from Althofen (Corinthia), Guttenbrunner is the author of poetry and essays. He was wounded during the war but also politically persecuted; his first volume of poetry, *Schwarze Ruten* (1947), was followed by others equally critical of social developments in Austria. *Ungereimte Gedichte* (1959); *Die lange Zeit* (1965).

Ulla Hahn (1946–)

One of the most controversial success stories in recent years, Hahn catapulted to literary prominence with *Herz über Kopf* (1981), which earned her the *Leonce-und-Lena-Preis*. Born in Brachthausen (in northern Germany), she grew up in the Rhine region, and, after an office internship, studied literature, history, and sociology in Cologne and Hamburg. Her early poetry from the 1970s was political, in sharp contrast to her recent verse with its use of occasional rhyme and traditional forms. While some have dismissed her poetry (including numerous love poems) as merely clever or subjective and sentimental, others view Hahn as combining "inwardness" with a considerable talent for wit. *Spielende* (1983); *Freudenfeuer* (1985); *Unerhörte Nähe* (1988).

Margarete Hannsmann (1921–)

Born in Heidenheim a. d. Brenz (southern Germany), she lives in Stuttgart and has published poems, prose, novels, radio plays, and documentary works, since 1967 often in collaboration with the painter Hap Grieshaber. Her autobiographical writings document her development from early Nazi to later left-wing engagement. *Schaumkraut* (1980); *Rabenflug* (1987).

Rolf Haufs (1935–)

Born in Düsseldorf, Haufs studied business, later moving to Berlin where he began to support himself as a writer. Beginning in 1972 he worked for the radio station Freies Berlin. The author of poetry, prose, and radio drama, his verse typifies the approach of "New Subjectivity" with its personal focus, everyday subject matter, and political resignation. *Grösser werdende Entfernung* (1979); *Felderland* (1986); *Allerweltsfieber* (1990); *Augustfeuer* (1996).

Helmut Heissenbüttel (1921–1996)

One of the important avant-garde authors on the postwar literary scene, Heissenbüttel became interested in creating texts that are not simply representational. Born in Rustringen (near Wilhelmshaven, north Germany), seriously wounded in 1941, he studied architecture, German literature, and art history, then worked as an editor in Hamburg in the 1950s. From 1959 to 1981 he was affiliated with the radio station Süddeutscher Rundfunk. His literary roots lie in the experimental modernist tradition (including Benn, Dadaism, and Gertrude Stein); he worked with fragment forms, the mechanics of syntax, sequences, and occasional verse. He began writing at the age of fifteen, publishing his initial volumes of poetry after the war, *Kombinationen* (1954) and *Topographien* (1956). Often grouped with the "Concrete Poets," Heissenbüttel's work (poetry, experimental prose, criticism, radio plays, essays) is extraordinarily diverse; his late verse again returned to the use of more traditional subject matter. Büchner Prize (1969). *textbücher, 1–6* (1980); *textbuch 11* (1987).

Stephan Hermlin (1915–)

Since 1958 Hermlin has published no new poetry and has rarely, except in essays and autobiographical sketches, broken the public silence he adopted in reaction to criticism leveled against him within the GDR. Born in Chemnitz (later GDR), he joined the Communist youth group in Berlin, engaging in illegal political activities, then emigrated to France in 1936. After the war he returned to work as a writer, living in East Berlin after 1947. His poetry from the 1940s and 1950s powerfully fuses political commitment with traditional aesthetic technique, using hymns in the spirit of Hölderlin or ballads with meter and rhyme. *22 Balladen* (1947).

Wolfgang Hilbig (1941–)

A worker who became a writer (yet not merely the author of "workers' literature"), able to frankly depict everyday life, Hilbig seemed almost the ideal synthesis once promoted by official GDR culture. Yet he was detained by security police in 1979 for publishing his work *Abwesenheit* in the West. Born in Meuselwitz (near Leipzig), he grew up in the house of his illiterate grandfather, a miner, and was himself employed as a stoker before being selected to join a seminar for writing workers in 1967. Hilbig authored poetry and autobiographical prose. His works have also been well received in the FRG, where critics have hailed them for their freshness. *Abwesenheit* (1979); *Die Versprengung* (1986).

Walter Höllerer (1922–)

An indefatigable promoter of contemporary literature, born in Bavarian Sulzbach-Rosenberg, he studied in Erlangen, Göttigen, and Heidelberg after serving as a soldier in the war. He went on to teach German and Comparative Literature (in Frankfurt, Münster, Berlin, and at the University of Illinois), became a founding member of *Gruppe 47*, organized the Berlin Literary Colloquium, publicized American literature in Germany (particularly the Beats), and edited the prominent literary journal *Akzente* from 1954 to 1959, all the while writing his own poetry and experimental prose. The unadorned language of his early verse was succeeded in the 1960s by long poem forms (styled, in part, after American models). *Der andere Gast* (1952); *Neue Gedichte* (1969).

Peter Huchel (1903–1981)

One of the most accomplished German poets of the midcentury, Huchel crafted rhythmical, evocative nature poetry, initially employing traditional forms (including ballads), later abandoning these formal stanzas while retaining their powerful cadences. Born in Berlin, where he spent much of his life, he studied literature and philosophy in Berlin, Freiburg, and Vienna, traveled, and published before the war. From 1940 to 1945 he served in the army, becoming a Soviet prisoner of war, then worked as an editor, managing the foremost GDR literary journal *Sinn und Form*, 1949–1962, until he was forced to step down. Barred from publishing and socially isolated, he eventually moved to West Germany (1972) and entered a productive period of writing that lasted until his death. Three major collections of poetry date from this time: *Chauseen Chauseen* (1963), *Gezählte Tage* (1972), and *Die neunte Stunde* (1979). *Werke*, 2 vols. (1984).

Ernst Jandl (1925–)

Sprechgedichte (poems to be read aloud), "Concrete Poetry," and dialect verse have earned Jandl an international recognition. Born in Vienna, he served in the army, was released in 1946 as an American prisoner of war, and taught German and English literature in Viennese high schools. His literary publications (1952–) include poetry, prose, drama, film, essays, and translations. Though not a member of the *Wiener Gruppe*, it (and Dada) influenced him; he collaborated with poet Friederike Mayröcker on award-winning radio plays. His poetry, which revels in the sound of language and its aesthetic potential, lies between traditional and experimental verse. Büchner Prize (1984). *Gesammelte Werke*, 4 vols. (1985).

Yaak Karsunke (1934–)

Born in Berlin, where he resides, Karsunke studied law and acting for a time, working for seven years before beginning his career as a writer. His oeuvre encompasses poetry, several plays and adaptations, and essays; he was also the editor of the left-oriented journal *Kürbiskern*. With *Kilroy & andere* (1967), he made his debut as a political poet who combines a sense of historical irony with firm command of diction. *Da zwischen* (1979); *Die Guillotine umkreisen* (1984); *Gespräch mit dem Stein* (1992).

Marie Luise Kaschnitz (1901–1974)

She began writing in the late 1920s, though her first volume of poetry did not appear until 1947 *(Totentanz und Gedichte zur Zeit)*. Born in Karlsruhe (southern Germany), Kaschnitz was trained as a book dealer and married an Austrian archaeologist, with whom she traveled widely. She lived for many years in Rome, and later in Frankfurt. Kaschnitz was honored with the Büchner Prize (1955) and a doctorate from the University of Frankfurt. Her poetry shows affinities to German writers from Trakl to Rilke. She moved from rhyme and meter to succinct poems in free verse (*Neue Gedichte*, 1957), and ultimately to longer line forms (*Kein Zauberspruch*, 1972). A chronicler of her times, she never longed for a "heile Welt" (safe and snug world) as did many of her more conservative contemporaries. *Überallnie. Ausgewählte Gedichte 1928–65* (1965).

Annerose Kirchner (1951–)

The author of poetry, opera libretti, prose, and radio plays for children, Kirchner, born in Leipzig (GDR), studied at the Becher Institute (1976–1979). *Mittagsstein* (1979); *Im Maskensaal* (1989).

Sarah Kirsch (1935–)

Deceptive in its apparent simplicity and magically evocative language, her poetry is among the finest by a living German author. Born in Limlingerode (the Harz mountains, later the central border region between East and West), Kirsch studied biology in Halle before attending the Becher Institute. She was married for ten years to fellow writer Rainer Kirsch. At first, GDR critics regarded her verse as too personal, but *Landaufenthalt* (1967), *Zaubersprüche* (1973), and *Rückenwind* (1976) earned her increasing acclaim. After protesting Biermann's expulsion, life in the GDR became increasingly difficult for her; she moved to West Berlin (1977) and then to the FRG. Kirsch's poems, often in a seemingly naive tone, are intricate, multilevel weavings of biographical, political, naturalist, and literary allusions. Since leaving the GDR she has published several volumes of poetry and prose poems. Her work also includes reportage and children's literature. *Katzenkopfpflaster* (1978); *Landwege* (1985); *Bodenlos* (1996). Büchner Prize (1996).

Wulf Kirsten (1934–)

He first studied business in Meissen, near Klipphausen (later the GDR), where he was born, then German and Slavic languages in Leipzig, before joining a publishing firm in Weimar. His verse first appeared in the late 1960s. Kirsten's poetry about the rural landscape and its people is written in a plain, clearly defined voice. *die erde bei Meissen* (1986); *Stimmen Schotter. Gedichte 1987–1992* (1993).

Karin Kiwus (1942–)

In West Berlin, where she was born, Kiwus works at the Academy of Arts. She studied German, political science, and journalism, and published two strong volumes of poetry in the late 1970s (*Von beiden Seiten der Gegenwart*, 1976; *Angenommen später*, 1979). Adept with both succinct, short-line verse and long-line descriptive poetry, Kiwus has a sharp sense of verbal irony, and a keen eye for detail. The ambiguity of contemporary male-female relationships enters into her numerous love poems. *Zweifelhafter Morgen* (1987); *Das chinesische Examen* (1992).

Barbara Köhler (1959–)

She studied textile manufacturing, then attended the Leipzig Literature Institute. Köhler has written for children and published poetry in anthologies. *Deutsches Roulette* (1991).

Uwe Kolbe (1957–)

The author of poetry and translations, and born in East Berlin, Kolbe began writing in the early 1970s. By age 19, he had been recognized by Franz Fühmann for his unmistakable talent and he has subsequently been widely discussed as the leading figure among the younger generation of GDR poets. His autobiographical, free verse poetry (*Hineingeboren*, 1980; *Abschiede*, 1981; *Bornholm II*, 1986) shows highly developed command of language and debts to Walt Whitmann, Gottfried Benn, Bertolt Brecht, and the Expressionists. In 1987 he moved to the FRG. *Nicht wirklich platonisch* (1994).

Alfred Kolleritsch (1931–)

A founder of the Graz artist group *Forum Stadtpark* and editor of the literary journal

Manuskripte (1960 –), Kolleritsch was born in Brunnsee (Styria, Austria). He has taught high school, and at the University of Graz began publishing in the early 1960s; his first volume of verse, *erinnerter zorn*, appeared in 1972 (also his novel *Die Pfirsichtöter*), but his second collection, *Einübung ins Unvermeidbare* (1978), established him as one of the important poets of his generation.

Hertha Kräftner (1928–1951)
Of the postwar poets, she was among the first to reestablish a productive relationship with the Expressionist and Surrealist generation (Trakl, Lichtenstein, van Hoddis, and Kafka—about whom she was writing a dissertation). She wrote poems and short prose sketches before committing suicide in Vienna, her birthplace. *Das Werk* (1977).

Ursula Krechel (1947–   )
A keen feminist perspective and abundant, rapidly shifting images characterize Krechel's verse. Born in Trier (FRG), she studied German, theater, and art history in Cologne, and served as a dramaturge in Dortmund before she began her career as a writer in 1972. She has worked in many genres. *Nach Mainz* (1977); *Rohschnitt* (1983); *Vom Feuer lernen* (1985).

Karl Krolow (1915–   )
Krolow's exquisite, magically evocative nature poetry is informed by his copious knowledge of modern literature (particularly French and Spanish Surrealism). Though he started his writing in the early 1940s (born in Hannover, northern Germany), *Die Zeichen der Welt* (1952), *Wind und Zeit* (1954), and *Tage und Nächte* (1956) established his reputation as a poet. Krolow's early verse employs rhyme and meter; later he progressed to laconic poems written in powerfully simple language, briefly returning to traditional forms in the 1980s. In addition to dozens of volumes of poetry (including erotic verse issued under a pseudonym, Karol Kropcke) and translations from the French and Spanish, he has published autobiographical prose, influential literary essays, and anthologies. Büchner Prize (1956). *Gesammelte Gedichte* (1965; 1975; 1985).

Günter Kunert (1929–   )
A highly prolific and multifaceted writer, born in Berlin, Kunert was prevented from pursuing an education because his mother was Jewish. His first poems and stories were published in 1948; Kunert was subsequently discovered by Johannes Becher and Brecht (whose influence is evident in his dialectically constructed and epigrammatic verse). Like many GDR authors of his generation, after 1965 Kunert was increasingly criticized; having protested Biermann's expulsion, he himself left for the FRG in 1979, where his reputation was already firmly established. His poetry evinces a deep skepticism about politics and history; he commands a full range of techniques (from traditional forms to free and experimental verse). *Abtötungsverfahren* (1980); *Berlin beizeiten* (1987); *Stilleben* (1992); *Mein Golem* (1996).

Reiner Kunze (1933–   )
Born in Oelsnitz (eastern Germany), he studied philosophy and journalism in Leipzig

(1951–1955), then, under political attack, left the university shortly before graduation to work in Czechoslovakia, where he met his wife and started translating Czech poetry. In 1962 he began his career as a writer. GDR authorities, however, impeded publication of his works; he moved to the FRG. His laconic verse offers barbed comments, as the title *Zimmerlautstärke* (1972, poetry), a commentary on state censorship, suggests. Büchner Prize (1977). *auf eigene Hoffnung* (1981); *eines jeden einziges leben* (1986).

Elisabeth Langgässer (1899–1950)
Born in Alzey (Rhine-Hessen), she lived in Darmstadt and Berlin. She taught school, and was racially persecuted; she died of multiple sclerosis. Her unique nature poetry combines strong mythic (classical and Catholic) elements, most of it in intricate cycles. She also authored novels, short fiction, essays, and radio plays. Büchner Prize (1950). *Gesammelte Werke* (1959–1964).

Christine Lavant (1915–1973)
Born in Gross Edling (Carinthia, Austria), she made her debut with the Rilkean *Die unvollendete Liebe* (1949). She eked out a meager living as a farm worker and by knitting. Her work with its use of form and rural imagery is unique in postwar German poetry, yet very Austrian. Reflections on life's hardships and religious dilemmas abound in her fiction and autobiographical prose. *Gedichte* (1972); *Kunst wie meine ist nur verstümmeltes Leben* (1978).

Wilhelm Lehmann (1882–1968)
In the 1920s, Lehmann won recognition as the author of narrative prose, but after 1945 he became the father of a contemporary line of mythical nature poetry. Born in Puerto Cabello (Venezuela), he served as a soldier in the First World War, then assumed a position as teacher in Eckernforde (northern Germany), where he remained until retirement. *Antwort des Schweigens* (1935), his first volume of poetry, appeared when he was already fifty; four books from 1942 to 1954 were later collected as *Meine Gedichtbücher* (1957). In addition, Lehmann published two other volumes of verse. Rhyme, playful mythical allusions, and concrete biological details characterize much of his stylistically subtle verse.

Kito Lorenc (1938–)
Though of the second generation of GDR authors, Lorenc by virtue of the experimental quality of his poetry shares affinities with younger avant-garde writers. Born in Schleife/Lausitz, he studied Slavic languages in Bautzen, near the Czechoslovakian border, where he still lives. He has written verse both in German and in Sorbian, publishing his works since the late 1960s. *Flurbereinigung* (1973); *Poesiealbum 143* (1979); *Wortland* (1984).

Rainer Malkowski (1939–)
Born in West Berlin, he is the author of poetry and prose. His first volume of verse, *Was für ein Morgen*, appeared in 1975. *Was auch immer geschieht* (1986); *Ein Tag für Impressionisten und andere Gedichte* (1994).

Kurt Marti (1921–)

A minister in Bern, where he was born, Marti has authored numerous slim volumes of poetry as well as narrative prose. His first collection of poems, *boulevard bikini*, appeared in 1958; his dialect poems (*rousa loui*, 1967) were a great critical success. Marti's verse is a congenial combination of his theological perspective and a playful sense of language (influenced by the Concrete poets and at times reminiscent of nonsense verse); short forms and precisely chosen language predominate. *Gesammelte Gedichte* (1982); *Mein barfussiges Lob* (1987).

Georg Maurer (1907–1971)

One of the most influential poets in the GDR—he taught at the Becher Institute (1955–1970) and was the mentor to an entire generation of younger authors, many of whom surpassed his own hard-won accomplishments—Maurer has not been highly regarded in the West, in part because his work fell within the older tradition of *Gedankenlyrik* (philosophical poetry). Born in Reghin (Rumania), he served in the army (primarily as a translator in Bucharest, where he grew up), then worked in radio broadcasting after the war before he assumed his post as a teacher of literature. *Poesiealbum 43* (1971); *Gedichte* (1972); *Unterm Maulbeerbaum* (1977).

Friederike Mayröcker (1924–)

A highly original author of poetry, prose, and award-winning radio plays (in collaboration with Ernst Jandl), Mayröcker (born in Vienna, where she taught English 1946–1969) began to write at age fifteen. She published her first verse in 1946, turning in the early 1960s to long poem forms (such as the sequence *Tod durch Musen*, 1966). Her texts, a patchwork of linguistic scraps, evocative images, and distilled impressions, are constructed associatively via what Mayröcker terms the *Bewusstseinsmaschine* (consciousness machine) of her mind. *Ausgewählte Gedichte 1944–78* (1979); *Ausgewählte Gedichte* (1986); *Notizen auf ein Kamel. Gedichte 1991–1996* (1996).

Christoph Meckel (1935–)

The son of a writer, born in Berlin, Meckel grew up in Freiburg (the Black Forest region), and was trained as a graphic artist, a career he has successfully pursued in parallel with his writing (he has produced a number of editions that combine work in the two fields). He began publishing poetry in the late 1950s (*Tarnkappe*, 1956) and has also authored prose and radio plays. His early verse reflects an interest in Expressionism; vivid, visual images predominate throughout his oeuvre. *Ausgewählte Gedichte 1955–1978* (1978); *Hundert Gedichte* (1988).

Karl Mickel (1935–)

Somewhat skeptically regarded in the GDR as a willful poet, Mickel made his debut with *Lobverse und Beschimpfungen* (1963), a work critical of capitalism. Born in Dresden, he studied economics, then edited the journal *Junge Kunst* before taking a job teaching economics (1965–1971). Later he became a dramaturge for the Berliner Ensemble (1971–

1978) and worked as an editor and anthologist. *Vita nova mea* (1967); *Poesiealbum* (1981); *Gedichte 1957–1974* (1990); *Palimpsest* (1990).

Franz Mon (1926–)

One of the leading members of the "Concrete Poetry" movement, Mon was born in Frankfurt, where he lives. He studied German, philosophy, and history, then began publishing in the mid-1950s (*Articulationen*, 1959, poetry). Mon has created visual, aural, and automatic texts. As distinct from other Concrete writers, he proceeds from the position that literature should be anti-ideological and skeptically examines the substance of language itself to debunk the assumptions made about language and its worn-out clichés. *herzzero* (1968); *hören und sehen vergehen* (1978).

Inge Müller (1925–1966)

Drafted into the air force as a helper during the war, Müller worked later as a secretary and journalist. She authored radio plays and children's verse prior to her suicide. She was married to dramatist Heiner Müller, with whom she collaborated on theater pieces. *Wenn ich schon sterben muss* (1985).

Helga Novak (1935–)

Long ignored in the West, though her works were published there (*Ballade von der reisenden Anna*, 1965; *Colloquium mit vier Häuten*, 1967; *Margarete mit dem Schrank*, 1978; *Grünheide Grünheide, Gedichte 1955–1980*, 1983; *Legende Transsib*, 1985), Novak is an accomplished poet who writes in an unmistakably firm voice and economic style. Born in Berlin (Kopenick), she studied journalism and philosophy, then held various jobs before marrying (1961) and moving to Iceland, where she worked in factories until 1965. After a brief stint at the Becher Institute, her GDR citizenship was revoked and she moved to the FRG. Novak, who also writes prose, shows a predilection for narrative poetry. Ballad and rhymed forms are prevalent in her early work (which often articulates social criticism); free verse dominates later, as does more autobiographical subject matter.

Brigitte Oleschinski (1955–)

An emerging writer who has published poems in journals and anthologies, Oleschinski was born in 1955 in Cologne and lived in West Berlin, where she studied political science. *Mental Heat Control* (1990).

Oskar Pastior (1927–)

A German born in Hermannstadt/Sibiu (Rumania), Pastior spent 1945–1949 in a Soviet work camp before returning to Bucharest to study literature (1955–1960). After a stint as a radio editor, he moved to the FRG (1968), settling in West Berlin to begin his career as a writer. His numerous volumes of poetry and translation from the Rumanian, such as his collection of palindromes *Kopfnuss Januskopf* (1990), test the limits of linguistic and literary convention and have earned him a considerable reputation among fellow writers. *Wechselbalg* (1980); *Anagrammgedichte* (1985).

Christa Reinig (1926–)

In Berlin, where she was born, Reinig endured an impoverished childhood; after the war she attended night school (1950–1953) and the Humboldt University to study art history and archeology. From 1954–1963 she worked at a museum in East Berlin. Her first poems appeared in 1948, but from 1951 on she was not allowed to publish in the GDR. Her work did, however, come out in the West (beginning in 1960). In 1964 she went to the FRG to receive the literary prize of the city of Bremen, never to return to the East. Biographical and existential themes (flight, isolation, anxiety) and a strong commitment to outsiders, the disadvantaged, and downtrodden play an important role in her work. *Gesammelte Gedichte 1960–1979* (1984).

Friederike Roth (1948–)

With a sharp ear for distinct types of speech (occasionally her Swabian background reveals itself in diction or themes—she was born in Sindelfingen), Roth insistently reveals the discrepancies that exist between language and reality, particularly in matters of love. Thus, female-male and mother-child relations have often been the subject of her poetry and successfully performed plays. *Tollkirschenhochzeit* (1978); *Schieres Glück* (1981); *Schattige Gärten* (1987); *Wiese und Macht* (1993).

Gerhard Rühm (1930–)

A cofounder of the *Wiener Gruppe* and a composer, Rühm was born in Vienna and lived there until 1964. He later taught in Hamburg and resided in Cologne. His first book was a collaborative effort with Artmann (*hosn rosn baa*, 1959); more poetry, drama, and prose followed in the 1960s and 1970s. Like others with whom he is associated, Rühm rejects conventional notions of literature, writing instead sound poems, Concrete verse, and dialect poetry and automatic texts. *konstellation* (1961); *fenster* (1968); *Gesammelte Gedichte* (1970).

Peter Rühmkorf (1929–)

This literary nonconformist, born in Dortmund, began writing while still in school, but not until the 1970s did the cultural establishment begin to take him seriously. Rühmkorf became involved in various literary and theater projects while a student in Hamburg, then broke off his studies (1957), later working as an editor (1958–1964). He has been politically active throughout his career. His poetry is anarchic and often satirical; he gleans inherited forms and vocabulary from the entire history of German verse and uses them for his own ends. His first volume of verse, *Irdisches Vergnügen in g.* (1959), puns on a title by the Baroque poet Brockes; *Kunststücke* (1962) contained potent literary parodies; *Haltbar bis Ende 1999* (1979, "Durable until 1999") hints at his disinterest in creating permanent and "beautiful" works of art. *Gesammelte Gedichte* (1976).

Nelly Sachs (1891–1970)

Winner of the 1966 Nobel Prize for literature, Sachs wrote visionary poetry inspired by the Cabbala, Old Testament, and mystical writings, much of it in reaction to the Holocaust. Born in Berlin, the daughter of Jewish parents, in 1940 she fled to Sweden, where she lived until her death. *In den Wohnungen des Todes* (1947), her first collection, contains many poems addressed to her fiancé, who died in a concentration camp. With *Fahrt ins Staublose* (1961, which includes new poetry and work from previous volumes) and *Glühende Rätsel* (1963), Sachs won a wider audience. Isolated, strong images densely pack her work; the style becomes increasingly elliptical in her later verse, where short poems predominate. She also wrote drama and translated extensively. *Suche nach Lebenden* (1971); *Gedichte* (1984).

Sonja Schüler (1950 –)
Born in Meissen (GDR), she studied agrarian technology in Leipzig (1969–1973). After 1977 she lived in Potsdam and published several volumes of poetry. *Poesiealbum 50* (1971); *Zwischen Donnerstag und März* (1975); *Schimmel werden schwarz geboren* (1982).

Peter Schütt (1939 –)
His work is unequivocally political, an example of the New Left realism that developed at the end of the turbulent 1960s, when his first book publication, *Sicher in die Siebzigerjahre* (1969, poetry and prose), appeared. Schütt was born in Basbeck (Niederelbe), studied German and history, and lives in Hamburg. He writes poetry, songs, essays, narrative prose, and reportage. *Zur Lage der Nation* (1974).

Julian [Jutta] Schutting (1937 –)
The author of poems, stories, prose, essays, and radio plays, Schutting was born in Amstetten (lower Austria) and resides in Vienna. The volume *Liebesgedichte* prompted considerable critical acclaim when it appeared in 1982. *Lichtungen* (1976); *Traumreden* (1987); *Flugblätter* (1990); *Das Eisherz sprengen* (1996).

Eva Strittmatter (1930 –)
Born in Neuruppin (later GDR), Strittmatter studied German, Romance languages, and pedagogy in Berlin (1947–1951), and in the 1950s worked on the staff of the literary journal *Neue Deutsche Literatur.* She has produced a steady stream of poetry and children's books. Her first volume of verse, *Ich mach ein Lied aus Stille* (1973) contains elements typical of her work: restrained, private tone, themes traditional to nature or rural poetry, and rhyme. *Die eine Rose überwältigt alles* (1977); *Zwiegespräch* (1980); *Einst habe ich drei Weiden besungen* (3rd ed. 1995); *Heliotrop* (1996).

Brigitte Struzyk (1946 –)
A native of Steinbach-Hallenberg (Thuringia), Struzyk studied theater in Leipzig (1965–1969) and has worked as a dramaturge and editor. Since 1982 she has been a free-lance writer, living in East Berlin and publishing poetry and prose. *Leben auf der Kippe* (1984); *Der wildgewordene Tag* (1989).

Hannelies Taschau (1937 –)
The author of poetry and narrative prose, Taschau was born in Hamburg. Her first volume of verse appeared in 1959; subsequently she published *Gedichte* (1969), *Luft*

zum Atmen (1977); *Doppelleben* (1979); *Gefährdung der Leidenschaft* (1984); *Wundern entgehen. Gedichte 1957–1984* (1986); *Weg mit dem Meer* (1990).

Jürgen Theobaldy (1944–   )

Perhaps the foremost representative of "New Subjectivity," Theobaldy published his first poetry in the 1970s (*Sperrsitz*, 1973, and *Blaue Flecken*, 1974), though individual poems in these volumes date back to the late 1960s. Theobaldy was influenced by American verse (Frank O'Hara and others); parlando tone and spontaneity counterbalanced with reflection characterized his early work. In 1977, while in Rome, he began experimenting with classical poetic forms (odes, distichs); the product of this was *Drinks* (1979), later heavily revised and reissued with additions as *Midlands, Drinks* (1984). This radical transformation marked the beginning of recent debates in Germany over metrical verse. Born in Strasbourg, he resides in Bern and remains an articulate critic, anthologist, and author of prose. *Der Nachbildsammler* (1992).

Ilse Tielsch (1929–   )

Born in Auspitz (Czechoslowakia) and displaced to Austria in 1945, Tielsch lives in Vienna. She studied journalism and German literature, has published several volumes of poetry, short fiction, essays, radio plays, and is best known for her novels about World War II and the postwar era. *Herbst mein Segel* (1967); *Regenzeit* (1975); *Nicht beweisbar* (1981); *Zwischenbericht* (1986).

Guntram Vesper (1941–   )

In 1957, Vesper left the GDR for the FRG. Many of his poems reflect a nostalgic longing for Frohburg (where he was born) that has allowed him to develop his own elegiac and descriptive style. Later, Vesper was active in the Agitprop scene (agitation and propaganda literature) of the late 1960s. In the 1970s he began publishing poetry again. *Die Illusion des Unglücks* (1980); *Nordwestpassage* (1980); *Frohburg* (1985); *Leuchtfeuer auf dem Festland* (1989).

Richard Wagner (1952–   )

Born in Lowrin (Rumania), he emigrated to West Berlin in 1987 with his wife, writer Herta Müller. Wagner began writing as a student and by age sixteen had published poems. In Rumania he worked as a German teacher before being forbidden to publish. He was also imprisoned, fired as editor of the *Neue Banater Zeitung* (the newspaper of German speaking Rumanians) for printing an article on former Stalinists. He has authored several volumes of poetry, including *Rostregen* (1986).

Silja Walter (1919–   )

In Switzerland (her birthplace was Rickenbach), she studied literature, then worked with the Catholic youth movement for two years before she entered the Benedictine convent near Zürich in 1948. Many of her works are religious (plays, hymns, oratorio, prayers). Walter's poetry, first published in 1944, has a tone reminiscent of the folk song tradition in German verse. *Die ersten Gedichte* (1944); *Gedichte* (1950); *Gesammelte Gedichte* (1972).

Paul Wiens (1922–1982)
Born in Königsberg (now Kaliningrad, Russia), Wiens studied in Switzerland from 1939 to 1942 because as a Jew he could not continue his education in Germany. From 1943 to 1945 he was held by the SS in a detention camp near Vienna. Here he came in contact with Marxist thinkers; after the war he moved to East Berlin (1947), working as an editor, then as a writer. *Vier Linien aus meiner Hand. Gedichte 1943–1971* (1972).

Gabriele Wohmann (1932–)
A native of Darmstadt, she studied German and music in Frankfurt and worked as a teacher before beginning her career as a freelance writer in 1958. In addition to novels, short stories, and radio plays, she has authored several volumes of poetry. *Ausgewählte Gedichte 1964–1982* (1982).

Wolf Wondratschek (1943–)
In the early 1970s, Wondratschek (born in Rudolstadt, Thuringia) rapidly made a name for himself with his sassy poems à la pop songs about the banalities of everyday life, collected in *Chuck's Zimmer* (1974). His influences include Bob Dylan and R. D. Brinkmann. He has also written narrative prose and radio plays, and lives in Munich. *Männer und Frauen* (1978); *Die Gedichte* (1992).

Peter-Paul Zahl (1944–)
Born in Freiburg (southwest Germany), Zahl grew up in the GDR, then moved to the Rhine area (1953), where he learned offset printing. He moved to Berlin as a conscientious objector (1964). In 1967 Zahl founded a small publishing firm in the service of political opposition groups. From 1969 on he was under police surveillance, subjected to repeated searches. While he was attempting to flee police conducting identity checks in 1972, shots were exchanged. Zahl was sentenced to four years, then (as "a warning to others") to fifteen years. His work (1972–1982, when he was granted early release) was written in prison. Literature, in Zahl's view, should both witness and affect events; the descriptions in his poetry are skillfully spare, resolutely political. *Schutzimpfung* (1975); *Alle Türen offen* (1977); *Aber nein sagte Bakunin und lachte laut* (1983).

Select Bibliography

Collections Available in English

Bjorklund, Beth. "Austrian Poetry: 1945–1980." *Literary Review* 25, no. 2 (Special Issue, Winter 1982).

Cocalis, Susan L. *The Defiant Muse: German Feminist Poems from the Middle Ages to the Present.* New York: The Feminist Press, 1986.

Deicke, Günter, ed. *Time for Dreams: Poetry from the German Democratic Republic.* Trans. Jack Mitchell. Berlin: Seven Seas, 1976.

Friebert, Stuart, et al., eds. *Field. Contemporary Poetry and Poetics. Special Issue: Contemporary East German Poetry.* Oberlin: Oberlin College, 1980.

Gutzschahn, Uwe-Michael, ed. *Young Poets of Germany: An Anthology.* Trans. Raymond Hargreaves. London: Forest, 1994.

Hamburger, Michael, ed. *East German Poetry.* New York: E. P. Dutton, 1973.

———, ed. and trans. *German Poetry 1910–1975.* New York: Urizen Books, 1976.

Hamburger, Michael, and Christopher Middleton, eds. *Modern German Poetry 1910–1960.* New York: Grove Press, 1962.

Holten, Milne, and Herbert Kuhner, eds. and trans. *Austrian Poetry Today/Österreichische Lyrik heute.* New York: Schocken, 1985.

Ives, Rich, ed. *Evidence of Fire: An Anthology of Twentieth Century German Poetry.* Seattle, Wash.: Owl Creek Press, 1988.

Rothenberg, Jerome, trans. *New Young German Poets.* San Francisco: City Lights, 1959.

Schwebell, Gertrude C., ed. *Contemporary German Poetry: An Anthology.* Norfolk, CT: New Directions, 1964.

Willson, A. Leslie, ed. *Dimension: Contemporary German Arts and Letters* (1968–   ). A journal published by the Department of Germanic Languages, University of Texas, Austin.

Secondary Literature in English

Allemann, Beda. "Non-representational Modern German Poetry." In *Reality and Creative Vision*, ed. A. Closs. London: Butterworths, 1963. 71–79.

Arnheim, Rudolf. "Visual Aspects of Concrete Poetry." *Yearbook of Comparative Criticism* 7 (1976): 91–109.

Bender, Hans. "Letter from Germany. Ever-New Mutations: Theories and Postulates of Today's German-Language Poetry." *Dimensions* 7 (1974): 317–23.

———. "Letter from Germany. The Myth of Kahlschlag." *Dimensions* 5 (1972): 395–401.

Bienek, Horst. "German Poetry Since 1945." *United Asia* 12 (1960): 47–48.

Bjorklund, Beth. "Tradition and Innovation: Austrian Poetry at the Opening of the Eighties." *World Literature Today* 55 (1981): 592–96.

Bloom, Harold, ed. *Modern German Poetry*. New York and Philadelphia: Chelsea House, 1989.

Bushell, Anthony. *The Emergence of West German Poetry from the Second World War into the Early Post-war Period*. Frankfurt: Peter Lang, 1989.

Closs, August. "German Poetry after 1945." In *Medusa's Mirror: Studies in German Literature*. London: Cresset Press, 1957. 213–21.

Demetz, Peter. *After the Fires: Recent Writing in the Germanies, Austria and Switzerland*. San Diego: Harcourt Brace Jovanovich, 1986.

———. *Postwar German Literature. A Critical Introduction*. New York: Pegasus, 1970.

Enzensberger, Hans Magnus. "In Search of the Lost Language." *Encounter* 3 (1963): 44–51.

Exner, Richard. "German Poetry 1963." *Books Abroad* 38 (1964): 123–27.

———. "Tradition and Innovation in the Occidental Lyric of the Last Decade, VII. German Poetry 1950–1960: An Estimate." *Books Abroad* 36 (1962): 245–54.

Flores, John. *Poetry in East Germany: Adjustments, Visions, and Provocations, 1945–1970*. New Haven: Yale University Press, 1971.

Geist, Peter. "Voices from No Man's Land: Recent German Poetry." Trans. Friederike Eigler. In *Cultural Transformations in the New Germany: American and German Perspectives*, ed. Friederike Eigler. Columbia, S.C.: Camden House, 1993. 132–53.

Glenn, Jerry. "Approaching the Contemporary German Lyric: A Selected, Annotated Bibliography." *Modern Language Journal* 51 (1967): 480–92.

Grimm, Reinhold. "More Poetry from Germany." *Pembroke Magazine* 26 (1994): 126–30.

Gumpel, Liselotte. *"Concrete" Poetry from East and West Germany*. New Haven and London: Yale University Press, 1976.

Haenicke, Diether H. "One Nation Divisible: The Divided Germany as a Theme in the Poetry of the German Democratic Republic." *World Literature Today* 55 (1981): 582–88.

Hartung, Harald. "Lyric Poetry in Berlin since 1961." Trans. Lorna Sopcak and Gerhard Weiss. In *Berlin Culture and Metropolis*, ed. Charles W. Haxthausen and Heidrun Suhr. Minneapolis and Oxford: University of Minnesota Press, 1990. 187–205.

Holthusen, Hans Egon. "German Lyric Poetry Since 1945." *Poetry* 88 (1956): 257–66.

John, David G. "Emancipation Through Poetry: Consequences of 1968." In *Crisis and Commitment: Studies in German and Russian Literature in Honour of J. W. Dyck*, ed. John Whiton. Waterloo: University of Waterloo Press, 1983. 117–26.

Keith-Smith, Brian, ed. *Essays on Contemporary German Literature*. London: Oswald Wolff, 1966.

Kramer, Jane. "Letter from Europe." *The New Yorker*, 25 May 1992: 40–64.

Kudszus, Winfried. "Lyric Poetry in German Since 1945." In *Contemporary Germany: Politics and Culture*, ed. Charles Burdick et al. Boulder, Colo.: Westview, 1984. 340–52.

Leeder, Karen J. "'Poesie ist eine Gegensprache': Young GDR Poets in Search of a Political Identity." In *German Literature at a Time of Change 1989–1990: German Unity and German Identity in Literary Perspective*, ed. Arthur Williams, Stuart Parkes, and Roland Smith. Bern: Peter Lang, 1991. 413–27.

Newton, Gerald. "'Ick snack Platt, du ok': The New Generation of German Dialect Writers." *German Life and Letters* 34, no. 4 (July 1981): 415–29.

Prawer, S. S. "Reflections on Recent German Poetry." *German Life and Letters* 13 (1959): 18–26.

Raulet, Gerard. "The Logic of Decomposition: German Poetry in the 1960s." Trans. Sheila Elizabeth Keene. *New German Critique* 21 (1980): 81–107.

Rolleston, James, ed. *Studies in Twentieth-Century Literature* 21 (Special Issue on Recent German Poetry, Winter 1997).

Rosellini, Jay. "Poetry and Criticism in the German Democratic Republic: The 1972 Discussion in the Context of Cultural Policy." *New German Critique* 9 (1976): 153–74.

Ryan, Judith. "'Your Life Jacket Is Under Your Skin.' Reflections on German Poetry of the Seventies." *The German Quarterly* 55 (1982): 296–308.

Sax, Boria. *The Romantic Heritage of Marxism: A Study of East German Love Poetry*. New York: Peter Lang, 1987.

Schmidt, Siegfried J. "Perspectives on the Development of Post-Concrete Poetry." *Poetics Today* 3, no. 3 (1982): 101–36.

Schulte, Rainer. "The Emergence of Multiple Voices: Contemporary German Poetry." *Mundus Artium* 11, no. 2 (1979): 8–12.

Scrase, David A. "Dimensions of Reality: West German Poetry of the Seventies." *World Literature Today* 55 (1981): 568–72.

Spycher, Peter. "Contemporary Swiss-German Poetry." *Dimension* 10 (1977): 7–15.

Subiotto, Arrigo V. "Poetry in East Germany." *Modern Languages* 42 (1961): 21–24.

Waidson, H. M. "Some Contemporary Swiss Poets Writing in German." In *Modern Swiss Literature: Unity and Diversity*, ed. John Flood. New York: St. Martin's Press, 1985. 127–36.

Wickham, Christopher J. "The Old, the New and an Empirical Investigation into the Appeal of 'Mundartdichtung'." *German Life and Letters* 35 (1982): 343–54.

Index of Authors

Index of First Lines

University Press of New England publishes books under its own imprint and is the publisher for Brandeis University Press, Dartmouth College, Middlebury College Press, University of New Hampshire, Tufts University, and Wesleyan University Press.

Library of Congress Cataloging-in-Publication Data

German poetry in transition, 1945–1990 / edited and introduced with translations by Charlotte Melin.

   p.   cm.

Introd. in English, poems in English and German.

Includes bibliographical references.

ISBN 0–87451–914–4 (alk. paper). — ISBN 0–87451–915–2 (pbk. : alk. paper)

1. German poetry—20th century translations into English.

I. Melin, Charlotte.

PT1160.E5G433   1999

831'.91408—dc21   99-24866